A British Fascist in the Second World War

A MODERN HISTORY OF POLITICS AND VIOLENCE

Series Editor: Paul Jackson

A Modern History of Politics and Violence is a new book series that scrutinises the diverse history of political violence in the modern world. It includes original studies, edited collections and reference works that explore the cultural settings and key actors that have allowed violent solutions to become seen as desirable somehow at certain points in history.

Forthcoming:

British Fascist Antisemitism and Jewish Responses, 1932–40,
Daniel Tilles (2014)
The Comparative History of Fascism in Eastern Europe,
Constantin Iordachi (2014)
A Comparative History of Persecution and Victim Experience,
Kitty Millet (2015)
Transnational Fascism in the Twentieth Century,
Matteo Albanese and Pablo del Hierro (2015)

A British Fascist in the Second World War

The Italian War Diary of James Strachey Barnes, 1943–45

*Edited by Claudia Baldoli
with Brendan Fleming*

B L O O M S B U R Y
LONDON • NEW DELHI • NEW YORK • SYDNEY

Bloomsbury Academic

An imprint of Bloomsbury Publishing Plc

50 Bedford Square	1385 Broadway
London	New York
WC1B 3DP	NY 10018
UK	USA

www.bloomsbury.com

Bloomsbury is a registered trade mark of Bloomsbury Publishing Plc

First published 2014

British Library Cataloguing-in-Publication Data
A catalogue record for this book is available from the British Library.

ISBN: HB: 978–1–4725–0579–8
PB: 978–1–4725–1042–6
ePDF: 978–1–4725–0582–8
ePub: 978–1–4725–0789–1

Library of Congress Cataloging-in-Publication Data
A catalog record for this book is available from the Library of Congress.

Typeset by Fakenham Prepress Solutions, Fakenham, Norfolk NR21 8NN

CONTENTS

LIST OF FIGURES

PREFACE AND
ACKNOWLEDGMENTS

This project first took shape some eight years ago, when Professor David Bradshaw (Worcester College Oxford) received a typescript section of the diary of James Strachey Barnes from Barnes's daughter-in-law, Lena, then resident in Stockholm. Our first thanks are therefore due to David Bradshaw, who passed those pages on to us, and without whom this publication would have never seen the light of day. We thought that the diary could be a valuable historical document, and we decided to dig in the archives in search of more evidence. We were lucky enough to find the whole handwritten diary in the Archivio Centrale dello Stato in Rome. The archives do not hold just the diary, but also a considerable quantity of Barnes's personal papers: four files of documents, which include more of his unpublished works, a photographic album and correspondence, both private and public. To complete our research, we consulted the files of the Italian Ministry of Popular Culture (also in the Archivio Centrale dello Stato), where Barnes was employed to broadcast programmes aimed at a British audience; the correspondence between Barnes and Camillo Pellizzi held at the Fondazione Ugo Spirito in Rome; and the files of the War Office at the National Archives in Kew, which contain papers from the Allied Commission Headquarters in Rome as well as Intelligence material relating to Barnes's work in Italy as a pro-Axis collaborator during the war. Published work by Barnes and by other Italian Fascists and British fellow travellers can be found in libraries across Italy and the UK, in particular the Biblioteca di Storia Moderna e Contemporanea in Rome, the British Library in London and the Bodleian Library in Oxford. As a result, we have been able to provide a historical context for this extraordinary source, which illuminates both the day-to-day activities and the state of mind of a British citizen who supported the Italian Fascist regime during the final years of its decline. The transcription of the diary was undertaken by Brendan Fleming with the help of Amy Hill and Claudia Baldoli. The introduction and annotations are by Claudia Baldoli with the help of Brendan Fleming. We are also grateful for the assistance we received from Luigi Petrella, Martin Farr, and Claudio Mancini, author of a detailed reconstruction of the main events in Barnes's life and career. In our efforts to discover the copyright holder of Barnes's papers we eventually came into contact with his closest descendants, his grandchildren Lucia Filhage and Richard Barnes. We wish to express our gratitude to them for granting us the right to publish the diary and excerpts from the papers. Our final thanks go to Paul Jackson, editor of the series 'A Modern History of Politics and Violence' at Bloomsbury, for his interest in and support for this project.

NOTE TO THE DIARY

Despite the difficult legibility of Barnes's handwriting, we have achieved an accurate transcription of the diary. However, there are still words which we have not been able to recognize, and we have signalled these in the text. When uncertain, we have situated the words in square brackets. The diary contains a great many names of individuals and places; while in most cases these have been identified, in some instances it has been impossible, in particular when Barnes referred to relatives or close friends where we have no further information. We have left mistakes, underlined and deleted words as they are in the original. When we have been unable to decipher a deleted word, we have indicated it by entering '[deleted word]'; when the word was recognizable, we have transcribed it with a line through as in the original. At some points in the diary, Barnes used coloured asterisks and arrows; we are unable to explain what they might signify. All translations from Italian into English are by Claudia Baldoli.

At some points in the diary Barnes revealed the intention to insert separate documentary evidence in order to support his views. However, the extracts he proposed to add were not eventually included. Although no clear evidence exists to confirm it, we believe that this may be due to his wish to publish some version of the diary at some point in the future. It also seems to us that some passages appear to be written with an eye to justifying himself in the event of being captured by the British.

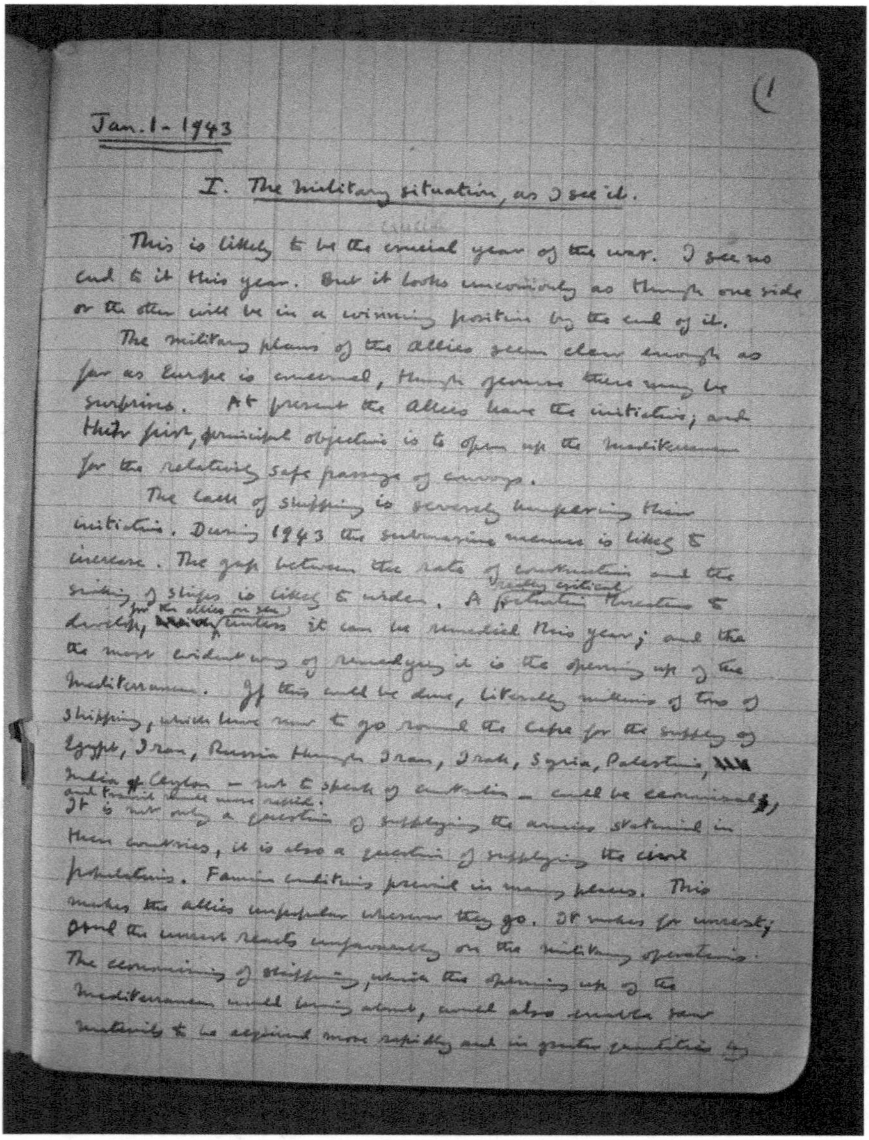

Jan. 1 - 1943

I. The military situation, as I see it.

This is likely to be the crucial year of the war. I see no end to it this year. But it looks uncommonly as though one side or the other will be in a winning position by the end of it.

The military plans of the allies seem clear enough as far as Europe is concerned, though perhaps there may be surprises. At present the allies have the initiative; and their first, principal objective is to open up the mediterranean for the relatively safe passage of convoys.

The lack of shipping is severely hampering their initiative. During 1943 the submarine menace is likely to increase. The gap between the rate of construction and the sinking of ships is likely to widen. A really critical threatens to develop for the allies on sea unless it can be remedied this year; and the the most evident way of remedying it is the opening up of the mediterranean. If this could be done, literally millions of tons of shipping, which have now to go round the Cape for the supply of Egypt, Iran, Russia through Iran, Iraq, Syria, Palestine, India & Ceylon — not to speak of australia — could be economised; and tonnage would thus become more available. It is not only a question of supplying the armies stationed in these countries, it is also a question of supplying the civil populations. Famine conditions prevail in many places. This makes the allies unpopular wherever they go. It makes for unrest; and the unrest reacts unfavourably on the military operations. The economising of shipping, which the opening up of the mediterranean would bring about, would also enable raw materials to be acquired more rapidly and in greater quantities by

FIGURE 1 *First page of the manuscript* Diary 1943

FIGURE 2 *James Strachey Barnes in Rome in the 1920s*

FIGURE 3 *James Strachey Barnes in Rome in the 1920s*

FIGURE 4 *James Strachey Barnes in Rome in the 1920s*

FIGURE 5 *James Strachey Barnes's grave at the Verano cemetery (Rome)*

FIGURE 6 *'9 May 14th year of the Fascist Era – Italy has finally its empire'. Fascist imperialist mosaic at the Foro Mussolini (now Foro Italico, Rome)*

FIGURE 7 'To S. S. Pius XII/Eugenio Pacelli/ Roman Pontiff/who, here, with the comfort/of faith/assisted the bombed city/ 19–7–1943'. Monument unveiled in the Verano cemetery, Rome, on 19 July 1967

FIGURE 8 *Image of the battle for Florence between July and August 1944*

FIGURE 9 *Pro-Allied and anti-German graffiti in bombed Bologna at the time of the city's liberation in 1945*

Introduction

On 29 August 1955, *The Times* commented on the death of Major James Strachey Barnes (1890–1955), who had died in Rome four days before, by describing him as *Inglese italianizzato*, something the conservative newspaper regarded as the incarnation of the devil.[1] Five years later, a right-wing Italian newspaper published a commemorative article on Barnes by the Fascist propagandist Luigi Villari (1876–1959), one of Barnes's closest friends, who had written of him: 'no Italian worthy of this name will ever forget dear Jim, his sacrifices for the Italian cause, and the terrible risks he ran in order to serve it'.[2] Villari was thinking about the years of the Second World War, and particularly the period from the fall of Mussolini in 1943 to the end of the war in 1945, two years in which Barnes lived in Italy as a 'traitor'. Like the British Fascist William Joyce in Germany, known by the nickname 'Lord Haw Haw', Barnes too was involved in propaganda activity directed at the country of which he was formally a citizen, even though he did not feel, and had never felt in his life, British.

Born in Simla in India in 1890, James Strachey Barnes was the son of a British civil servant there, Sir Hugh Shakespear Barnes, and his wife, Winifred Strachey. The death of his mother, when Barnes was only two years old, changed the course of his life. James and his sister Mary were sent to Italy, where Winifred's parents lived. They were brought up by their upper-class English grandparents, who had retired to Tuscany, and educated in an Italian environment until they were sent away to boarding school in England. Mary remained in England, where she married the lawyer John Hutchinson and became a writer and member of the Bloomsbury group;[3] but James returned to Italy, choosing it as his own country. His father, who had remained in India after the death of his wife, and from whom James had been separated as a young child, was a stranger to him; he objected so strongly to the idea of James taking Italian citizenship that the latter applied for it only after his father's death in 1940. By then, Barnes had become a well-known Fascist writer and propagandist.

From the beginning of 1943 to the end of the war, Barnes kept a diary, which was finally deposited in the national archives in Rome.[4] Written in the midst of dramatic events, the diary is an extraordinary source which bears witness to the difficult choices that a Fascist enthusiast, officially British but at heart Italian, had to make when confronted by sudden turning points in history. It shows how great international events could have a disruptive impact on the lives of individuals, and how those individuals react to them; in the case of Barnes, the diary reveals how events in Italy gradually brought about the collapse of his ideological hopes, and how those events affected his ideas about Fascism, Italy, civilization and religion. It tells, through the eyes of a British Fascist Italophile, much about Italian society under the strain of war and Allied bombing, and about the behaviour and actions of different Fascist leaders and ordinary Italians alike between the fall of Mussolini's regime in July 1943 and the end of the war in Italy in April 1945.[5] It also prompts reflections on the shifting relationship of British Fascists and sympathizers towards both German Nazism and Italian Fascism. Although Barnes was not a profound intellectual, his meditations on religion and nationality have a notable documentary value for the study of such a crucial moment in European history.

The small world of British Italophiles

Although the most extreme case, Barnes was not unique; he was one among a number of British Fascist sympathizers who loved Italy and admired Mussolini. Among the British conservatives who appreciated Fascist Italy, there was indeed a minority which went beyond a simple respect for Mussolini as the man who 'disciplined the Italians', and genuinely looked at Italy during the 1920s and 1930s as an example of a higher civilization. Their affection for Italy distinguished them from members of the British Union of Fascists (BUF), who held Italy as a model until the mid 1930s (when their Italophilia was replaced by admiration for Nazi Germany), but always put their Britishness first. The Italophiles were journalists and writers such as Francis Yeats-Brown, Douglas Jerrold, Charles Petrie, Harold Goad and Muriel Currey, or military men such as John Frederick Charles Fuller (the only one who was also a member of the BUF) and Edward William Polson Newman. Some Conservative MPs (like George Ambrose Lloyd, Leo Amery and John Edward Bernard Seely – from 1933 Lord Mottistone) collaborated in London with the Italian Ambassador (particularly with Dino Grandi in the 1930s),[6] though they could not risk exposure by expressing their opinions in Italian newspapers. Instead, the Italophiles wrote books and articles praising Fascist Italy and regularly travelled there, where they were personal friends of many members of the National Fascist Party and of the Fascist Grand Council.[7] They (Barnes included) were active members of the Royal Institute of International Affairs, which, among other public activities, published the *Bulletin of International News* and a number of pamphlets which all favoured a pro-Italian and anti-German foreign policy based on the idea that British foreign policy had to support an Anglo-Italian axis as joint guarantors of the Locarno treaty of 1925.[8] Their publications became openly philo-Fascist during the Ethiopian war, praising Mussolini and supporting the idea of an Italian empire in east Africa.[9]

The British Italophiles were convinced imperialists who accused the British government of neglecting the empire and pursuing an allegedly feeble policy in India. They believed the parliamentary system could not continue to work as it did, and that Britain, although not suited for dictatorship, needed a stronger government and a corporative system based on the Italian model, both adapted to the British constitution. They were strongly anti-Bolshevik and worried about the perceived growing Russian threat to Europe: Fascist Italy showed them an alternative. Some of them were Catholics rather than Protestants, which marked an important difference between them and the members of the BUF. Some were strongly anti-Nazi, while others were worried by German expansionism; but they did not altogether reject Hitler, because they perceived him too as an alternative to Bolshevism.

Unlike Nazi Germany, Italy was not, for these Italophiles, just a Fascist country of corporativism and squad violence, but also the perfect realization of a compromise between Fascist radicalism and conservative forces such as the monarchy, the Church and the industrialists. They promoted a pro-Italian British foreign policy which was designed to allow the development of Italian imperialism alongside that of Britain. However, their support for Fascist Italy was not limited to foreign policy issues, but was spiritual, often religious, and cultural. They had studied Italian history and were admirers of the Roman and Renaissance civilizations; they had also studied Fascism, which they saw as the rebirth of those once glorious eras. In their eyes, Italy was a rising nation, as opposed to decaying Britain.[10] None of these Italophiles, however, went as far as James Strachey Barnes whose devotion to Italy led him to apply for Italian citizenship and to live in Italy for most of his life.

A universal Fascist

While Charles Petrie, the Italophile and ardent monarchist (and, interestingly, biographer of Locarno's very own Austen Chamberlain), distinguished Fascism from Nazism mainly by emphasizing the role of the crown in Italy,[11] Barnes was first of all a Catholic and a proselyte of 'clerical-Fascism', an ideology he believed could be fully realized only in Italy. The term 'clerical-Fascism' had in fact been coined in 1922 by an anti-Fascist Catholic priest, the leader of the Italian Popular Party Luigi Sturzo, to define Catholics who supported Mussolini's first government. It continued to indicate, throughout the duration of the regime, those Catholics who, like Barnes, believed in a convergence between Catholic theology and the Fascist doctrine.[12] The turning point in the relationship between the Vatican and the Fascist regime came at the end of the 1920s, when (for the first time since the occupation of Rome by the newly unified state in 1870) the Pope's diplomacy decided to settle the breach with the Italian government. Although Fascist squads had destroyed the Catholic peasant unions by 1922, and Christian democratic leaders had had to flee

Italy to avoid persecution by 1926, in 1929 Pope Pius XII signed a treaty with Mussolini in the Lateran Palace to resolve the 'Roman question'. In addition to financial advantages for the Church and the civil recognition of sacramental marriage, the pact validated Roman Catholicism as the only state region and granted the Pope temporal rule of the Vatican City. While in the eyes of many Fascists this concordat appeared to curb the regime's totalitarian aims, it also increased Mussolini's prestige both at home and abroad.[13] In 1929 Barnes thus welcomed the Lateran Pacts as a proof of the 'triumph of the sounder forces within the Fascist party ... Italy, always profoundly Catholic in heart and in tradition, has at length been given the seal and outward visible sign of Catholicity by Mussolini'.[14]

Brought up in a largely Anglican family (even his grandfather Sir John Strachey, who became attracted to Catholicism, never formally became a member of the Roman Church),[15] Barnes only became a Catholic at the age of 23; however, he saw his childhood in Italy as the most influential factor on that decision. In an unpublished memorandum written in 1947, he recalled that his whole childhood was spent in Florence, where he developed a 'huge love for Italy, a kind of love which, instead of diminishing, continued to grow after I was sent to college in England'. There, first at Eton and then at Cambridge, he found himself in an alien environment, where nothing conformed to his Italian taste: 'perhaps it is because I already felt, even though I was not yet a Catholic, to belong to that part of Europe that had never abandoned its universal traditions of which Rome was the mother'.[16] Barnes described his British experience in his first autobiographical volume, *Half a Life*, published in 1933; a second volume, *Half a Life Left*, followed in 1937 which took the story up to the Ethiopian war, after which he began writing what might have become a third volume (though it was never published), *Life Made Whole*. The manuscript of this third volume, held in the Archivio Centrale dello Stato in Rome, was dedicated to Barnes's sister Mary, 'in the hope that she will read it conscientiously' and to his wife Buona, 'who is alone the keeper of my heart'. It was divided into three parts, the first entitled 'Belief in God', the second 'Belief in Christ', and the third, on his first love experience at the time of the First World War, 'An epilogue concerning a love affair'. In this manuscript, not dated but written after the Second World War, he recalled some of the themes of *Half a Life Left*, explaining the links between his rejection of Britain and his Catholicism, and the importance of his holidays in Italy while he was studying in England in preventing the development of his 'Britishness':

> If I had stayed at Eton another two years and then translated myself immediately to Cambridge ... I should have been reconciled to English life ... in all this I see clearly now the finger of Providence; for otherwise I might have never become a Catholic.[17]

He described, as an adult, his first impressions of England when he was sent there to school, comparing them with an idealized view of Italy:

> With what horror I viewed the white cliffs of Dover, the rows of dingy little houses, the drizzling rain, the fog and the blasting east wind, unrelieved like our Florentine *tramontana* by the presence of bright sunshine, and the English food and the drilled English servants. What a ghastly country I thought it![18]

His identification of everything he loved with Italy was to influence his later decision to become a Catholic. He read D'Annunzio, whom he considered the best poet in the world, and Nietzsche, both of whom taught him, he claimed, the sense of leadership and the principle of authority. Like his close friend, the American poet Ezra Pound, he believed that culture had degenerated in Britain when the aristocratic tradition had become undermined by the forces of democracy and liberalism, when, as it were, quantity had replaced quality.[19] British culture now allegedly produced intellectuals who were atheist, pacifist, feminist and sexually ambiguous: he identified the Bloomsbury circle, of which his sister, to his regret, was a member, as an example of that decay.[20]

His unhappy early years in England persuaded him that he was at heart Italian, and therefore had to apply, as soon as it was possible, for Italian citizenship; however, once his grandparents died, his father returned to England from India, and asked Barnes not to give up his British citizenship as long as he was alive. Barnes made the promise to his father, but refused to pursue a political career or accept public office in Britain because serving 'another government' would have clashed with his feelings for Italy. His experience as a King's Indian Cadet at the Royal Military College of Sandhurst in 1909 and his subsequent attempt to prepare for a diplomatic school were indeed short-lived. Before beginning university, in the summer of 1913 he travelled around Italy and wrote a diary dedicated to his sister. Even parts of Italy where he could not find anything special to see were idealized. Turin, for example, was described as 'nice' because he could always see 'the dear people'.[21] He returned to England in early October, feeling 'like a dynamo' after his journey, and simply noting in his diary: 'Rain as usual in England'.[22]

In June 1914, while a student at the University of Cambridge, he was formally accepted into the Catholic Church. In 1915, only after he was certain about Italy's entry on Britain's side in the First World War did he serve in the British army as a cavalry officer and then as a pilot in the Royal Flying Corps, rising to the rank of major. Abandoning the opportunity to carve out a military or political career in post-war Britain, he moved to Rome in 1923 to work as a freelance journalist.[23] At the same time, he was employed by the Anglo-Persian Oil Company in Italy. His Italianness remained more important to him than political ambition, for he later declined an invitation from Harold Nicolson in 1931 to stand as a parliamentary candidate for Mosley's New Party, precursor of the British Union of Fascists.[24]

Living in Italy in the 1920s, he soon became a close friend of various Fascist personalities, and a supporter of the regime. Among his closest friends were two Italians whose activity had been instrumental in expanding Fascism among the emigrant communities in Britain: Luigi Villari, whose propaganda there took the form of numerous conferences, articles and books (challenged with limited success by anti-Fascist exiles like Gaetano Salvemini);[25] and Camillo Pellizzi, one of the intellectuals of Fascist universalism and the founder of the London *Fascio* in 1921.[26] Pellizzi, who had perhaps the strongest impact on Barnes's ideas, began investigating the relationship between idealism, Fascism and religion in the early 1920s.[27] Brought up in a lay environment, he became a Catholic through a spiritual and philosophical crisis, and came to recognize the central role of the Roman religion as a strong identity element in the Italian cultural tradition. According to him, idealist philosophy had brought religion into history; in the same way, Fascism was bringing Catholicism into the essence of the state.[28] In 1928 Barnes published his first book, entitled *The Universal Aspects of Fascism*, in which he explained why he believed that Fascism had an Italian origin but a universal mission:

> For this reason alone Fascism has come to stay in Italy. For Europe it stands at the cross-roads looking back towards the two Romes, Imperial and Catholic, that made her civilisation, and pointing to its straight continuation as the only safe road by which to advance. Thus its historical function and mission is simply this: to prepare the ground for a new European political and social synthesis, founded on the sure traditions of the past, when Europe was yet one.[29]

The book had two important consequences for Barnes's life: it caused him to lose his job at the Anglo-Persian Oil Company; and it brought him closer to Mussolini, who decided, following a suggestion by Luigi Villari, to employ Barnes as director of the *Centre International d'Études sur le Fascisme* (CINEF) based in Switzerland. The CINEF claimed that it provided an opportunity for the impartial study of Fascism, by classifying everything written on the subject through a card-index system. The claim of impartiality was immediately contradicted by the fact that Fascist personalities were asked to contribute to the Institute's Year Books, while national representatives were generally sympathetic to Fascism or even formally Fascists (the Italian representative was the regime's philosopher Giovanni Gentile).[30] Indeed the institute became an instrument of Fascist propaganda abroad, and was supported financially by the *Istituto Fascista di Cultura*.[31] The CINEF was not only concerned with Fascism in Italy, but also with the birth of Fascist movements in other countries. In an introduction to the work of the institute, Barnes defined Fascism as a 'revolt against the materialistic and individualistic thought of recent centuries', the principles of which were: a strong governmental authority, capable of promoting the 'highest collective good, the spirit of social solidarity, and respect for tradition'; and 'the principle of the *carrière ouvert aux talents* for all citizens, coupled, however, with an investiture of authority from above'.[32]

The belief that Italy had been the mother of European civilization and that Italian Fascism had created a new, just society, in which talent had replaced democracy, was shared by Ezra Pound who seemed to echo Barnes when he wrote, a few years later, that Italy's major contribution to the present world was the substitution of a sense of responsibility for the concept of freedom, which he considered the major cause of the decline of the West.[33] However, for Barnes a crucial element in any description of Fascism was Catholicism, and he sought to draw parallels between the ideals of the two doctrines:

> Prescinding *sic*] from the supernatural nature of the Church, there exist a definite parallel between the principles and traditional methods of the government of the Church, as a vehicle within which ... religion may be diffused among men, and the principles actuating Fascism in the building of the State and in the propagation of a civic sense and of abiding social values.[34]

Barnes believed that Fascism was not simply an Italian phenomenon, but he assumed it had found its perfect realization in Italy thanks to its special relationship with Italian Catholicism. His book on universal Fascism was indeed an interpretation of Fascism from a Catholic point of view; Mussolini, whom he met several times, liked his book (or perhaps the publicity that would result from it in Britain) and agreed to write a foreword. It was the presence of the Catholic Church and its central role in Italian history throughout the centuries from the Roman age onwards that made Italian Fascism, in Barnes's view, a universal doctrine. The aim of Fascism was to lead Italy and, through Italy, Europe, back to the millenary tradition of Roman civilization, so to reconstruct a spiritually, politically and economically united Europe which would be a real synthesis of the universal values represented by the three eras in which Rome was the centre of civilization: imperial Rome, the Medieval Catholic Church, and the Renaissance.[35]

Reflecting on this book almost 20 years later, after Fascism had fallen, he claimed again that his concept of Fascism was profoundly congruent with that of Catholicism, and argued that if such a concept could not be entirely realized under Mussolini it was not because of the dictatorship, but because the Italians were not yet ready to receive that idea. 'Indeed', he wrote then, 'the tragedy of Fascism lay in the fact that it has been ruined precisely by those vices and defects of the Italians, which Mussolini had hoped to eradicate and correct through Fascism'.[36] The origins of Barnes's Fascism also made it anti-German, for it was rooted in the experience of the First World War against Germany and Austria, and in the idea that Fascism was the expression of the national spirit unleashed by the conflict. His views were criticized by Fascist anti-clerical intellectuals, including Giovanni Gentile and his followers, who saw Barnes as mainly a Catholic interested in the religious policies of Fascism; clearly, for Barnes Fascism and the Church were on the same level, but for other Fascists they were not.[37]

In 1930, when the CINEF activity began to decline, Barnes became sales manager for Eastern Europe on behalf of Vickers Aviation Ltd, and the same year married Buona, the Tuscan daughter of General Margherito Guidotti and of Donna Lodovica Altieri (the cousin of a German prince). In 1933 he changed job again, and began to work for the Reuters press agency in India, where he moved with his wife and his son, Adriano (in the diary nicknamed 'Job'), born in Lucca in 1931. Following Italy's invasion of Ethiopia in October 1935, however, and worried that a war between Italy and Britain may have resulted, he sent his family back to Italy and moved, as a Reuters' correspondent, to Ethiopia. This was the first war of Fascist Italy. It was in defiance of the League of Nations (of which Ethiopia was a member) and was conducted by employing modern weaponry against the civilian population. More than 2,000 bombs containing poison gas (forbidden by the 1925 Geneva Protocol) were dropped to destroy Ethiopian resistance. As soon as Italian troops triumphantly had entered Addis Ababa on 5 May 1936, Mussolini addressed cheering crowds from his balcony at Piazza Venezia, saluting the rebirth of the Roman Empire. Barnes's reports from Ethiopia were entirely dependent on Italian propaganda and as a result, when his contract expired in May 1937, he lost his job. His attitude did not differ from that of other Anglo-Saxon right-wing conservatives, who believed that there was no necessary clash between Italian and British imperialism, and did not see the point of defending the independence of an African country. During the conflict, some of them, including writers and poets like G. K. Chesterton and Ezra Pound, wrote articles in a bulletin of the London *Fascio* created by Ambassador Dino Grandi, *The British-Italian Bulletin*, about the need to support Italy's cause. Beyond the usual propaganda on Italy's lack of space and overpopulation, one aspect commonly repeated was the recognition that Britain, and indeed the wider world, owed an 'immemorial' spiritual debt to Italy, 'for spiritual services whereby in law and letters, as in art and half the sciences, she has ever led the way to civilisation'.[38] Ezra Pound, writing in the *Bulletin*, advocated a strong Italy because he believed Italy represented the keystone in world civilization.[39] To wage war on Italy would have been like 'murdering our own mother'.[40] Barnes did not spend a long time in east Africa, nor did he take part in any major battle; he nevertheless attached much importance to his contribution as a journalist and complained to both Mussolini and Grandi that he had not been awarded the silver medal for military value he believed he deserved – and which he was finally granted in 1938.

Like all British Italophiles, he desperately sought from the Ethiopian conflict up to 1940 to prevent a war between Britain and Italy; in 1938 he travelled twice to the United States, delivering speeches in both large cities and small centres in support of Neville Chamberlain's policy of appeasement. He was convinced that the choice was between conciliation with Germany and a long war which might bring about the triumph of a much more dangerous power, the Soviet Union. He thought that if the outcome of any future war was a German victory, Nazi Germany might occupy the whole of Europe; if Britain won, then Europe up to the Elbe and the Adriatic could fall under the Bolsheviks, an outcome that would in turn threaten the whole world, causing Britain's ruin too.[41]

In 1939 he went to Spain as a correspondent for British Catholic newspapers like *Social Justice* and *The Universe*, but he was in Italy when the Second World War broke out.[42] In February 1940 his father died, making it possible for him to accomplish his dream of becoming officially Italian. He immediately applied for citizenship. Despite his personal connections, wartime difficulties postponed official approval until June 1943, but the crisis of the regime and the armistice between Italy and the Allies of 8 September that year delayed once again the completion of the paperwork; the process was only concluded 10 years later. Thus Barnes spent the war as a 'traitor' – a British subject in enemy country employed in propaganda activity against the Allies. In the Italian edition of the second volume of his autobiography, published in 1939, he added a foreword explaining his loyalty:

> I love Italy to the point that I desire to be Italian. This makes me suspicious to the British but also to the Italians. But there is nothing to be done. The fact remains a fact … On which things does patriotism depend? On two things. First, on all the intimate emotions which have their origin in the life of a happy child, and on the things that surround him: a home, the first language spoken, the landscape, the food and all the environment which penetrate into his soul and to which he becomes attached without knowing why; then, when the boy becomes a man, the reasoned recognition of the spiritual values that a Nation represents.[43]

He recalled that his affection for Italy had already been formed before he was sent away as a young boy to school in England; but only when he grew up and began to reflect on these feelings did he become aware of the alleged superiority of the spiritual values of the Italian Catholic civilization over those of northern Protestantism. Fascism brought new faith into these values, encouraging him 'to fight for the expansion of Roman civilisation in the world'. The Second World War provided him with a further opportunity to accomplish his mission, by writing, and particularly broadcasting, to the British in an attempt to persuade them that they were fighting a war against the most ancient European civilization. He was employed by the *Ispettorato per la Radio Diffusione e per la Televisione*, British section, giving commentaries on war news. In the Ministry for Popular Culture it was believed that Barnes's radio conversations in English were very effective:

> He is well known among a significant sector of the British public and his programme was listened to widely, when he broadcast last year from our microphones. We reckon that as soon as it is known in Britain that he has restarted his conversations, this would reawaken an interest among the British public and the number of British listeners would increase.[44]

Disappointingly, the content of Barnes's radio programmes has not been preserved,[45] perhaps because a large portion of his personal papers were lost in the post-war period. However, a list of programme titles was recovered in 1945 by the Rome Allied Area Command, which concluded, after searching the Italian records of the propaganda ministry, that there was 'sufficient evidence to charge JSB with collaboration'.[46] From these titles it is possible to find similarities with the programmes transmitted in Germany by the British Fascist and Nazi broadcaster to Britain, William Joyce, whom Barnes had probably sought to contact during the German occupation of Italy.[47] Between December 1940 and September 1941, Barnes compiled over 170 broadcasts in English for the Italian Fascist radio with the intention of countering the anti-Fascist propaganda of Radio Londra (the BBC service for Italy), a task for which, according to the Allied authorities, he received 33,000 lire.[48] The Allied report provides a list of the programmes' topics, which suggests that Italian propaganda in English was indeed similar to its German counterpart: both focused on undermining the credibility of the British government, in particular, Churchill; on reporting Axis military victories; on condemning British 'hypocrisy' and 'plutocracy'; and on representing the Axis as the last stronghold of European civilization. Here are some of Barnes's titles:

'Gleanings from the British press' – 5–8–1941

'Thank God for the blunders of our enemies' – 18–7–1941

'What are respectable people thinking in England' – 30–7–1941

'Pride cometh before a fall' – 19–7–1941

'India's real masters' – 25–7–1941

'The saving of European civilization' – 17–7–1941

'Gt Britain's war aims' – 2–4–1941

'The logic of Churchill's inner thoughts' – 10–1–1941

'The British plutocracy' – 24–1–1941

'Resist or die' – 31–1–1941
'On lies' – 2–2–1941
'The answer to De Gaulle – Traitor' – 5–2–1941
'Short-lived Lies' – 9–2–1941
'An answer to Churchill' – 10–2–1941.[49]

A Fascist during the collapse of the Italian home front

Although Mussolini's propaganda had managed to create a festive climate in favour of the Italian declaration of war on Britain and France on 10 June 1940 (when France was already close to defeat at German hands), the continuation of the war, for a weak economy with few raw materials and a badly equipped army, soon exasperated a population asked to endure sacrifices on behalf of the regime. The Italian attack on Greece, launched on 28 October 1940, was halted and then reversed in November with the loss of southern Albania; by May 1941 the Italian army had been defeated by the British in east Africa, resulting in the loss of the empire in Ethiopia. The correspondence sent by prefects from all over Italy to the Ministry of Interior revealed growing criticism and complaints from women about the difficulty of supporting their families, while the bombing campaign, which hit Italian cities from the very start of the war, exposed the lack of appropriate anti-aircraft defences and contributed to the psychological detachment of the home front from the war effort.[50] As early as autumn 1941, the press and radio began to comment critically on episodes of defeatism, and several party newspapers suggested that the reason for the military defeats was to be found in the weakness of the Italian people, though such polemics were limited in order to avoid the impression that there were divisions within the country.[51] From the end of 1942 it became evident that the majority of the population no longer responded to propaganda attempts to instil hatred of the enemy, and instead began to morally dissociate itself from the Axis. By the time Barnes began his diary in January 1943, it was widely regarded as grotesque to continue publicly to support the idea of a Fascist 'empire'; only an Axis victory could have mitigated popular resentment, but it was no longer expected – in fact it would have worried many, since it was by then clear that victory would result in German control over Italian society. The Allied decision to intensify the bombing of Italian cities was based on evidence of declining war-willingness, and motivated by the belief that under the strain of the bombs the Italian people would finally collapse, sue for peace and bring about the end of the regime.[52]

On this major question – the resistance or collapse of the Italian people – Barnes's views were divided, at least at the beginning of 1943. He thought that the British were wrong in assuming the Italians had all turned pacifist, but at the same time realized that there were 'some ugly symptoms' on account of the defeat in Africa. After all, no war could be popular unless it was victorious, and Barnes, despite his almost romantic belief in the fighting courage and ability of the Italian soldier, knew well that the Italian armed forces had not been adequately prepared to fight a long conflict. Moreover, the reason for the series of defeats suffered by Italy was due not only to the condition of the Italian military, but also to the discrepancy between their actual capacity and the grandiosity of the ambitions of Mussolini's foreign policy.[53] This contradiction is evident in Barnes's diary, which moved between what Barnes saw and heard ('the Italian people cannot easily be induced to hate their enemies') and a wishful image of the 'people of heroes' celebrated by Fascist hymns like *Giovinezza* ('if defeat comes to stare them in the face, they will wish to fight doggedly to the end').[54] At that stage, what worried Barnes was not the anti-Fascism of ordinary Italians, but the behaviour of the Fascist party authorities. Italians, he believed, had stood up to bombardment 'calmly and cheerfully', a fact he attributed to their very nature:

> Their nervous system is magnificent. Freud could have never been an Italian ... They suffer from no complexes. Of all peoples they are the least subject to neurosis. They grumble, they criticise, they are exasperatingly temperamental; but they are astonishingly patient and resilient. Behind a soft exterior, they possess the toughest core. If the British count on an Italian collapse, they will be disappointed.[55]

However, Barnes regretted that Italian life was characterized by a *mafiosa* mentality which allowed the party to be run by various corrupt and privileged groups; he believed that a rebirth, a second March on Rome, was needed to purify Fascism as soon as the war was over.[56] Italians had not yet acquired a 'responsible civic sense' and did not regard it as shameful to cheat the government.[57] He recognized that this lack of civil sense was weakening the war effort. He hoped a 'second March on Rome' would complete the Fascist and modernist attempt since 1922 to eliminate nineteenth-century positivism, agnosticism, liberalism and anti-clericalism – the elements of what he perceived to be a world in decline. Pellizzi's vision of an 'endless revolution' and the 'sense of a new beginning' at the heart of Fascist ideology had always remained a feeling shared by a minority of pioneers rather than by the masses;[58] Barnes's vision of the post-war period was one in which that feeling would be understood and shared by the majority of the population. The *mafiosa* mentality, he believed, was particularly prevalent in Rome, despite the presence of the Vatican. For many British Italophiles, the best of Italy's spirit and culture was to be found in Tuscany. Barnes never mentions trips to southern Italy, and although he liked Rome and was enthusiastic about cities in the north when he moved there after the armistice, Tuscany always remained his ideal of Italian perfection.[59]

The personal fortunes of Barnes's family were inextricably linked with those of the war: a defeat threatened financial ruin as well as probable death if the Allies ever caught Barnes in Italy and treated him like a traitor – as later happened in Germany to Joyce, who was executed for treason in January 1945. In May 1943, worried by the course of military events, he met the Spanish Ambassador to Italy, Raimundo Fernández Cuesta, and the Italian Ambassador to Spain, Luigi Lojacono, an old friend of his and a supporter of universal Fascism.[60] They decided that the two ambassadors should discuss the matter in Madrid to see if Barnes and his family could be allowed entry into Franco's Spain with the help of the Vatican.[61] Anxiety about possible defeat runs throughout the diary and punctuates the correspondence between Barnes and his wife during the periods when they happened to be apart. Until 1943, and particularly in the war years, the couple had succeeded in continuously increasing their wealth, partly thanks to Barnes's earnings from the Ministry for Popular Culture for his radio programmes. Clearly, if the war was lost his salary would come to an end; his wife had a property she let in Rome and possessed shares and treasury bonds, all of which might be lost in the case of defeat. In her letters to Barnes, Buona continued to worry about money, which was clearly a highly important aspect of their relationship.[62] Nevertheless, daily life during the war (at least until the situation suddenly became dramatic after the armistice) continued to include tea with friends, among them Villari and Pellizzi (who was also Adriano's godfather), as well as visits to church. Barnes also visited the Vatican often, and had contacts with powerful personalities there, to whom he wrote to ask for advice and, in case things went wrong, protection.

Pellizzi continued to be a regular and stimulating source of political discussion. He noticed the spread of Communism among Italian intellectuals – something that had in fact begun after the racial laws of 1938 among groups of university students, who had previously belonged to the Fascist University Groups.[63] The prospect of an American invasion of Italy prompted Pellizzi to suggest that even Communism might be a better option – for it was at least the expression of an Italian movement capable of challenging American occupation, evidence of a will to continue existence as an independent nation. This view at first disturbed Barnes, worried by the consequences of a possible Communist Italy for the Church. After all, Pellizzi had always seen the alliance with Germany as good only so long as Italy's primacy was respected, to the extent that he thought even defeat preferable to victory on German terms.[64] Although Barnes never cast doubts on his own Italianness, as Italy's military disasters continued and Germany became the only hope left, he increasingly inclined towards philo-Germanism.

Barnes's negative view of the Allies never changed throughout the war: when they bombed they were the 'Anglo-Assassins', and generally their image corresponded perfectly with Mussolini's anti-British propaganda of the late 1930s. The Allies went to war 'as into a speculative business', with 'no ideals but only economic interests'.[65] American cynicism was perfectly displayed with the violation of Italy by bombing.[66] However, a great many letters written by British and American soldiers who landed in Italy expressed surprise over the festive welcome they received from the Italians, who appeared eager to be 'liberated from war, from Fascism and from themselves'.[67] The Italian reaction was such that in the autumn of 1943 Radio Londra had to make it clear several times that the Allies had not 'landed in Italy because of love for the Italians', and that the latter were supposed to contribute to their own liberation and to make it faster by acting themselves.[68] At the time of the invasion, Barnes's loss of hope was replaced by religious feeling: 'We must have faith and pray. Communion this morning. Pray and be worthy of the prayers'; just like Catholics at the time of the invasions in the Middle Ages, he adds: 'Out with the barbarian!', as if praying could stop them.[69]

In Barnes's view, the climax of the criminal behaviour of the Allies was reached with the bombing of Rome on 19 July 1943. The case of Rome was a peculiar one, for it was the city of the Vatican, the Fascist city, the 'cradle of world civilisation' and centre of Western Christianity; there was a general idea that the enemy would not really dare to bomb Rome. This attitude is also confirmed in the outrage shown by Fascist newspapers after the city was bombed. It was, they argued, one of the most significant events of the Second World War.[70] As early as August 1940, a papal intervention to persuade Britain that Rome should not be bombed, 'in view of its sacred character', had been received by the Italian authorities with optimism.[71] However, for the Allies Rome was first of all the capital of a philo-Nazi state, and with the invasion it became an important communications centre and therefore a military target.[72] For Barnes the raids on the 'eternal city' remained the most evident example of the barbarism of the Allies. He nevertheless hoped that the bombing in July would finally bring Italians together again, to stand up to the enemy.[73]

With the war almost lost, at a meeting on 24 July 1943, the Fascist Grand Council voted in favour (with 19 votes out of 28) of the agenda proposed by Dino Grandi, which asked for the end of the dictatorship and a return to the monarchic Statute (the pre-Fascist Italian Constitution, created in Piedmont in 1848 and extended to the rest of Italy after unification).[74] The Duce was arrested and King Victor Emmanuel III appointed Marshal Pietro Badoglio as the new Prime Minister.[75] Mussolini's was a silent fall, imposed from above, but it was immediately welcomed from below: as the radio announced the news, the summer evening saw massive crowds in the streets and piazzas, cheering and shouting that the war and Fascism were over. Although the radio made clear that the war would continue, the population could not see any reason to go on fighting once the regime had fallen. There was a mass reaction against the symbols of the dictatorship: images and statues of Mussolini were taken down; images of the *fasci* on public buildings destroyed and streets renamed.

Mussolini's fall, anxieties about his personal fate and about the destiny of Italy, but most of all the scandal of the way the Italians had behaved on 26 July shocked Barnes, who confided his feelings to his diary, almost incredulous, disgusted and humiliated. Now convinced by Pellizzi's views, he admitted that 'a British or American occupation, even if it saved us from Bolshevism, would be even worse – because it would mean the corruption and the death of Italy'.[76] For a few weeks, although constantly worried by the fate that could have befallen Mussolini, he found hope in the House of Savoy, thinking that the Badoglio solution might unify the Italians once again. By September it became clear that nothing had divided them so deeply. At the end of July Barnes was aware that the continuation of the war and the Italians' will to fight were mostly propaganda, the same propaganda he sought to export to the British who listened to his radio programmes. And what about Mussolini? Barnes identified what he believed were erroneous foreign policy choices in 1939–40 as one of the reasons for Italy's crisis, and these he blamed mostly on the Foreign Secretary (and Mussolini's son-in-law), Galeazzo Ciano, rather than the real source, Mussolini. For Barnes, the Duce's greatness could never be denied whatever moments of weakness he may have shown.[77] Mussolini's name, he was sure, would be 'bracketed with Augustus', vindicated by history. Barnes's heart bled when he heard 'the cowards [sic] toadies throwing mud on him'. What Fascism needed in order to resuscitate itself, Barnes believed, was a 'greater saturation with the Catholic spirit'. Fascism had been betrayed by 'Italians calling themselves Fascists'. However hard it was for him, he had to admit that the Italians were 'an easily corruptible people', who proved to be unworthy of Fascism. Barnes soon began to doubt that Badoglio could persuade Italians to continue supporting the war effort; only one hope appeared to be left: 'pray God that Germany would prove strong enough'. The diary continues to move between these contradictions, from hope for a last-minute rescue by the Germans to the calls for a Catholicized Fascism, a 'Fascism based unequivocally on the encyclicals of the Popes', a 'March towards Rome'.[78]

The new March on Rome was needed precisely because the capital and its political elite had, in his view, become a typical nest of Italian opportunists, which eventually came to influence fundamental choices in foreign policy. In Barnes's view, Italy had not been ready for war before spring 1941, and should have tried to postpone entering the conflict until then, or, if that was not possible, at least until September 1940. But Italy's major weakness, from every point of view, was not having strengthened its bond with the Vatican. At this point of painful disillusion with the Italians, he recognized that 'just as Italians have generally failed as yet to develop a high civic sense, so they have failed to develop a really deep rooted faith'. Italy was full of fake Catholics 'who only go to Church to please their wives'. But how to march on Rome again, to accomplish a moral Fascist revolution, if the war was lost? Italians in the streets, Barnes saw everywhere, would have been ready to cut Mussolini's throat; from time to time he asked himself hopefully, 'will there be a miracle'?[79] Was a second Piave coming to vindicate the shame of July, just as it had come after Caporetto in the First World War?[80]

Barnes's painful frame of mind continued to move between disillusion with the Italians, hope that the Germans would rescue Italy and Europe, and fear for his family's destiny and for the fate of the country he continued to love even if it now appeared to be full of traitors and opportunists. Contradictory sentences run through his dairy in the months after July. On 18 August he wrote: 'yet I still love Italy and trust in her resurrection. My hope, however, is in Germany'; if Italy, helped by Germany, continued to fight and suffer, then she might 'redeem herself'. The rhetoric of the Italians resisting well against bomb attacks was now abandoned; it was evident that attacks were made to terrorise Italians, and Italians were not standing up to them: 'especially as the Italians have a congenital incapacity to organise'.[81]

Towards the end of August, fearing the worst also for his own personal safety, he decided to visit the German SS authorities in Rome to see if they might be a possible help in case of emergency. For the first time, he admitted in his diary that at that point he felt greater familiarity with the Germans than with the Italians, and when he suggested that he might be prepared to serve Hitler if Italy made a separate peace, the SS officer replied: 'Well, you see Nordic blood counts'. Torn between his sense of belonging to Italy and disappointment with what he saw as the Italians' lack of loyalty, he concluded with a prayer for the day: 'May my lack of confidence in the Italians' will and capacity to fight hard be betrayed by events'.[82]

In the Salò Republic

During the summer of 1943 secret bargaining between the Allies and Badoglio led to an armistice on 3 September (announced publicly five days later), and Germany became Italy's enemy.[83] Again, the popular reaction was a delighted but misplaced belief that the war would be over. The army collapsed and everyone who could escaped, starting with the King and Badoglio who abandoned Rome to German vengeance and sought refuge in Allied-liberated southern Italy. Soldiers left the field without orders in a large-scale repeat of Caporetto, pursuing what seemed the only sensible idea: to go home. It was difficult to cross Italy and escape from the Germans; some 600,000 Italian soldiers were deported to German internment camps. Women took on a major role in defending, feeding and helping Italian and Allied soldiers, demonstrating that civil society continued to function and a country named Italy continued to exist despite the absence of a state to give out orders. But which Italy? Fascist Italy had died and the army and the state had collapsed. Some have claimed that 8 September represented the 'death of the fatherland'.[84] This was certainly the way that Fascists felt,

Barnes included: one of them, the young Carlo Mazzantini, expressed these feelings in his wartime memoir *A cercar la bella morte* ('Looking for the beautiful death'): 'There was no more Italy; there was no more government, no more army ... Italy had become nothing more than a territory with a population occupied by a foreign army'.[85]

Just one day before the armistice was announced, the day of his birthday, Barnes received the 'finest birthday present' he had ever had, his long awaited Italian citizenship. A passionate love for Italy was reawakened by the event.[86] Italy's strength was that she was a 'land of extremes'. If the majority was corrupt, the virtuous minority was made up of saints, heroes and geniuses – a 'land of saints and sinners and therefore of hope. Only the individuals and communities who are neither good nor bad have no future – like the Swiss, the Swedes and the mass of English'. On the very eve of 8 September 1943, he concluded his diary with the question: 'civil war is certainly in the air. And where is Mussolini?'[87]

The following night, as events unfolded and the formal documents for citizenship were not yet ready, he began packing against the sound of gunfire. Even though his papers were still not available, he received some money from the Italian Foreign Office, and the Vatican arranged for him and his family to escape to a convent. On 11 September they resolved to go to the German embassy. They were told they could not come in, but Barnes explained his personal situation and was allowed to enter after he had proclaimed that he wanted to continue the fight and told them that he was 'the Italian Lord Haw Haw'. He thought that the Germans had the situation in hand, but they were occupying a land where Italians, all cowards and traitors, were ready to welcome the Allies and even to blame the bombs on the Germans.[88] The worst traitors were Badoglio, the King and other military and naval chiefs. And where was Mussolini? 'Nobody knows the fate of Mussolini. My heart bleeds for him ... will he be rescued?'[89]

Thanks to the Vatican, Barnes and his family obtained fake passports to go to Switzerland, but they chose nevertheless to remain in Italy with the onset of the civil war.[90] Barnes and his wife had met Pius XII in the spring to ask for his protection; the Pope put them under the custody of Cardinal Giovanni Battista Montini, who was entrusted with providing escape and safety for the Barnes family in case the Allies entered Rome. However, as there seemed to be no immediate danger, Barnes decided to stay and to follow Mussolini, who was indeed rescued by the Germans on 12 September from his prison in the Gran Sasso mountain in the southern Italian region of Abruzzo. He agreed with Hitler to establish a Fascist Republic in central and northern Italy. The Republic's ministries spread out between different cities in northern Italy, but the capital was at Salò on Lake Garda, headquarters of the Ministry of Popular Culture. Barnes's motives for joining the Republic reflect those of many other Fascists, infuriated with the King and Badoglio, humiliated by the Italian surrender, refusing to believe that the Fascist experiment, in which many of them had been brought up, had failed. Echoes of this argument can be found in the more recent revisionist version of the Republic's history, particularly in the work of Renzo De Felice, who justified Mussolini's protracted cooperation with the Germans in 1943–5 on the grounds that the dictator, by continuing the fight at the side of Germany and complying with the worst aspects of the German occupation, including collaboration in the Holocaust, did so in order to save Italy from German vengeance.[91] Barnes indeed argued that all those Italians who followed Mussolini had rescued Italy from Hitler's fury; furthermore, he explained his participation in the civil war of 1943–5 as an act of personal loyalty toward the Duce, a way of dissociating himself from the 'betrayal' of many Italians.

Escaping from Rome on 21 September 1943, Barnes and his family moved to the north, via Florence and Ravenna, reaching Venice on 7 October. The journey by train was difficult because of the effects of Allied bombing in central Italy as far north as Bologna.[92] In Venice they felt a 'glorious relief' when they sat on a gondola which took them to the Canaletto hotel; they had an aperitif at the historic bar Florian in Piazza San Marco; the days that followed brought various practical difficulties, but never prevented them from enjoying the city. However, orders and counter-orders made life unstable, until it became clear that the Ministry of Popular Culture, for which Barnes continued to work, was going to be established on Lake Garda – good news, Barnes recorded, because of the milder winter climate there. Excited by the opportunity of being close to the new government, on 21 October Barnes joined the Fascist Republican Party and three days later moved from Venice to Salò. Although they settled there, from April 1944 Barnes worked in Milan broadcasting programmes to the British troops in Italy, while Adriano studied in a college at Riva at the northern end of Lake Garda.

Despite Barnes's regular remarks on the defects of the Italians (easily bribed, disorganized, unfaithful, without a sense of civic responsibility, morally shameless, and too weak to control their women's will), the diary continued to express his love for Italian landscapes and towns in the new part of Italy in which he now found himself, as well as his enthusiasm for Fascism, prompted by the prospect of re-establishing links with Mussolini and men like Marshal Rodolfo Graziani and Alessandro Pavolini, who were among the founders of the Republic.[93] Sometimes his passion for Italy resembles the love for a woman who has broken his heart ('better to have loved and lost, than never to have loved at all'); despite everything, he could not stop believing that Italy still was, spiritually, the essence of European civilization.[94]

The Barnes' first months at Lake Garda were often pleasant enough; they were given comfortable accommodation and enjoyed discovering the landscape and a few trips by bicycle to the nearest city, Brescia. As the military events continued to favour the Allies, however, the correspondence between James and Buona became increasingly anxious, particularly in the case of Buena (who wrote to him from Salò to Milan on the headed notepaper of the Minister of Popular Culture). She worried about the military situation and about their personal position, particularly the fear of having to cope without money and the problem of Adriano's poor performance at school, made worse by the difficulty of sending him packages across the lake to Riva where boats were commandeered by the Germans to carry wounded soldiers or simply lacked sufficient fuel. From the liberation (Barnes called it the 'fall') of Rome on 4 June 1944, Barnes lost any remaining faith in a possible recovery of the morale of the Italians and began to sense the coming of the end. If the war was lost without any resistance to the Allies from the population, Italy would be despised by the rest of the world as it had been before its unification in the nineteenth century; Italy, he wrote in June 1944, 'would cease practically to exist'.[95]

During the 20-month period of the Salò Republic Barnes was again employed as the 'Italian Lord Haw Haw'. Until the end, he continued to broadcast programmes destined for American and British radio listeners. The content of his speeches had to be approved by Mussolini and the German authorities, no longer just by the Ministry of Popular Culture. For Barnes, the experience of the civil war was an adventurous one, particularly when he fled Rome with his family, but also one which would allow him to bring forward, though well aware of the desperate military conditions, his plans for a Catholicized Fascism. Clerical-Fascism was indeed resumed during the Republic, particularly by a Fascist priest, Don Tullio Calcagno, who published the newspaper *Crociata Italica*, to which Barnes contributed. The newspaper expressed the views of Italian Catholics who supported the Salò Republic both spiritually and ideologically; their choice was determined by their belief in the religious policies of Fascism and their instinctive indignation against the betrayal of their ideals on 25 July and on 8 September. Some of the journalists of *Crociata Italica*, mainly priests, were already well known for their articles in the intransigent Fascist newspaper *Il Regime Fascista*, founded in Cremona in 1926 by the Fascist leader Roberto Farinacci (head of the Fascist Party in 1925–6) and which was now more clearly pro-German and anti-Semitic. After the fall of Mussolini, Farinacci had appeared to many, Barnes included, as a possible new leader of what remained of Italian Fascism; indeed, in July 1943 Farinacci was the only important Fascist leader in German-occupied territory, and he presented himself to the Germans as the man who could rebuild Fascism (although, as Goebbels explained in his diary, his lack of solidarity towards Mussolini lost him Hitler's support).[96] Don Calcagno, like Farinacci, lived in the small northern city of Cremona in the Po Valley. He too was an anti-Semite, and anti-Semitism was one of the features of *Crociata Italica*. Farinacci's anti-Semitism, like a great part of Fascist anti-Semitism, shared much of the Catholic rhetoric of anti-Judaism.[97] Indeed, from 1931 onwards the publishing house Cremona Nuova produced, together with Farinacci's daily *Il Regime Fascista*, the anti-Semitic periodical *La Vita Italiana*, founded by the main voice of Italian anti-Semitism, Giovanni Preziosi. Fascist anti-Semitism thus pre-dated the promulgation of the racial laws in 1938, although it was at that point that fundamental changes in the life of the Italian Jewish population took place. The racial laws established that foreign Jews must be deported; they forbade marriages between Aryans and Jews; they decreed that Jews could no longer hold public office; and they outlined strict limits on the Jews' right of property.[98] While between 1938 and 1943 anti-Semitism took the form of an attack on the civil rights, during the Salò Republic it extended to deportation to German extermination camps and death on a mass scale.[99]

Like most British right-wing conservatives and British Fascists, Barnes was also anti-Semitic. Throughout the diary, and particularly in the last months, the Jews are seen as responsible for the war, for the betrayal of Fascism, and for the corruption of British and European society, while the Allies are described as instruments of the Jews. Barnes's anti-Semitism, like that of Farinacci, preceded his philo-Germanism; only briefly after the armistice, and later in the weeks before the final defeat, did Barnes express real admiration for the Germans. However, unlike Barnes, Farinacci was not a Catholic, and from at least 1939 onwards he had been accusing the Catholic Church of anti-Fascism.[100] Crociata Italica also attacked the Church's hierarchies and their timid wait-and-see policy during the years of the civil war. The newspaper became increasingly schismatic and abandoned the attempts of Republican ministers like Fernando Mezzasoma (with whom Barnes was in close contact as he was Minister Of Popular Culture) who sought, unsuccessfully, to draw together Catholic orthodoxy and what historians have called 'intransigent' Fascism.[101] The newspaper's attacks on the Vatican forced Mussolini to keep a deliberate distance from it – he supported Don Calcagno's project, but could not go so far as to endorse it officially, for fear of coming into conflict with the Church – and he encouraged Barnes to stop collaborating with it. Barnes did, though not in spring 1944 as he later claimed in his recollections,[102] but only the following autumn. A signed article (with his signature Italianized, as he often chose to do, as 'Giacomo Barnes') can still be found in the newspaper on 2 October 1944.[103]

According to his own recollections, Barnes spoke to Mussolini for the last time on 9 April 1945. He might well have been with him until the violent end at Dongo (the village in the Como province where on 27 April the partisans caught Mussolini while he was trying to escape to Switzerland), but until the 24th he was working in Milan with Mezzasoma to broadcast conferences on 'peace with justice', and returned to Salò the same day. Barnes was therefore in Salò and not in Milan on 25 April when Mussolini began his journey towards the north with a few Fascist leaders and his mistress Claretta Petacci. In the weeks that followed, described by Barnes as a time of 'terror', he and his family remained hidden in Meran in South Tyrol; then they split up, James moving to Bergamo while Buona stayed in Meran with Adriano. He had to remain hidden, hosted in Catholic convents between Bergamo, Florence, Rome and Sicily, in order not to be caught, tried and hanged by the British. He still did not have official Italian citizenship (which could have been granted only if he had been able to take a particular oath within six months following the first approval of his application in September 1943) and he therefore remained a traitor to his country. After the war Barnes had to reopen the case by applying for Italian citizenship once again, but the whole process was delayed by the lengthy time it took for the British authorities to acknowledge his loss of British citizenship; the Italian authorities thought that this was due to British hostility towards Barnes for his anti-patriotic propaganda during the conflict.[104]

At the end of the war, the correspondence between James and Buona did not mention either politics or ideology, but remained very practical. They professed to miss each other and hoped to meet again soon; a number of friends managed to see them from time to time. They discussed money issues and the names of priests to contact in order to receive help. Although Buona was always worried by lack of money, it seems clear from their letters that even during the war they had continued to have servants, to travel first class or by taxi; and even when Buona was looked after by nuns in November 1945, where she complained about having lost everything, a cousin sent her money through the mediation of nuns from Rome. One of the nuns wrote to her, in response to her constant complaints: 'I know that you have suffered much, but many others have suffered a lot more, and still do not appear so demoralized. They have lost everything, and they do not know how to start again, they have not seen their dear ones for years, if they are not dead'; on the contrary, continued the nun, Buona had lost only part of her fortune, and still had her family.[105]

From the fall of Mussolini onwards, Barnes continued to be tormented by his attempt to find out 'who betrayed' Fascism, becoming convinced that there had been a conspiracy ever since the time of the alliance with Germany. Despite his admiration for Grandi (particularly for his anti-British stance in London at the time of the Ethiopian war), he finally persuaded himself that his disapproval of the Axis had led Grandi to organize a plot against Mussolini, together with Badoglio and the King. Up to this point Barnes's ideas seem to coincide with those of Farinacci's supporters of intransigent Fascism. However, it would not be appropriate to call Barnes a *Farinacciano*. It is true that he praised the Cremonese leader several times in the diary, and in January 1944 he appears to have shared Farinacci's criticism of Mussolini's Fascism. Farinacci was right, he thought at that point, when he claimed that Mussolini's main mistake had been 'his attempt to make a revolution without bloodshed', compromising with the moderate establishment 'instead of sweeping the whole opposition away'.[106] However, Barnes's Catholicism could never bring him too close to a man who had begun his political career as an anti-clerical during the First

World War and had compromised with the Church only for opportunistic reasons during the regime. Moreover, Barnes's occasional critical remarks directed at Mussolini could never diminish his admiration towards, love for, and loyalty to the Duce. The Duce, he repeated until the last months of the diary, was good and wise, comparable with a saint. The coming of the end brought Barnes nearer to him. He portrayed their final meetings in minutely detailed descriptions of Mussolini's words and gestures, with that infatuation for the Duce's body which never died in Barnes. Consciously differentiating himself from the majority of Italians, Barnes continued to insist on the concepts of honour and loyalty, central to the memorialization of those who fought for the Salò Republic.[107] On 10 April 1945 he proudly recorded that he had obtained confirmation from Mussolini himself that, if they all had to move from Salò, Barnes and his family would be allowed to follow him.

At the beginning of May, as refugees in Meran, he and his family heard about the death of the Duce, of Petacci and of the other Fascist leaders, executed on 28 April by the partisans who caught them at Dongo and who hanged their corpses in a central square of Milan, Piazzale Loreto – the same square where in August 1944 the Fascists had murdered 15 partisans and exposed their bodies. The macabre scene of 28 April 1945 represented the last act of a ferocious civil war, but also the difficult beginning of a new democratic Italy.[108] Mussolini was once more the prime actor – no longer addressing the crowds and hailed by the masses, but this time dead and hanging upside down, with the masses shouting insults at him. Barnes's family prayed for him; Barnes believed the Duce had now become 'almost a saint', whose ideas would live on and triumph after his death, and who would be avenged by history. The drama in the Piazzale Loreto, he wrote in Italianized English, was 'the greatest crime since the Crucifiction [sic]'.[109]

This final comparison between Christ's crucifixion and Mussolini's hanging, the cathartic event that brought Barnes's diary to an end, should be contextualized in the light of Barnes's perception of the two men. When he 'described' Jesus in *Life Made Whole*, in a physical and homoerotic way, he was suggesting the corporeal and moral model which he found incarnated in Mussolini's body, and which had been used to construct the cult of the Duce during the regime. Jesus, he argued, 'was no pacifist'; he was 'no sentimentalist'; every one of his words was 'the word of an uncompromising leader of men'; 'he stated facts and issued commands'. In 'the real Christ' there was 'no trace of effeminacy': he was 'a tremendous He-man', with an athletic body, 'tireless in energy and ever maintained in proper fitness'. It is easy to recognize Fascist descriptions of Mussolini in this portrait, particularly as Barnes suggested that every great man could be, 'in the measure of his greatness, a pattern of the Christ'.[110]

After the war

The British authorities in Italy made efforts to find out where Barnes was hiding. In fact, as soon as Italy entered the war in June 1940, the British government asked the Ambassador to Rome, Sir Percy Loraine, to control Barnes, in case he decided to return to Britain.[111] However, dangerous times for Barnes only came with the arrival of the Allies, and particularly with the liberation of Italy. His complex dual role as a British subject living in Italy and as an enemy of his own country made him suspect not only to the British, but also to the Italians. During the last two years of war, rumours spread (and reached the Allies) that Barnes was in fact a British spy who pretended to be pro-Italian. In August 1945 news came to the Allied authorities through the Rome police that immediately after the arrival of the British and Americans in Rome in 1944, Barnes had been employed by the Allied Psychological Warfare Branch. A possible origin of this rumour was a protest by British civilians resident in Rome, who had written to Allied headquarters in July 1944 to express their indignation at the alleged employment of Barnes by Allied forces, and had described him as 'a principal Quisling and anti-Allied broadcaster'.[112] The Allies did not appear to take the complaint seriously, and concluded: 'they believe him to be employed by Welfare', and at the time never confirmed the rumour.[113] However, in November of the same year, the Allied authorities in Rome and the Rome police did carry out an enquiry, coming to the conclusion that no evidence existed that Barnes ever carried out activities in favour of British Intelligence: the police files on Barnes were, according to the report, 'sufficiently damning to need safeguarding ... They prove that Barnes was an Englishmen [sic] anti-English and carrying on propaganda against his own country'.[114]

Barnes's position was particularly complicated when he lived in northern Italy during the Salò Republic, because the political atmosphere of the civil war increased the number of rumours on both sides about the existence of spies. The fact that he was British, taken together with his close relationship with the Church authorities, raised suspicions about his real role. Archival documents prove that Barnes was in northern Italy, employed by the Ministry of Popular Culture between October 1943 and the end of the war, except for two weeks in November 1943, when he was driven to Florence and Rome by Pavolini's private secretary to pick up some boxes left there in September. It is unlikely that he could have easily moved between Rome and Salò to work as a spy at a time when that half of Italy was occupied by the Germans and bombed by the Allies. As both Italian and Allied documents suggest, there could have been a mistake in Rome due to a confusion of names, which generated the idea that Barnes had been employed there; in fact, it was probably someone else, with the same or a similar name.[115]

After the war, the British continued to look for Barnes with the intention of charging him with collaboration. In February 1946 he was believed to be hidden in the Vatican at College Beda, which was therefore put under observation.[116] In September of the same year, the British interrogated Buona, who pretended not to know where her husband was. Because she was married to an Englishman, she was formally a British subject; but there was no evidence of her activities against the British government during the war and she was released.[117] The search for Barnes continued until 1947, when he was deemed to be either hiding in the Vatican, or, in July of that year, to have escaped to Austria 'with an Italian passport and under one of his assumed names'.[118] In fact, between September 1946 and August 1947, Barnes and his son were accommodated in a convent in Sicily.[119] In September 1947 the Peace Treaty came into force, and the British began to leave Italy. According to a treaty signed between Britain and Italy in June 1947, within the 90-day period in which the British forces had to withdraw, the British could continue to bring to trial anyone who had committed a crime before the Peace Treaty. Barnes remained sheltered in convents in Lazio and in Piedmont until September 1949, when he returned to live in Rome. By then, the British, now allied with Italy in the new geo-political context of the Cold War (and more worried by the growth of Italian Communism than by the extreme right) had lost interest in him. In the years that followed, he took on a job with an oil company and mingled with neo-Fascists.[120] In 1953, two years before his death, he officially became an Italian citizen. His grave in the Verano cemetery in Rome carries his Italian name, Giacomo Barnes.

Barnes's peculiar position in the history of Italian Fascism has meant that there has been little historiographical interest in him. Nevertheless, his role as a propagandist during the Salò Republic was not a minor one: his work was highly regarded by the Ministry of Popular Culture, and he was, even more than he had been under the pre-1943 regime, in close contact with the Fascist hierarchy. Among British Fascist sympathizers and Italophiles, he was the only one to reject his own nationality in order to be Italian and the only one to play the kind of role William Joyce had played in Germany. However, he has remained largely forgotten. Many Fascists regarded him with suspicion because he always appeared a Catholic first. For the Catholic Church in the post-war period, he was one of the many embarrassing examples of the way in which the Vatican protected Fascists and Nazis both during and after the end of the war.

A recent attempt to honour his memory has occurred with the online edition in 2006, by a neo-Fascist publishing house, of a pamphlet Barnes wrote in 1944, first published in Venice by the Ministry of Popular Culture. The pamphlet was on the issue of social justice through monetary reform, a subject that fitted in well with the propaganda on the so-called socialization of the Republic, which aimed to attract workers by suggesting the idea of a third way between the enemy capitalist plutocracies and Soviet Communism. The fact that no socialization of the means of production, involving both capitalists and workers, was ever put into practice did not prevent many Fascists from believing in it, nor did it prevent the drafting of a *Carta della socializzazione*, which listed the norms of the supposedly new economic system within the Manifesto of Verona of November 1943 (the official act of constitution of the Salò Republic). The term Italian Social Republic, the formal title of the Salò Republic, originated from the same idea of socialization of the means of production within an economic corporativist order. One of the architects of the *Carta* was Manlio Sargenti, Undersecretary of the Ministry of Economy of the Republic and later one of the first members of the neo-Fascist Italian Social Movement (MSI), although he left the party in the 1950s because it had become, in his view, too liberal. Barnes's interest in the idea of socialization, at times mentioned in the diary but never discussed, appears in this pamphlet, which is also further testimony to his anti-Semitism:

> The war against the American, British and Jewish plutocracies, which form a single block that intends to subject Europe – at least economically –, has its own revolutionary aspect. In other words, it is not enough to save the economic independence of Europe; it is also necessary to trash within Europe itself the financial, monetary and banking system run by the British and the Jews, because until it lasts ... it will render impossible the creation of a true system of social justice.[121]

To Fascists of the next generation, Barnes became, together with his friend Ezra Pound, a representative of that 'Fascism of the origins' which some Fascists had hoped to revive at the time of Salò; for them his example is still relevant today: 'for all those have not yet surrendered to the perverted logic of the dominant economy'.[122]

Although the extreme right never developed a historiography of any interest, it produced a culture that aimed at legitimating its subversive activity within Republican Italy. Only by this neo-Fascist right could Barnes be acknowledged and remembered. Like others who left testimonies of their journey through the Salò Republic, he was instrumental in the construction of an alternative memory to that of the Resistance; one which exalted the opposition between a heroic image of the Salò martyrs and the Italy of the grey zone, of Badoglio, of the 'barbarians' who, they believed, sold their country to capitalism in exchange for cigarettes and chewing gum. To these nostalgic militants, even the MSI was a corrupted party: the right had to be, in their view, an autonomous political area, 'exiled within the fatherland',[123] and completely alien to democracy.[124]

Diary 1943

1 January 1943 – 1. The military situation, as I see it

This is likely to be the crucial year of the war. I see no end to it this year. But it looks [*illegible*] as though one side or the other will be in a winning position by the end of it.

The military plans of the Allies seem clear enough as Europe is concerned, though of course there may be surprises. At present the Allies have the initiative; and their first principal objective is to open up the Mediterranean for the relatively safe passage of convoys.

The lack of shipping is severely hampering their initiative. During 1943 the submarine menace is likely to increase. The gap between the rate of [*illegible*] and the sinking of ships is likely to widen. A really critical situation threatens to develop for the Allies [*illegible*] unless it can be remedied this year; and the most evident way of remedying it is the opening up of the Mediterranean. If this could be done, literally millions of tons of shipping, which have now to go round the Cape for the supply of Egypt, Iran, Russia through Iran, Irak, Syria, Palestine, India [and] Ceylon – not to speak of [Australia] – could be [economized], and transit made more rapid. It is not only a question of supplying the armies stationed in these countries, it is also a question of supplying the civil populations. Famine conditions prevail in many places. This makes the Allies unpopular wherever they go. It makes for unrest; and the unrest reacts unfavourably on the military operations. The [economising] of shipping, which the opening up of the Mediterranean would bring about, would also enable [*illegible*] materials to be acquired more rapidly and in greater quantities by the centres of industry in Britain and the United States. The food situation in Britain is none too good. The shipping there of greater quantities of foodstuffs is an urgent matter. More shipping is also required to ensure adequate supplies for North West Africa.

We may expect therefore a great effort on the part of the Allies to clear us out of Tunisia. So long as we hold Biserta and Tunis and Cape Bon, together with a certain, if limited hinterland, the Sicily channel must remain a death trap to both merchant ships and warships attempting to pass. [*illegible*] also important to us. [*Illegible*] is negligible.

The allies hoped to accomplish this first objective by the New Year. They have failed to do so. But they have still time to do so before it is too late.

I expect they will launch their big offensive in March – or at the latest in April. This will be a very critical time for us. Unless we can hold on, the war may be lost. If we can succeed in holding on throughout this year, we should on the other hand, be able to reach a winning position ourselves.

If the Anglo-Saxons get through in April, or even as late as September, the situation would become exceedingly dangerous.

I doubt if the plan is to invade the mainland of Italy, though doubtless there would be attempted the invasion of Sardinia and Sicily and Corsica (Perhaps also Puglia). Overwhelming bombing raids would also certainly be developed against us, especially with a view to [illegible] our air activity in the channel of Sicily, Lampedusa, Pantelleria, Sicily, Southern Sardinia and southern Italy would get it hot and thick. Amphibious action, backed by a preponderant fleet, would also be progressing developed [illegible] the Greek islands. But I am convinced that the Allied invasion of Europe is, at present planned to place through <u>Turkey</u>. It is moreover [illegible], I believe that since the Mediterranean is opened Turkey would land herself under pressure to [smash] our enterprise; If this invasion could be initiated before or even during the coming German summer offensive against Russia, the fat would be in the fire. Over a million men, well backed by all the [murderous] longing of war, would be concentrated within a relatively short time in European Turkey. Bulgaria's attitude would in such circumstances become equivocal, because of the widespread communist & [illegible]. An invasion of Bulgaria could be undertaken, and soon all the Balkans would be aflame. The Germans would need to detach vast numbers of troops and aeroplanes from the Russian front to withstand the shock. Russia as a military power would consequently survive the summer and be in a position to undertake a fresh devastating winter offensive.

The aim of the Allies would be to reach the Adriatic coast and [cut] out both Greece and Albania, rouse Serbia and the [illegible] Croats, strike terror into Roumania, bomb the oil fields, progressing [illegible] with Dalmatia + Roumania itself and establish a front along the Danube as far as Belgrade and along the borders of Transylvania.[1]

It is not to be [illegible] that all this <u>might</u> be accomplished within the next 12 or 15 months; and then our position would become more and more desperate. We should fall with honour; but we should fall; and although Germany could hold out longer, I think her fate in such circumstances would be sealed.

This is probably the actual Allied plan and its present [illegible] mainly depends on our holding the Tunisian ports.

There is as yet no indication that Russia will succeed by her present offensive in paralysing the [illegible] German offensive due to start as soon as the winter is over. I do not think that Russia will meanwhile secure either Charkov or the major port of the Donatz basin. She probably will skupper the Germans in Stalingrad.[2] But I am confident she will not rout the Germans; and, unless she can be aided the invasion or at least by a very serious threat of invasicn of Europe in the manner suggested, her colossal losses during this winter, should greatly facilitate the German [*illegible*] summer.

Since the menace of invasion is likely to come through Turkey, the situation needs to be watched with the greatest care. If the General Staff at any time comes to the conclusion that the chances of our holding out in Tunisia are slight, probably the only way to prevent the situation getting out of hand would be to anticipate the British move into Turkey and [*illegible*] Turkey [*illegible*] combining this invasion with a spring offensive from [*illegible*] in a drive to the Caspian Sea and the River Volga. We might then still save the situation, though it would remain very problematical whether we should be able to do so.

On the other hand, if the Anglo-Saxons were held in Tunisia, there is an excellent chance of Russia being <u>laid low</u> during the summer. By this I mean <u>paralyzed</u> and unable to develop another winter offensive. Then the Germans could turn their attention to Africa and the Middle East with all their resources. We should have the [*illegible*] of operating on interior lines and the submarine campaign would make things more & more difficult for the Allies to withstand the initiative which would be once more entirely in our hands.

The war cannot be won, however, until Europe is freed from the pressure of the barbarians – and by Europe I mean a good deal more than political Europe. The real boundaries of Europe are the Sahara Desert right across Africa from [Rio] del Oro to the Egyptian-Sudanese frontier. The whole Arabian peninsula is really also part of Europe. We have therefore not only got to lay Russia low, but oust the Anglo-Saxons from the whole of North Africa, from Egypt, Palestine, Syria and Irak, and this means ousting them from the greater part of Persia.

We must have the Caucasian, the Irak the Anglo-Persian oil fields in our hands. Then England is beaten; and America even if she thinks – in her present mind – of fighting, if necessary, a 30 years war, would soon learn that such a war would not be worth the candle.

If we are going to win, the decisive battle of the war [*illegible*] will be fought at the foot of the Pyramids.

The situation in the Far East appears to be good. Japan has almost if not quite completed the essential task of consolidating, fortifying and organising her [*illegible*] of last winter. It looks as if she was about to resume the initiative. The Americans and the Australians have accomplished very little (and that at great cost in warships) since they started their offensive in august in the Solomon Islands and New Guinea.[3] The Japanese should now be able to retaliate effectively.

The declaration of war by Nationalist China on Britain and the United States is important in that it means that both Wang and Tojo believe that the time has come to liquidate Chiang Kai Check.[4] It also means that Nanking is sure of itself; and no doubt in due course the great potentialities of Nationalist China will be developed as a tremendous war reserve. I am inclined to prophesy that this year will see Chiang Kai Check laid low. But I doubt if Japan will be able to do much against the British in India until the [fall] of the year. If things go well with us, Japanese action against India should then put the kybosh on the British.[5]

1 January 1943 – 2. The internal situation in Italy

The British are completely mistaken in their obstinate belief that Italian public opinion is dead against the war and in fact defeatist though there are some ugly symptoms about on account of our African defeat.[6] No war is popular unless it is victorious. The British should also have learnt by now that the fighting qualities of the Italian soldier, sailor and airman are second to none. I should even go so far as to say that they are the best individual fighters of the lot. We have few scientific generals, however; and the technical training of the army officers is deficient. Nor have we the resources to equip our army with the necessary quantity of modern armaments. That is our great handicap.[7]

The Italian people cannot easily be induced to hate their enemies. They understand fully, however, that the war is their fifth war of national independence,[8] that victory will give them a vital space sufficient to provide the economic uplift which is needed to potentialise[9] their great national talents and vital energies, and that defeat means servitude, the end of all the promise of a new cultural renaissance as well as stagnation and poverty for all but a favoured few.

If defeat comes to stare them in the face, they will wish to fight doggedly to the end. If the Anglo-Saxons continue their bombing with intent to terrorism, the Italians will give way to hatred, which will last generations.

I have no fear that they will not stand up to even the worst bombardments. The Neapolitans have taken things very calmly and cheerfully up to now. Italians may be highly strung, but their nervous system is magnificent. Freud could have never been an Italian. Because the Italians never hesitate to let off steam, they suffer from no complexes. Of all peoples they are the least subject to neurosis. They grumble, they criticise, they are exasperatingly temperamental; but they are astonishingly patient and resilient. Behind a soft exterior, they possess the toughest core. If the British count on an Italian collapse, they will be disappointed – as they have been disappointed before.

There is strong amount of discontent, however, in Italy today with the Fascist Party. This is quite a different thing to saying that the majority of the people are anti-fascist. On the contrary, Italians are fascist in overwhelming majority. But they want a complete renovation of the party members. They want the whole [*illegible*] to be given the chance of becoming members of the party, except for a small black list. They are sick of the various camorras which unfortunately exist and which are unfortunately still characteristic of Italian life. They are against the existence of a privileged minority. There has been a good deal of corruption in the Party too; and the people are not satisfied that the various purges that have taken place have done more than skim the problem. There has been also considerable profiteering and scandalous hoarding by the well-to-do. The bureaucracy has become heavy, slow and uselessly expanded. Above all else perhaps the people are determined, sooner or later, to see to it that the organs of government and the vocational organisations are simplified and organised as they should be. When the war is over, there will be a second March on Rome, unless sweeping changes are made in the government itself.[10] Probably the Duce realises this as well as anyone and will take the necessary action at this right moment. If he fails to do so, he will lose his popularity and position of authority. But whatever happens, far from ending fascism, fascism will be strengthened, because the ranks will be purified and its doctrines applied to better purpose. Besides, the modern world has no choice except between some form of Fascism and some form of Communism; and Communism has no standing here at all. At present there are as many good fascists outside the party as there are in it and as many bad fascists in it as outside it. That won't do. But the chief remedies can only come when the war is over, provided we win it.

The persistent idea current for years in the so called democracies (better described as plutocracies) that fascism is not a popular form of government, that criticism and dissention are suppressed and permanently discouraged is completely at variance with the facts. Fascism rests on popular consent; and it is patently ridiculous to imagine that it is possible to stop criticism and discussion in Italy. The expression of individual personality is the essence of the Italian character, for Italians are all, in a sense, artists. This is recognized by the regime and it is in fact a postulate of fascism to enhance personality.

When Italy came to be united, Cavour pronounced his famous dictum: 'We have made Italy. Now it is necessary to make Italians'.[11] Fascism has completed the making of Italians. The national consciousness is now universal and radicated.[12] But we have not yet acquired a responsible civic sense. To cheat the Government and public utility companies is not regarded as a shameful thing; and this makes it very difficult to set up efficient organisation of the country's collective life. People recognise and demand this reorganisation as necessary to modern condition of life, but, individually, they do little to help it and make worth it. This lack of civil sense weakens our war effort. People are ready enough to die for their country, but few are ready to sacrifice their individual advantage. Italians are also a jealous lot. They have little sense of fair play towards their rivals.

Finally it must not be forgotten that Italy has been suffering from growing pains. Popular education and increased economic opportunities are forcing quantities of people up from the bottom to the top. This means the uprooting of quantities of people from their natural soil, so that they lose their traditional <u>style</u> and have not yet had time to acquire a new one suitable to the new position they occupy.

Rome, which is undergoing a monstrous growth, is full of such people – semi educated upstarts from all over Italy in all ranks, ill-mannered, greedy, frightened of falling back when they came. Very disreputable people.

But they are not defeatists. The defeatists are a small but exasperating minority composed of snobs and the language of snobs and there are some unscrupulous [illegible] who believe that an Allied victory will give them the opportunity to grow rich ([illegible] at the expense of their neighbours). The Anglo-Saxons can also count on the friendship of the freemasons, who are still hidden among us, and this is the big danger, on the Jews (taken as a whole) and on those who regret the [illegible] days when they were all to profit in the service of international finance. They can also count on a residue of sceptics, positivists, agnostics, and anti-clericals. But all these people belong to a world in decline, a world already dead – the world of 19th century Liberalism, which can never be resuscitated.[13]

The war is not popular in one sense. The Italians are too civilized and too universally minded to regard it otherwise than as a grim necessity. It is not an adventure, this war and we did not will it. It is a fight for freedom and for the survival of European civilisation. The Jews are the aggressors and the Anglo-Saxons want to keep their hegemony. The crises as far as we are concerned, begin and end there. We have no choice but to face them with all our courage, fight and hope. But with enthusiasm? No. Matters involving life or death are not faced with enthusiasm but with anxiety.

3. <u>My personal situation</u>

The fortunes of myself, my wife and only child are bound up with victory or defeat.

Our actual situation is not unfortunate. We are united. We have sufficient for our needs. We enjoy good health. We have many friends. We are spared the anxieties which so many others had to endure – for I am over military age and my son is below it.

Our only anxiety is the possibility of defeat. Goodness knows what would happen to us then.

During the war I have constantly improved my financial situation. I earn rather more than 5000 lire a month at the Ministero della Cultura Popolare.[14] The work is agreeable and not heavy. I have 3 broadcasts a week (two registered,[15] one direct to the microphone) and I compose 2 news commentaries a week, which are generally read by either Principe Tasca di Cutò or by prof. Morelli (Ranieri di S. Faustino is unfortunately ill).[16]

My pay is for what I do and therefore ceases if I go away. It is sufficient, however, for my purposes even if I absent myself for 2–3months in the year – always counting also the interest on my government securities, of which I possess 650.000 of 5%. Buona in her name, has a small apartment in Rome which is let and brings in 700 Lire net a month – enough to give her a dress allowance. She has also 25.000 treasury bonds and a fair share in a linen cotton yarns factory (all [that she] ever got in the way of a dote[17]).

Well, that is all very well if we win the war. There may be a measure of inflation in that event, but it need not be serious if we take the right course, and it should not be serious in any case always provided we win. But if we lose the war, government securities will have little value: and it would be silly to refuse to look the possibility of defeat in the face. I have faith in the causes that we have at stake and therefore my faith in victory remains. But I have not got that English mentality which does the ostrich. Therefore I must take thought for the moment and take precautions against all eventualities.

Defeat would also place me in a very awkward situation. I am still a British citizen. I had promised my father not to ask for Italian citizenship until after his death. He died in February 1940 and I immediately saw the Duce. I omitted however to make any formal demand for Italian citizenship until after the outbreak of war between Great Britain and Italy, partly because I did not see any reason to hurry, partly because I contemplated the possibility of a visit to England to settle up my inheritance. Anyhow, as things turned out, there was cause for hurry; for [illegible] unfortunately collapsed and immediately after Italy's entry into the war, a law was passed which held up all applications for Italian citizenship by enemy subjects. Consequently, things are at standstill.

True, I have not been treated as an enemy subject. But technically I remain one. My money was at first sequestrated, but later was released. I still have to ask permission to travel. It is always given me, but it always means delay. I am endeavouring to obtain free pass and I am undertaking to obtain a special decree in my favour granting me Italian citizenship. The Duce, however, is now unapproachable and the military authorities are slow to move (a free pass depends on them). I hope for the best, however, and am pulling every string at my disposal. But if a crash comes and the English arrive in Italy, I should technically be a traitor. There will be no alternative but to become a refugee. I would leave my son with Buona's cousin, Camilla Pasolini,[18] and the rents from Buona's flat could pay for him. They would go up, if inflation came. But Buona and I would have to flee; for we are determined not to surrender, come what may.

We have a charming little apartment in Rome, belonging to [illegible] Busini (nee [illegible]), who furnished it with taste. We have a dream of a little home in the country near Florence, also rented and furnished and where we keep such belongings as we possess. Adrian goes to school at the college of S. Giuseppe, which is run by the Christian Brothers.

My activities are multiple. I hope to take a degree in Political Science at the Rome University next June or the year after. I have been composing some music (military marches and songs) and some of it is being played. I write articles, mainly in economics. I do a little business and so supplement my income. But the situation is as such that I must rebuke my activities with an eye on the possibility of defeat. Pray God that the Gates of Hell shall not prevail. The Gates of Hell are the Jews.[19]

1 January

A jolly New Year's Day. Tea with Francis [*illegible*] and Mariano Frasso who live in the flat of Signor[a] [Tornaghi] as paying guests. Francis is a Scotswoman; was a member of Tom Mosley's British Union and very naturally in the circumstances preferred to stay here when the war broke out. She is on our sides of the barricades; and the authorities therefore don't worry her. Mariano is a magnificent fellow – an old squadrista,[20] now employed by Ala Littoria.[21] The two are engaged to be married but cannot ~~do so~~ unite owing to the present regulations. But true love never did run smooth – that is, not until the Fairy Godmother comes along. May the Fairy Godmother be Peace with victory.

2 January

Tea with Signora Paoli-Pogliani who paints & sculpts [.]

3 January

Tea with Andrea and Laura Malcangi. She is my great friend Nello Maraini's sister.

14 January

Look up Emanuela and Don Jaime (Duke of Segovia) on my way back from the EIAR.[22]

16 January

Carmine Auristi lunches with me chez Archimede, and we talk business. Carmine and I have various irons in the fire together and the time has come to think about new plans.

Afterwards I visit [Maestro Triventi] at the Foro Mussolini, Commando Generale G.I.L.[23] He is head of the G.I.L. bands who have 2 of my marches. The difficulty is to get them performed. [Triventi] is willing to help, but advises me to get Camillo Pellizzi to write to [Buonamici] about them. Camillo is Adrian's Godfather & one of my best friends [.][24]

18 January

Signora Lombardi and Gino Villari came to us after dinner. Gino is my oldest existing friend.[25]

19 January

Betty & Cyril Rocke came to tea [.]

21 January

Call in on Vicky [*illegible*] at the Grand on my way back from the EIAR. Meet a Marchese Spreti, whom I hope to meet again.[26] A good man, I should judge and possibly helpful.

22 January

The news is sad. The fall of Tripoli is enough to make one weep. I think of the happy days I spent there as the guest of Balbo and of all the wonderful things he did for Libya.[27] It is heartbreaking. But it was expected. The evacuation is however all according to plan, and does not alter the main military situation. Everything must be concentrated on the defence of what is essential in Tunisia. But the news from Russia is also bad today, though nothing has actually happened yet to upset the strategical situation.[28]

Conte e Contessa Ottieri came to tea. Civilized Toscani.

23 January

I go to the Vatican & hand Mgr. Cippico a letter for the Pope. I am a Privy Chamberlain of Cape & Sword of the Pope's and I have written to ask him for his advice and, in certain circumstances, his protection.[29] I shall follow up the letter with a request for an audience.

I also go to the Ministero dell'Educ. Nazionale[30] to explore the possibility of taking one of my examinations in February. I had already written to Bottai[31] about this, who referred me to Dott. [*illegible*]. [*Illegible*] is helpful; but the matter has now to be followed up at the university[.]

Confession & mass in St Peter's[.]

24 January

Communion.

A long business talk with Auristi. I decide gradually to dispose of my bonds with a view to turning over my money with greater profit & preserving a more liquid situation.

Fine concert at the Adriano with Edwin Fischer playing Brahms's concerto (B flat) & D'Albert's concerto (D minor).

Went round and headed to Camillo Pellizzi's in the evening and had a long interesting talk. He does not share my view that the actual loss of our positions in Tunisia would make it very much more [easy] for convoys to go through the Sicily Channel. If the Allies could obtain mastery of the air, they would be able to press the convoys through even if we continued to hold the Tunisian ports. If they So long as they have not the mastery of the air, on the other hand, the convoys would have difficulty in getting through even if we lost Tunisia. That is his argument. I do not think it is altogether sound, because there are so many intermediate considerations positions. At present neither side has mastery of the air. The position is one of defence and offence; and (it seems to me) the possession of the Tunisian ports by the Anglo-Saxons would enormously help the passage of convoys, other things being equal. The Allied bombers moreover would be able to concentrate activity on bombing our bases in Italy, instead of now having to be largely employed for use against troops in the field, while the fighting planes based on numerous [*illegible*] would be able to [*illegible*] the convoys.[32]

Pellizzi did not appear to have envisaged the possibility of Turkey coming in with the Anglo-Saxons and he admitted that if this occurred, it would instead be serious.

He says there is a strong Communist movement here among the young intellectuals; and that there have been a considerable number of arrests. These young Communists apparently are also strong nationalists in a sense. They feel Russia is the only hope against the Plutocracies, and that Fascism has lost its original dynamism. Rather Russia than America. Well, there is something to be said for this attitude. There might be more national self-expression under Moscow than under American financial control. But what of religion? What of the small owner? Pellizzi says that anyhow if the Americans came here, they would find themselves immediately up against a strong communist movement, which would in a sense be the expression of our will to continue to be an independent nation and to take an important part in the forging of a new world order. He adds that probably a long war would solve all problems. Economic Liberalism would die everywhere and communism would become more moderate, so that we should end up all more or less thinking alike and all more or less fascists. It is certainly an interesting thought.

Personally, I am convinced that ~~the only~~ one way to galvanise Fascism is [*word deleted*] to breathe into it more of the spirit of Catholicism. Why is not this done? The Catholic Church is our great trump card. We do not use it, though we are a profoundly Catholic people. Fascism is far from being anti-Catholic, but it [*word deleted*] refuses to come out straight on the Catholic ticket. Yet Italy ~~will only lead in~~ can only hope to take a lead in the New Europe, if she unequivocally puts herself at the head of the Catholic nations. This I told to <u>Pavolini</u> the other day and he seemed to agree.[33] Italy is always doomed to decay in so far as she detaches herself from Catholic civilisation.

25 January

Saw Dott. Cipolla[34] of the Duce's <u>Segretario</u> & told him that[35] Pavolini had handed just before ~~Christmas~~ the New Year a letter of mine to the Duce and that the Duce, after reading it, had said: 'Yes, Yes – I ought really to see Barnes again.' Nothing having happened since then, I said I wanted to see the Duce's Private Secretary, De Cesare, with a view to seeing what might be done to obtain an interview with the Duce about my getting my Italian citizenship.[36]

Yesterday Buona saw her cousin, Camilla Pasolini (Altieri) who agreed, in the case of disaster, to look after Job (Adrian).

The food situation by the way is not so bad. It is definitely better than last year. There is an increased ration of bread and abundance of potatoes. But this year dried figs and raisins, which were a great stand-by, are scarce and difficult to procure. However we managed to get 5 kilos of figs from B's[37] brother Emiliano who is at Susale (Firenze). There were plenty of <u>torroni</u> & <u>panforti</u>[38] at Christmas & we laid in a store. They make excellent calories. The one thing lacking badly is fats. One can buy castor oil on the black market, but so far we have abstained from doing so. It is a pity there is not some cheese & <u>ricotta</u>[39] available in Rome. In some other places there is plenty of it. The toilet soaps are very poor, but we have still some good pieces left – and we have an entire stock of beans. So there is nothing serious to worry about. Vegetables are [of course] abundant & at half last year's prices. Fruit – at present, oranges & alternatively apples, not to speak of lemons can be had, though the oranges are until lately have been somewhat sour. Actually we do not spend more than 1740 lire all told including rents & other outgoing per month, which works out at 580 lire per head or, say £6.10.0, which isn't bad, considering we do not stint ourselves. I get an excellent red wine from Palestrina which costs 6.50 lire per litre.[40] I reckon this alone would [make] the envy of the English, where even the most synthetic, watery beer costs a fortune. There is also plenty to smoke, though my Tuscan cigars now cost 1.30 each. Before the war they cost 0,80.

I saw Marchese Spreti who is legal adviser to the Republic of San Marino, at the Circolo degli Scacchi.[41] I wanted to know if there was any means of wrangling S. Marino citizenship. As I expected, however, such a thing is impossible. It is an extremely difficult thing to become a citizen of S. Marino. One can become an honorary citizen, but that means nothing at all, except perhaps a title. In fact there are numerous families who have been resident in S. Marino for centuries and yet the citizenship is refused them.

The Marchese Spreti was nevertheless very helpful. He suggested that I should see Senise Chief of the Police, who has wide discretionary powers.[42] In the event of a crash he would help [word deleted] me. It was interesting to see Senise anyhow about my liberty to travel in Italy as I liked without having to get each time the permission of the Police & Military Authorities (which is always a long business) and I shall therefore take the opportunity of tackling him on this question also.

I also suggested to Spreti whether I might not be attached to the S. Marino Embassy to the Holy See & so receive a diplomatic passport in that way. This he says is a possibility as the Ambassador or Minister [illegible] can do what he thinks fit in the matter, since the job would of course be unpaid. I shall accordingly follow the matter up in due course.[43]

26 January

A wasteful morning at the University in a typical Roman fashion. Endless anti-camera.[44] Wafted on from one person to another; and then, in the end, nothing definitely settled. But I have found out what to do: Pay 6 lire to the Fisc.[45] and send in a formal demand to be admitted to one [illegible] in February, which, now that I have established a personal contact with the Powers that be, will probably be accorded.

I have discovered however that there was a formality to perform when passing out of the 3° into the 4° year of my university studies – and I have omitted to perform it. Of course nobody told me. Consequently I am still in the 3° year &, to put matters right, I must now pull strings at the Ministry again. What a world!

Monsignor MacDaid, Rector of the Irish College, came to tea. We both of us love the Irish and we had a lovely talk. Afterwards an Indian Moslem student turned up, a Mr Hassan, who asked me what I thought would be the position of England after the war. My answer is: If she wins it: a [*illegible*] & destitute Dominion of the United States. If she loses it: a poor but respectable member of the European family. These things in the long run, anyhow. Meantime I feel like saying with the Irish: God damn England! What fools the people have been and what knaves the Government.

28 January

A rush all day. Vatican & Min. Educ. Naz.[46] in the morning and EIAR in the afternoon, not to speak of having to declaim at the Min. della Cul. Pop.[47] my talk for India by 7.30 a.m. – an unearthly hour. I had worked at it until 1.30 in the morning & I am one who cannot do without sleep.

At the Vatican I asked for a private audience with the Pope for myself & family; and I withdrew my certificate conferring my appointment under the present Pope as Privy Chamberlain of Cape and Sword. 400 lire have to be paid!

At the Min. Educ. Naz.[48] I tackled the question of my inscription[49] for the 4th year at the University, which by an oversight I omitted to do within the prescribed time. I was told the only chance lay in a personal appeal to Bottai, which I must write tonight. Otherwise I lose a year, which would be a bore. Not that there is any chance of the [year] ending before June 1944. But one never knows. If it did I might miss the bus. Or I might be a refugee by then?

29 January

Another busy day with a nice, quiet evening in the end, listening in to Beethoven's 13th.

I had an interview with the Duce's Secretary De Cesare, explained the whole situation & expressed my desire to see Mussolini again [*illegible*] and in order to obtain my Italian citizenship. As far as it went it was a successful interview. I feel I gave the right impression and made him interested. We parted with genuine cordiality; & he promises to communicate with me in due course, after doing what he can. He looks the ideal secretary: a man of detail & industry & loyal – but always the secretary. For that very reason he might succeed where more domineering personalities would fail. Before tackling the Duce, he ~~will~~ wishes to speak to Buffarini.[50] But I fear Buffarini will not be helpful. He is one of those persons it is impossible to pin down. But he might be worth [*illegible*]. He is a Tuscan.

30 January

A day of comparative rest – mostly spent in bed suffering from an incipient cold. Yesterday evening I called in at the Grand Hotel to see Vicky [Ruspoli] and the Princess (who was in bed) and we discussed the war. She shares my views & says that every soldier should have assigned to him a Holy Soul in Purgatory for [*illegible*] prayers. It would be an excellent idea. But she is not depressed any more than I am. The latest gossip is that Japan is pressing Russia to make a separate peace, saying: 'Now is your opportunity, as you have been having some success, to get good terms. Otherwise you will be in the soup next summer, especially as we (Japan) may jump on your back.' Who knows if it be true? And if so, will Stalin be tempted? Such an event would certainly cook the Anglo-Saxon's goose.

Beatrice & Gigi Miami came in as I left, and Frank [Ruspoli's] young son. I am angry with life in <u>general</u> because (a) Maestro d'Elia has not the time to orchestrate my music 'Passo Romano' – (b) Maestro Spaggiani of the EIAR, who was to hear my song 'Lamento oltre Mare'[51] sung on Sunday and go into his regular programme, has been called up. His successor will now have to be approached and this means endless delay – (c) The EIAR has refused to pass the words of my Hymn-March 'Asse in Marcia'[52] (words by Guidobaldo Mazzoni) on the grounds that ~~things being~~ the military situation being critical, the words are too jubilant. I ~~believe this is~~ shouldn't be surprised if this is not merely an excuse; and that the <u>Camorra</u> which [monopolises] the music world in Italy (programmes by official [toadies]) want to see it suppressed: anyhow Mazzoni is offering to change the words and we shall therefore see what we shall see. What a business it is, however, to get anything done in Rome. Eternal Rome! I suspect the EIAR [too] of being [honey-combed] by freemasons – defeatists.

31 January

Stay in bed all day & leave Buona to have tea with the Ottieri. Sorry particularly to miss [*illegible*] Thaon di Ravel ([*illegible*]) who was to be there & whom I have not seen for a long time.[53]

Job got into an awful row yesterday, because for the nth time he did not come back straight from school. He has no control over himself & has no sense of responsibility. Besides, he is not [*illegible*] brave. He can be charming, but with these defects, he is a difficult subject to deal with. He needs the steady discipline of a college; & I mean next year to send him (probably) to Farfa.[54] In many ways he is very English, always ready to deceive himself. Superficially he is Italian – voluble & volatile. But he lacks logic & artistic sensibility. Unlike his father, moreover, he seems to have no particular interests except adventure stories – though like most modern children he has a knack for mechanical devices. He is extremely lazy & in spite of a [mature] intelligence, refuses to concentrate on anything for more than a few minutes at a time. But he is improving slowly, I think.

2 February

Buona & Job have gone to Florence for a week (<u>beati loro</u>)[55] and I am left alone. My cold is better & I shall have more time to work; but I shall be bored. I have arranged, however, to dine each evening with Francis [*illegible*] & Mariano Frasso; and this will be a comfort.

German lesson [*illegible*] [*illegible*] to talk business.

4 February

Back to the Vatican to see Mgr. Mella di Sant'Elia about the audience. I explained to him why I wished to see the Pope & that I had written to ~~the Pope~~ him. He promised me that we should see the Pope alone & be able to talk to him freely. He also advised me to see Mgr. Montini, the Sostituto of the Cardinal Sec. Of State & discuss details of what might be done for me, should things go wrong.[56]

Back again to the Min. Educ. Naz. But (eternal Rome!) nothing has yet been done about my university predicament. There may be news on Saturday.

The good news of the day is that my song ('Lamento oltre mare') has been taken up by Maestro Spaggiari's successor at the EIAR, Maestro [*illegible*], and will be put in the programme on Feb. 11th or in another. We shall see.

5 February

The Russian front news is bad. The fall of Stalingrad I took for granted; but it looks really as if the Germans might lose all they gained in the summer; and this is not what anyone expected. The best parts of the [*illegible*] are already lost. As long as Kursk, Charkov, the line of the Drutz and Rostov are solidly held, we need not get too flustered, however. All the same, the

D[*illegible*] [*illegible*] [*illegible*] a [dangerous] [salient] as things stand and there seems no end to the Russian thrust. I fear Rostov is doomed.[57] It is also doubtful if the Germans will be able to keep a footing in [*illegible*] (with [*illegible*]). One cannot help feeling extremely anxious. All the more do things depend to my mind, on the successful defence of Tunisia. So far so good. But the big Anglo-American thrust is to come.

Churchill has no doubt prepared the way for cooking the Turkey. Otherwise Casablanca was no great success for him.[58] Roosevelt gave nothing away. Not for nothing did he describe the meeting as the 'Conference of Unconditional Surrender.' It was Churchill's unconditional surrender; but, like a true Britisher, he doesn't know when he is beaten.[59]

7 February

Confession & Communion.

The comfort in the military situation is that of the total Russian population of 175,000,000 – some 60,000,000 or more are under German occupation still. Thus the population of Germany, Hungary, Slovakia & Roumania (not to speak of Finland) is considerably greater than that of Russia now, and the German resources must be considerably larger. Consequently it is difficult to believe that, taking into consideration the appalling Russian losses in men and material (and the far smaller percentage of experts & educated persons), Russia is in a position to stand up to a third German offensive. Her only assets are the distances & the short summer – & the increasing [American/ammunition] supplies through Persia.

One is apt to forget the enemy's difficulties when our own difficulties loom large. Tunisia is still firmly held. The submarine campaign is an ever growing menace to the country's lines of communication; & Japan is winning more important victories. So we must not get down in the dumps.

The new Italian Cabinet contains ~~2~~ one first class name: Bastianini; ~~and~~ while Acerbo's appointment is a good one – with round pegs in round holes, both men of [*illegible*] and [*illegible*] brains.[60] That is their reputations anyhow. I don't know them personally. The disappearance of Ciano is not to be regretted, though I hold him to be a much libelled man.[61] Nevertheless in the popular mind he has become the symbol of the upstart passive element, accused of personal ambitions and graft. Consequently Ciano's going should strengthen ~~the~~ [*words deleted*] Fascism; and reassure the country. I am sorry Pavolini, who is an intelligent & charming man, has had to go too – especially as my relations with him are particularly cordial. He has gone presumably because he is a great friend of Ciano's.

Bottai & Grandi[62] are also out. But they will come back. Grandi will not be sorry to remain still more in the background. This is the game he wants to play and, if things go badly, he may be the man who more than anyone else will be able to save [*illegible*] [*illegible*] he saved for Italy.

Polverelli, Pavolini's successor, is an excessively nice and honest person, but he is not distinguished by a reputation for either first class brains or experience of the wide world.[63] I shall need to cultivate him for my own interests; ~~but I fear he is not the best man for the job~~ and it may be that I shall discover him to be much abler than is generally supposed; for he is a shy man, and therefore possibly [*illegible*], all the same. I should have liked to see Ezio Maria Gray Minister of Popular Culture.[64] That would have been a really good appointment & Gabry Paresce ought to be made Under Secretary.[65]

Thaon di Ravel was a good administrator, but not a great Finance Minister. [*illegible*] should be [*illegible*] in time with [*word deleted*] new ideas, and he is more of [*word deleted*] an expert. I wish De Stefani would be recalled in some way: but no doubt the government makes use of him a good deal behind the scenes.[66]

F[irstly/inally], I am not sorry to see Buffarini go. I have always felt that, though very able, he is a [*words deleted*] ~~Benini is back in office & for that I am glad~~ bit too much of a manoeuvre for the stern necessities of these times. I am glad to see Zenone Benini back in office.[67] He is a Toscano and one of our [*illegible*]. Biggini, as Minister of Education, is quite a good administrative appointment;[68] and I should <u>imagine</u> that Albini's and Tiengo's are also good, as Albini was a friend of Balbo's.[69] With Ambrosio Chief of the general Staff, we can say without hesitation that now we shall be better served than before.[70] It is a more forthright team than the old one.

8 February

Saw Senise, Chief of the Police – who was very cordial & nice. He said I could look upon him as a friend to come to in emergency; but the 'pratica'[71] for my free movement in Italy was still in the air. But he promised to do what he could to hurry it up – and, in fact, during the afternoon an officer of the Questura[72] called ~~& said~~ to say that I should be given immediately a pass to go to Florence, Leghorn, Bologna, Milan, Venice & Trieste & other places in north & central Italy. This at all counts is something.

Ciano's appointment to the Vatican I am very glad to see. It should guarantee a sound Church policy, for Ciano has always been in favour of cultivating the best possible relations with the Papacy.

Lunched very well with [Auristi] chez '<u>Cenci</u>'. Our business plans are in full development.

10 February

Job & B back from Firenze. ~~She has bought a flat for investment.~~ She has got some oil and figs. She has decided to buy on my behalf another flat for investment.

12 February

Churchill's speech is a good one of its kind. His [illegible] best for a long time and, alas, his most [illegible] confident. All the same he cannot be altogether happy. He worked for war for reasons of personal ambition. He has got his war and he has now good hopes of a personal triumph. But he must realise that to win means the destruction of European civilisation: and the eclipse of England in a grand Anglo-Saxon merger, dominated by the U.S.A. It also means Jewdom. I do not suppose, knowing him as I do and admiring him in many ways as I do, that he meant things to go like that. He is still gambling on the off chance of things going otherwise – on his own personality being able to prevent the worst. But I fear lord Beaverbrook is the greater realist.[73] When he says that 'perhaps the best solution after all is to let Europe fall into the hands of Russia', he is really admitting the inevitability of this in the event of an allied victory. But we shall fight; [*word deleted*] the decisive battles have not yet begun; and there is no convincing reason yet to be down hearted. It is interesting to note that Churchill says that the British plans will develop within the next nine months. This corresponds with my diagnosis of the situation.

A [small] party chez Gino Villari after [dinner]. There was [Ing.] [Migliorini] whom I had met in [*illegible*] in 1928 and had not seen since. A very nice man.

13 February

Madam de [*illegible*], widow of my old chief at Lausanne, is on a visit to Rome & came to tea. She is a woman of admirable faith.

But how difficult do I find it to love God and love my neighbour in a <u>personal</u> way! Apart from Buona I sometimes feel I love nothing in the whole world. For the rest, I only love what is admirable and good and beautiful and true. This is something, but I admit that it is not enough. I suffer fools and knaves very badly. I dislike people for what is foolish & [*illegible*] in them. I despise most people; and God, though <u>Feb 15</u> [*illegible*] true to me, is in some ways as remote as the law of gravity. I wish I had been brought up a Catholic and so acquired the [*illegible*] of [intimate] relationship which I find now so hard to establish. But at least I can say that I do not [hate] my enemies. This however is the quality of the same defect, which [prevents] me losing my friends.[74]

13 February

There was a young man of Aberystwith
Who banged his best girl on the waist with
a hammer, by Gad!
But now he is sad,
For he aint got no more girls to [tryst] with.[75]
There was a young [illegible] of Kildare
Who became, one day, strangely aware
that [word deleted] all life was quite [illegible]
and [word deleted] unmistakeably [illegible] –
So she gambled and [illegible] in the air
(She has now got a pair)[76]
There was an [word deleted] old man of Dundee,
Who was horribly [buzzed] by a bee. (pace Lear)
It sat on his nose,
(which it took for a rose),
and occasionally perched on his knee
(which it took for a tree)![77]
I know an old man of [illegible]
Who possesses a boat and he sits in her – (an [illegible] Lear)
His [back], it would seem
Is as broad as the beam
of the boat, where he sits in her
he fits in her ...
(and some people say that he shits in her!)[78]
Why did the [word deleted] whale [illegible]?
Because the Octopus's Plaice Smelt.[79]
You can give a horse a drink, but you cannot
always make him water.[80]

To continue yesterday's thought: – Of course there are a few people of
whom I am very fond, though there is nobody I love like Buona, which is as
it should be. I become more and more in love with my wife, as time goes on
and it is not only on account of the fact that she has grown more lovely as
her health has improved since her operation or because the war has brought
out all the more emphatically her admirable character. She is my very life.

It would be invidious to make a list of those I most care for – but
here are some, though the list is not complete: [illegible] [illegible], Bebe
[illegible], [illegible] [illegible], [illegible] & [illegible] [illegible], Francesca
and Mariano Frasso, Camillo and Raffaella Pellizzi, Gino Villari, Gabry
Paresce, Niccolò [illegible], [illegible] [illegible] and her [mother] ... and in
England, the Lytton family, the Plymouth family, [illegible] [illegible], Eddie
Marsh, Ralph Joyce, William [illegible], the John family, Mildred [illegible]

Ronnie [*illegible*] & even that old [*illegible*] [*illegible*], my sister Mary, though [*illegible*] [*illegible*] she [represents] a great deal of what I detest most in contemporary England – the [*illegible*] proves that I do not always love people only for their qualities.[81] I love Italy with all her defects. I love Mother Church. I love animals and children, because they are innocent.

I had a good talk with Mgr. Montini today at the Vatican. He struck me as an emphatically able man and also as a really good man – [positively], [actually] good which is the only sense of the word I make use of. I explained my position; and after I have spoken with the Pope, we shall doubtless have further conversations. Meanwhile he made a useful suggestion. He will tackle Ciano regarding my Italian citizenship and officially recommend that I, as a member of the Papal Household, should be governed by a special decree. I should not be surprised if this did not do the trick. We shall see.

17 February

I have obtained my permission to travel to a number of named towns in central & northern Italy.

Pavolini has sent me a signed photograph dedicated 'to the faithful fighter for good causes.' It was B's idea to ask him for a photograph & so here it is.

My song 'Lamento oltre mare' has not yet been sung. But Mazzoni has written new words for the [March] and will tackle the EIAR about it.

Charkov has fallen; and I certainly never bargained for that [*illegible*] though I had allowed for the loss of Rostov. All the same there is nothing to indicate that the German reserves are not in [*illegible*]. Better lose territory than reserves. The key to the situation is still, I believe, in Tunisia; and news from that quarter is so far good. The American troops are not showing up well. They have much to learn.

I have [now] got those deals going with [Auristi]:- a small government contract for telegraph poles; a salami deal; and a Ford lorry, which should cover its cost within 10 months. I should have begun buying things for resale a year ago. What profit I might have made!

There is nothing to be done about my getting inscribed now for the 4th year at the university & it is too late to give one of the examinations this month. So I must content myself to wait another year before being able to give my final examination. If Bottai had not left the Ministry just at the moment when I applied for a special order, I would probably have succeeded in getting what I intended. But as a matter of fact, as I have 8 exams still to go, another year gives me a certain relief from pressure of work, which I already find too much for me. So perhaps it is better thus.

20 February

Good news from Tunisia. The Americans have taken a severe knock and Rommel's [star] is now crossed. If we could take [*illegible*] and drive the enemy back [*illegible*] to south [*illegible*], the English will be turned out of the North; and we should have a line of defences from which it would be really difficult to oust us. But this would be almost too good to become true.

My song <u>was</u> performed the other day, but I missed it. Too bad!

22 February

Even if one is so obtuse as to regard Gandhi's 'fast unto death' as a suicide rather than as a sacrifice, it is against ethical principles and contrary to decent [*mark deleted*] common human instinct to sit back and watch him suffer and slowly die, when it is [*word deleted*] possible to save his life. The fact that he may survive has nothing to do with it.

No Catholic people would tolerate such a thing.

Besides, Gandhi is an honourable foe, a great man and a good man.

So was [*words deleted*] S^t. Joan of Arc. But the British burnt her. They have not changed much since then. They are always the same unimaginative, conscientious people, ready to commit any crime in the name of what is right.

Had another good chat with Camillo Pellizzi. He seems to like to use me as a help to turning things over in his mind. But until he reaches a positive conclusion, the process is a bit exasperatingly academic. Yesterday he turned over his doubts about whether the Germans are capable of smashing at the Russians in the course of the coming summer and whether it was therefore wise to try – because if the attempt fails, then there would be nothing to prevent the Russians battering their way in. Would it not be wise to dig in on roughly the present line and turn more attention to Africa, and at the same time make every effort to arrive at an honourable compromise peace?

But I doubt if digging in would stop the Russians; and I doubt if any honourable compromise peace is possible at present. Practically, it seems to me there is no other alternative but to play the game hard, all we can, during the next 9 months, just as the Anglo-Saxons mean to do. One side or other may then be in a winning position or both may realise that neither side can win. [*word deleted*] In the latter hypothesis, a comprehensive peace ought would become possible. But at present, whatever the risks, there is nothing to do but fight – unless the Pope could accomplish a miracle.

'She had an old bee in her bonnet
Which managed to crawl out upon it.

Deprived of its buzz,
What d'you think she does?
She refuses from that day to don it.'
(You may say such nonsense
Has no correspondence
With fact. All the same, it's a [*illegible*] –
-ary, cantering sonnet.)

26 February

The dear old vispa comare[82] di Roma – the [Boschitto] – came to tea, as full as energy, indomitable courage & faith as ever. Also Laura [Mallagi] & the Signora [Pasti-Pogliani], who is a very intelligent woman, as well as a clever artist. But deaf as a post.

Tomorrow B makes a rapid excursion to Florence to see about the new investment flat. Due back on Sunday. I always am bored without her.

Yesterday there was another distressful row with Job. He had been given a letter to register. Afterwards he said he had lost the receipt. The letter, however, has been brought back by a woman who found it in the street. Job had dropped it; feared to confess his carelessness; invented the rest of the story and pocketed the money. When confronted, he stuck to his lie, until the proofs were produced. But even then he was not frank & prevaricated about what he had done with the money.

Now, this is not the first time he has been caught stealing & lying. I really do not know how to deal with it. His punishment is the confiscation of the money he had saved up to buy an adventure story by Salgari, and the banning of all reading of adventure stories till Easter.[83] He deserves to be whipped, but this only makes him hysterical.

One trouble of course is that these Italian schools have no organised and competitive games, or any real esprit de corps. Job would really do much better in an English school – like Ampleforth, for example.[84] He would undoubtedly excel in games; and that would give him the means of letting off steam & a sense of responsibility towards others.[85]

9 March

I have been in Florence for the week [and] [*illegible*] to look into the various financial questions connected with the flat which we have bought as an investment. It seems O.K., though the price is high after adding the taxes. All the same, it is wise to take possessions of values which would rise if things went badly. On the other hand, we must try to sell it again at a profit at the psychological moment if things go well.

The wonderful weather has at last broken. But Florence was adorable as ever. I lunched and tea'd with Yoï & [Nello] ([Romaine] [Brookes] & her friend Natalie came in to tea), and dined with Elena [*illegible*] & [*illegible*] (Mario de [*illegible*] came in after dinner). Very delightful it all was. We discussed everything & everybody. [Ippolito] is well – a [prisoner] somewhere up in the hills near Kashmir. How sad & [*illegible*] it must be for both him & his little wife [*illegible*], left behind with her 3 little cherubs of girls. Yoi, thank goodness – who has been suffering from her heart – is better. She is my spiritual sister and as passionately loyal to the good causes as ever.[86]

12 March

Today I ran across my friend Sorrentino – a journalist, who has been in Russia 2 years. His view of the situation seemed to me very realistic. He compared it to river over which a dam had burst. The water was now completely out of control. The engineers could only look on and wait until the waters subsided. Will they return to the river bed or submerge the countryside? All we can do is to fight. All the enemy can do is to fight. The result is beyond the ken of man. Nobody knows or can foretell how it will all end or what the damage will amount to.

As for the future military operations in Russia, S. is doubtful if the Russians can be properly beat. If they avoid being caught by the new German offensive, they may only lose territory again and be able next winter to ~~advance~~ [*word deleted*] do as before. ~~Besides~~ Campaigns in Russia are like naval battles. It is a question of destroying the enemy's forces either by a series of smashing blows or by a favourable balance of wear and tear. The occupation of territory is of no particular significance. At present it is impossible to tell to what point the Soviets are worn & torn in comparison with the Germans. The latter smashed the Russian Northern Army in 1940. They only succeeded in wearing & tearing the Southern army in 1941. The Far Eastern army then came into the picture and carried out the recent offensive; but it has also undergone in consequence a process of wear & tear.[87] The coming summer therefore will [*word deleted*] reveal the extent to which the Southern & Eastern Armies can [*illegible*] destruction. If they can do this, the war is likely to enter into a phase of hide & seek, e.g. elastic defence on both sides – which, however, requires great forces, especially for the Germans who cannot afford to be too elastic; &, also American supplies for Russia will multiply as time goes on through Iran.

But, then, <u>also</u>, even if we hold Africa this year, we should come up against stronger & stronger forces in Africa next year – unless the submarine campaign turns out to be an even greater success than can be confidently hoped.

Can we hold [*word deleted*] in Africa this year?[88] It is, I think, an open [game] provided the Germans have understood its importance but there is no reason to be too pessimistic. At least we can delay the enemy's success.

Can we counter and destroy the Russian forces this summer? It depends a lot on the enemy's generalship. If we fail, it would be difficult to hold Africa next year, if we happen to be still there, & the Anglo-Americans would be in a position to open the second European front in the Balkans.

How far can the submarine campaign decide the day?

These are the great question marks.

England ought to be on our side. It is tragic that she is not – tragic for her and tragic for Europe. She wrecked the spiritual unity of Europe at the time of the Reformation. ~~She~~ Now, by a parallel blindness, she threatens to [crush/wreck] European civilisation.[89]

20 March

The retaking of Kharkov & Belgorod by the Germans is good. Probably the whole of the railway from Orel to Taganrog will soon be in their hands. & also [*illegible*]. This is the necessary jumping off ground for the spring offensive. But Rostov is also needed.[90]

Buona says she is <u>certain</u> that we shall be kicked out of Africa. Why, she does not say. She says it is her woman's intuition. She may be right, and she may be wrong. It seems to me to be absurd to be positive in a matter where we have no positive data to go on. We don't know what our intentions are yet or what means we possess. Personally I think it is a 100:50 chance [*word deleted*] that we shall have to go by June. The British now say they will be through by the end of May. But the British have often vainly boasted before.

The fat would be in the fire, if they succeeded – the only hope then would be in the submarine campaign which is going strong, and in the complete smashing out of Russia – or a route through Turkey & the Persian Gulf. But if we hold in Africa until the end of the year (Oh that it were possible!) the situation [*word deleted*] would be saved. By June, our European coast defences at least will be completed. [*word deleted*] is [*word deleted*] [*word deleted*] [*word deleted*] [*word deleted*] [*word deleted*].

Eden has failed in Washington.[91] Why should Roosevelt accept an electoral liability in order to play Britain's dirty game? He may have his own dirty games to play, but that is another matter. No need to follow Britain's example in <u>deliberately</u> and openly betraying civilisation.

Talking of religion, even as a child ([*illegible*] was an atheist) I had an instinctive and profound distaste for protestant civilisation, while I loved the Catholic; & being extremely sensitive, I have never been able to live in an [*word deleted*] antipathetic atmosphere without drooping. Hence my aversion from England. I wanted to become Italian in order to be able to flourish. Italy was my choice because Italy was my home. If it had happened to be some other Catholic country, I might have chosen that other country. This really explains everything in my life, my successes & above all my failures. But even though I have failed to become a great man in the eyes of the world (and I believe I had the talent to do so), I have succeeded in loyalty to my principles and to my [loves].

I have been trying to persuade my German professor, who is an Italian (I give him in return conversation in English) that it is only possible to understand English poetry by approaching it as music. Unless English nonsense rhymes (Carroll & Lear) are understood, the great & serious lyrics will probably remain a half closed book.[92]

24 March

So the Anglo-American offensive in Africa has begun. I cannot but feel very anxious and nervy. But few people here seem to realise how much depends on the result. Our men are sure to fight magnificently, but the odds will be against them. So far the enemy has suffered some very severe losses, but he has made some progress, especially in the centre which is our weak flank.

The Pope is indisposed, but we hope to see him next week.

Churchill's speech is an attempt to tranquilise public opinion, ever more insistent in England for social reform. The British government always makes bountiful provisions in war time, but it never seems to have any money except for bloody wars. The irony of Churchill's speech is that his programme of social reform is borrowed straight from Fascism, which his war is meant to destroy.[93]

What an absurd [illegible] it all is! How unique! Here we have blazed out the trail of a better world, only to be attacked and perhaps destroyed by those who have nothing better to do but to imitate us. Not that imitation in this case is [sincere/genuine] flattery – for Churchill is not sincere. His programme is [merely/mainly] dust in the eyes of the people – though of course he always allows his vivid imagination to carry him away in the exuberance of his own verbosity. But it is no use undervaluing the power of the man. He has made mistakes, but so have we – especially the Germans. We should never have allowed the opportunity of last August to pass, when we reached the gates of the Nile Valley. The Germans should have suspended everything to bring to bear at that point the decisive thrust. With proper support in aviation and petrol – even if the sending of it had cost us a fleet of ships – we would have reached the coast & the war would have been virtually won. Now everything hangs on a thread.

31 March

The battle is not going too well in Africa, but not yet too badly. The best line of defence in the South appears to ~~have been abandoned, but not without inflicting great~~ be still in our possession and we have inflicted severe losses on the enemy. We may be saved by the wear & tear which the enemy is undergoing. And it is too early yet to judge, though I am afraid they are too strong for us.

I have sent in a new official memo. regarding my citizenship. [Corrias], the new [Cabinet] Chief of the Ministry of Popular Culture is a very efficient person and a good friend of mine (he was my brother-in-law's chief in the Albanian dept. of the Foreign Office) and he is taking the matter up with the Minister. I got the memo. drafted by [*illegible*], who is a great lawyer and a very dear friend. So I hope for the best again.

Talking again of the war, the more I think of it, the more I am convinced that our great mistake was not to push through to the Suez canal at <u>all</u> costs from the Alamein last August, before the British received their reinforcements. That was our great opportunity & success would have been decisive. We should have thrown everything into the scales. As it is, we actually broke through, but were held up for want of petrol – for we had a convoy sunk. But we should have been prepared to lose 50 ships if necessary. Supplies should have been [rushed/pushed] through, ~~at all costs~~ sink or swim and the Germans should also have [*illegible*] strong reinforcements of aeroplanes down at the cost of the effort to take Stalingrad (which after all failed).

But neither the German nor the Italian command seems to have seen the crucial importance of the opportunity, which presented itself & was missed; and the Germans have always failed to understand that England can only be beaten in the Middle East.

We had [*word deleted*] Ezra Pound to dinner this week. He is, as Buona says, really a great pet. He is always stimulating too & we talked our favourite subject: economics.

Yesterday we lunched with [*illegible*] & ate magnificently. It is good to [*illegible*] magnificently & joyously from time to time in these hard times.[94]

1 April

The All Fools Day was celebrated by the B.B.C. this morning with the announcement that 'General Rommel was in full retreat towards [*illegible*]; that the Germans were commandeering all the available motor transport & that they had left the poor Italians, as usual, in the lurch to die or surrender.'

It is worthwhile [stressing] this lie. It is imaginary. The fact is that we have retreated behind the Mareth lines, after [*illegible*] General Montgomery's attempt to envelope our right wing & after causing the enemy to pay dearly for what we never have considered other than advanced positions. General Messe has done very well & could not possibly have been expected to have done better.[95] The British lie, which at first deceived us, is all the more ridiculous in that Messe is in command of the whole of the southern section.

2 April

B's birthday. [Tokay] & Old Orvieto for dinner. Stockings for a present.

7 April

Francesca & Mariano after dinner to celebrate. But, damn it all, I've caught a cold.

Zero hour at 4.30 yesterday on the Tunisian front. The B.B.C. has started off [at] full [cock], but so far the news is not to our disadvantage. All the same, the odds are terrific. If we hold this line solidly, it may be the equivalent of winning the campaign. If we lose it, all will not yet be lost – but I fear we shall lose it.

9 April

The British & Americans have joined hands, after forcing the lines North of [illegible]. Well, that's that. The only comfort is that we do not appear to have lost control of our tactical [illegible] & have not been trapped.

The [illegible] of the English knows no bounds. Mr Steer, Times correspondent in Abyssinia confesses that for propaganda purposes he besmirched the name of a [illegible] [illegible] [illegible] General [Lorenzini]. It now turns out that Mr Steer was the same man who invented the lies about the bombing of Guernica during the Spanish Civil War. What a specimen of humility! But the horrible thing is that he is typical of modern England – & so is the Times for [countenancing] these methods, which must make the old owners [words deleted] turn in their graves.

Mr Eden – to give but another example of [illegible] British turpitude – admitted gaily in the H. of C. yesterday that the Americans had kept up relations with Vichy, because it enabled them to send hundreds of agents to [illegible] [Africa] and therefore to prepare the invasion. In other words, treachery. But does any Englishman see it as that? Probably not. Their mind will have grown too thick.

14 April

The official account of the Battle for the Mareth lines published today makes interesting reading.[96] It shows our superiority over the country in every way except equipment. But why are we not properly equipped? If we had possessed more aircraft, it appears the British would never have got through. Why have we not more aircraft? The Germans continually boast of their war potential. Why don't they equip us? How are we expected to do anything effective with equipment much of which dates from 1918? We are not going to win the war by magnificent proof of our superiority as soldiers man for man. If we lose Africa, Italy will not be fighting on a single front. We shall be [illegible] manning our coasts & the Balkans & part of southern France.[97] Properly equipped we could do a great deal more. This seems to me to be the curious & at the same time damning fact of the situation. Properly equipped we could not only do infinitely more [two lines deleted].

Of course we are partly responsible. The mistakes made in 1939 are appalling. It is not as if I was judging things after the war. I repeatedly said at the time that we should have placed ourselves on a war footing – started rationing at once, and piling up reserves of modern war equipment & pouring it into Libya & East Africa. But we seem to have drifted for [nine] months – so that when we found ourselves at war, we were both materially & morally unprepared. The surprise of France's sudden collapse is no excuse.

Mussolini should have made a whole series of speeches, swiftly followed by a whole series of actions. The speeches should have been on the importance of Italy's part in keeping the peace in the Mediterranean – preventing the war spreading; but pointing out that this means sacrifices, vigilance, economy & above all the [illegible] possible expansion in armaments.

If I could have seen Mussolini in May 1940, as I tried, I could have told him that there was no hurry to declare war on England, because there was no chance at all of England giving way, even if invaded.

~~Perhaps if he had done this, he~~ Then he would have had that intuition of genius ~~which [?] could have kept~~ to keep us out of the war for a longer period – or else, as an alternative, have put us in position to attack England with success. One or the other. When France collapsed, we should have mobilized on the 2 northern frontiers, but not declared war. With the France of Pétain we should have negotiated, flattered, talked renouncing Nice, but insisting on Mentone, [illegible] – Corsica – & we should have tried for an arrangement regarding Tunis & Djibouti I am sure could at least have been secured – and an arrangement regarding the Suez Canal would have been secured during 1939. The latter arrangement would have been easy I believe [2 lines deleted] anyhow the military occupation of Tunis should have been made the essential objective. ~~Otherwise,~~ Then, we should have [illegible] [illegible] What a difference [word deleted] all this would have made! What a difference too it would have made to me. Our precipitous, unnecessarily precipitous entry into the war entirely dished me. Another couple of months & I should have [*word deleted*] bought for a wonderful bargain (£2000) that House at Careggi;[98] I should have got my boxes over from England; I should have secured most of Father's legacy; I should have had my [journey] to Albania, which would have led to certain excellent rewards & my application for Italian citizenship would have been filed before the outbreak of war.

Well, it's no use crying over spilt milk. We have now got to go on & fight & fight & fight for our lives – O God help us.[99]

What ought to be done? What have Mussolini & Hitler decided? The only positive hope is that Russia shall be liquidated during the summer. But it seems to me that we ought to take graver decisions. ~~We should~~ Could we, for example, anticipate British action through Turkey? ~~We ought to~~ Could we force Turkey onto our side and march through Turkey whether she likes it or not? Otherwise I fear the British will do this before the year is out. If we could take this initiative, we might succeed in rolling up the British right down to the Persian Gulf. This would smash the Russian supply route & cut the British supplies of petrol. It might, with a simultaneous drive through the [*illegible*], result in smashing Russia. Has this been decided upon?

I trust so. But I feel sceptical because I fear that from a military point of view (what with Russia on our backs, the bad communications in Turkey & the strength of the Turkish army) it is not practicable. All the same we seem to have lost our initial power of daring initiative. I am not secure in a position to say whether any such a plan is really practicable. I have not the data at my disposal.[100]

19 April

The Barnes family had its audience with the Pope; and we had a very useful conversation. The conversation will be continued with Mgr. Montini.

The notice came yesterday & I had the greatest difficulty in getting together the necessary clothes, because my dress suit is in Florence. Luckily I had my dinner jacket trousers & waistcoat. I tried Don Jaime, who is about my size. But his only coat was at the tailor's being re-lined. I tried Gabry Paresce, Ranieri di S. Faustino. But their things were packed away in the country. At last I got Tasca di Cutò to lend me his, as well as a shirt, collar & studs. They fitted me tolerably well. But he hadn't a white tie. Eventually I got one from a waiter at the Excelsior, [*illegible*] [*illegible*] & Alberto [*illegible*]. Then I had to get out my golden collar chain & medals from a box at the Collegio Beda.[101] In the end I was equipped and looked O.K. B. Borrowed a suit from Camilla Pasolini & we were lucky to get a taxi from Piazza Cairoli.

The wait in the Vatican was long but interesting, as we found people to talk to. There was among these B's cousins Campello & some of the Pellizzi family.

The Pope is an impressive figure. I was chiefly impressed by his immediate grasp of all the points I missed, his [stringent] & forthright manners & his great charm. He seemed extraordinarily on the spot & exceedingly brilliant. Most people are carried away by his spirituality, but we had business to talk & he responded as a man of practical good sense, rather than one of sympathy. But this is what I needed.

23 April

The massacre of 10,000 Polish officers by the Reds is still being passed over in silence by the BBC.[102] The fiction is still being kept up that it is a German lie. The Russians are trying one lie after another, however, in the vain effort to absolve themselves; and now the Polish Red Cross has made its first report which confines the date of the massacre as having occurred between March and April 1940 – that is, long before the Germans attacked Russia. [words deleted] ~~somewhat later even the English will have to be told the truth.~~

This atrocity is nothing special for the Bolsheviks. But it has caught the public imagination and may do more than anything else to unmask the wickedness of the Soviet Regime.

If General Sikorsky is the honest man I once took him to be (I used to meet him in Lausanne) he will resign.[103] But I expect he is completely corrupted by now.[104]

The British are now telling us that the Germans intend to use poison gas against the Russians.

This means they are contemplating using it themselves in their 'frightfulness' campaign from the air.[105]

We have been visited lately by an interesting young Frenchman who is working on the radio on behalf of the Germans here (attached to the German Embassy). He is a friend of Olga's & is a bright lad [illegible] by name. He says the British propaganda in France has been enormously effective; & that the lies told are beyond – I was about to say – 'beyond belief'. But unfortunately they are believed.

The Germans are, however, now doing useful counter propaganda. Our own on the other hand is very poor as far as France is concerned. It seems we are incapable of swallowing our pride in dealing with France. We make no attempts to flatter the good French; for this is what we ought to do. I am trying to convince the authorities to be more sensible & less provincial; but it is a hard & stubborn task.

Italy should also certainly win the Vatican to her side. Mussolini should make speeches like Franco & Salazar.[106] There need be no shadow of contradiction between Catholic Doctrine & Fascism. This fact should be accentuated at every opportunity & all the Pope's utterings should be given good publicity. I explained all this to Pavolini at Christmastime, when I saw him – and he agreed with me most about my suggestion to flatter & cultivate Petain's France.[107] Since he has taken over the <u>Messaggero</u>, the tone has definitely improved.[108]

Talking of the <u>Messaggero</u> I am now writing a series of small articles for it on England. I had another article the other day on India in the 'Vie del Mondo' with photographs.[109] I am now writing 2 articles on monetary reform for Alberto de Stefani's review 'Scienze Economiche'. De Stefani is sound. He also sees the importance of cultivating the Pope. We have plenty of good men, if we would only use them to better advantage. Recently I went to 2 lectures at the Angelicum by Senatore Orestano.[110] It was excellent. He has also the right point of view towards the war & the Catholic part that Italy ought to play with greater energy & perspicacity.

Emiliano is here for an Easter vacation. He was at luncheon on Easter day & was interesting with his accounts of guerrilla warfare & intrigues which infect the Balkans. One interesting thing he said was that Russia does not want to see the British in Constantinople & a second front in the Balkans. This recreates Russia's veto to the amphibious action planned with King Constantine against the Turks at the beginning of the last war. It fell through owing to Russia's veto & after that King Constantine proposed to try to keep Greece neutral. I wish it would turn out to be true that Russia has again vetoed Churchill's plan & thus my fears of an attack through Turkey by the British will consequently fail to materialise. In that case we may expect their attack against Sardinia & Corsica – with a view later to attempt an invasion of Italy in the Maremma. But this [c/w]ould be hazardous. We should fight like tigers, even more than we are doing in Tunisia.

On Easter night we spent the evening with the Pellizzi & had a long, long talk; but we concluded nothing.

Personally I'm glad that Scorza has been made Secretary of the Fasci.[111] We need to galvanize things a bit & to deal more efficiently with the effective element. These people are furious, which is the chief reason for us to be glad. Chierici instead of Senise as Chief of the Police may also be an excellent appointment.[112] But it is a nuisance for me, as I know Senise which was useful; & I had a lot of difficulty in getting to know him. Now I [shall/will] have to cultivate the new man; for it is very important for me to be known at Police H.Q.

26 April

My March 'Asse in marcia' was sung in 4 parts (Sabatini's score & Galli[n] o's orchestration) by the E.I.A.R. tonight. Quite a worthy programme. Sabatini's fast scoring was excellent.

This is the result of 6 months incessant pressure. At last!

Now I hope it will be from time to time regularly performed.[113]

28 April

The Principessa [Ruffo di Calabria] – [nee Torrigiani] – came to tea. Buona is to see the Queen.[114]

4 May

B. went to Florence – & [I] and Job, with Mariano Frasso went for a gita[115] (Friday to Tuesday) with bicycles from Viterbo – and a wonderful gita it was too. Job very gagliardo,[116] because the distances were long, the hills often very steep and the weather turned raining & wintry. But it was, despite the weather exceedingly enjoyable. From Viterbo we bicycled to Capo di Monte on Lago di Bolsena & had a trip on the lake. It was too threatening to venture to visit the islands, however, as we had intended to do. We had also intended to stay the night at Valentano, but the inn was closed – so on we went, in the rain, to Pitigliano, where we found rooms with difficulty.[117] In all 59 hours.

Pitigliano is perfect & the wine as good.

What a difference too between Lazio & Toscana, where the people immediately become cordial, civilized & engaging.

Next day we had Castell'Ottieri as our objective, via Sorano, which is perhaps the most magically picturesque place of all.[118] We could not do the gorge of the [*illegible*], as I was not certain it was practicable with bicycles. But the road was very beautiful too.

At Castell'Ottieri we were royally entertained by the peasants – relations of Lidia, who is [*illegible*]'s servant. Whole wheat meal bread, cheese, salami & wine – sausage, pane di Pasqua ....[119] Never ate more or better in my life. Cordial & charming types, with their cousins & aunts refined though poor peasants all of them. The girls beautiful.

Then on to Bolsena for the night. 55 hours in all & rain.

At Bolsena, famous for its [*illegible*] & for Santa Cristina, who is Job's birthday saint, we visited the church & admired the Della Robbias.[120]

The back trip to Viterbo was hard / 32 hours / against a head wind; but the woods of Monte Fiascone were gloriously pretty with the trees in full flower; and at Monte Fiascone we had a large meal with its famous wine (though nothing to my mind beats Pitigliano). The open country to Viterbo was a blaze of flowers (blood red clover [*illegible*] especially).

We managed to get some ricotta at a farm.

And so home the next day, very much improved in health & energy. Job's effort was splendid. He was good & brave.

9 May

The fall of Biserta & Tunis comes as an unexpected blow so soon. It had become obvious that it was only a question of time, but I hoped that we should have been able to hold out until the end of the month or even well into June.

The Italians seem to have fought better than the Germans. The latter are the best organisers, but we are the best fighters, man for man.

Now what is going to happen?

That we are in for a hard time goes without saying. That we shall go in fighting harder than ever also goes without saying. We are not down hearted. We are morally more determined and united than before. The closer the war comes to us, the more our people take the war seriously – the more they are determined to win. I still believe that if ever the Axis cracks, Germany will crack before us. But God forbid that it should crack at all.

Today, however, is the worst day of the war. It has come to a dead end. April was also a poor month for the submarine war, and Japan is still, relatively speaking, marking time.

Everywhere else our enemies have the initiative – & Africa is lost. It is difficult to understand why things have gone wrong, why things always just seem to misfire. The forces at our disposal all [though] would seem to have justified better results.

As Scorza said in his fine speech the other day: Those who will win the war are those who believe in the Catholic religion, those who recognise the glory of the House of Savoy, those who have faith in the glories of the Duce.

Well, those are my profound sentiments. Only sometimes I wonder if the Duce has not lost since the close of the Spanish war his wonderful intuition for right action at the right time. Our war has not been conducted with any brilliance. All we can say is that we have fought splendidly. Our people, however are only now beginning to take it seriously. The appointment of a man like Scorza as head of the party should have been made in 1939. It is rather late in the day to pull the nation & party together for a supreme effort. It should have been pulled together a year before we entered the war. Military opportunity after military opportunity has been missed. Part of the missed opportunity is the fault of the Germans for not understanding the importance of Africa. But we have failed to produce a general of first rank, except, perhaps, Messe. He is still holding on in Africa, but is of course doomed. I only hope he will be ordered to return before the capitulation occurs. We can ill spare him.

As it is, have we a plan for resuming the initiative?

Only time will show.

The danger is great, mainly because of the terrible menace of Soviet Russia and from Communism breaking out spontaneously all over Europe in the event of defeat.

We cant just stay put & await the ~~initiative of the~~ enemy's next move.

As Mussolini said in his speech the other day. We must win, because God is just; and we desire nothing else but justice. It was a good little speech; and Scorza's was magnificent – full of lapidary phrases, frankness, humility and humour. 'Friendship should be offered standing. It should be received kneeling.' This is worthy of la Rochefoucauld.[121]

If we look at the war as entering an entirely new phase now that Africa is virtually lost, things do not look so bad as a matter of fact. We have been through a bad patch; but that should not depress us. In the Far East, the situation is disastrous for Chungking & very unfavourable for the Allies.[122] In the western theatre, Europe is fortified and it is impossible not to believe that we have a big offensive plan, which we should be able to initiate before the Anglo-Saxons initiate theirs. As far as resources are concerned, ours are great, even if theirs are greater. But we have the advantage of [interior] lines, greater unity and greater necessity to win. The next 5 months should make it possible to gauge how things are likely to go – but now it is too early to predict anything. It would be a rash man who would say with any confidence which side is going to win.[123]

My application for Italian citizenship has been backed by the Vatican officially. Thus pressure converges through the Pop. Cult. Ministry & the F.O. I must now see Ciano. On Monday B & I will see Mgr. Montini. Then I must see De Cesare again. Meanwhile B hopes to see the Queen. [*illegible*] Altieri has arranged for her to see the Q's chief Lady-in-waiting on Monday – & I must ring up cousin Admiral Renzo Bonetti, with a view to seeing if I might not see the King. Had a good talk with Gabry Paresce.[124]

12 May

We had a grand talk with Mgr. Montini. He is a really sympathetic & brilliant man. I should not be surprised if he were not the next Pope.[125] He advises us to go to Spain if the worst comes to the worst & he will back us up with the Spanish Ambassador to obtain the necessary visas. Alternatively Switzerland.

I followed up this talk with a call on the Irish Minister, MacWhite, who has given me an introduction to Cuesta, the new Spanish Ambassador.[126] S. Faustino meanwhile is arranging for us to see Ciano.

Unfortunately the Queen (and King) cannot receive every subject. But the Contessa Leonardi (Chief Lady in Waiting) has spoken to the Queen about us & a copy of my memo which Polverelli is forwarding to the Duce (in due time – for everything in Rome is eternal) has been given to the Minister of course. So perhaps he may be able to do something about it. Cousin Renzo Bonetti will be on duty at the Quirinal in June, when I shall be able to follow the matter up.[127]

N.B. (Later)

The Contessa Leonardi said to Buona in an agitated voice: 'Oh, but you must flee, you must flee.' This remark seems significant now after the events of July 25. Evidently she knew something of the plot.[128]

In 1939 Balbo should have been brought back & made Under. Sec. for War, Navy & Aeronautics. Scorza should then have been made Party Secretary long ago. Ezio Maria Gray should have been made Propaganda Minister. Graziani Chief of the General Staff.[129] Nasi Governor in Libya.[130] Then we should have been more prepared; and if we had gone to war more or less when we did, we should have done so without warning like Japan – & only against England, with a descent on Malta. But all seems obvious now. Modern wars are not fought with the clarity of ancient times. Mussolini has been too generous and too honest.

Our delaying action in Tunisia has at any rate lost the British 5 months since Churchill made his 'Ivy Bells' speech and 2 months since the Casablanca meeting revised the Tunis talks.[131] Meanwhile the European coasts have been fortified & it is difficult to see how Churchill's 9 months baby (due to be born before November in the form of a 2ⁿᵈ European front) can see the light unless Turkey is violated. But doubtless we are prepared for this eventuality & I cannot but believe that the Germans mean business soon in Russia. Japan also looks like business in the Pacific.

Churchill has gone to Washington presumably to make new plans since the Casablanca plans are now out-dated.

All this is to the good.

We shall of course be badly bombed all this year. But baby killing will only infuriate us & stiffen our resistance.

Convoys through the Mediterranean should also prove very costly for the enemy. So we shall see what we shall see.[132]

14 May

Last night we went to the Pellizzi and talked. Pellizzi thought that an invasion of Italy was not to be excluded & that I must take steps against the possibility in order to save my skin. Well of course I am taking every possible step. My offensive in fact is now in full swing in the Vatican, Polverelli, Bastianini, Ciano, De Cesare, Chierici, Altieri ... for the first essential is to get my Italian citizenship, not because the English would recognise the change, but because, without it, I should not obtain without great difficulty permission to go abroad or to Germany or have, if I got over the frontier into, say, Switzerland, the protection of the Italian State. If I got my citizenship, on the other hand, I might even [now] get a job now in Switzerland or Spain, either on behalf of the Italian Government or privately (Gigi [Miami], for example). Otherwise, I am blocked &, if things suddenly precipitated themselves, I might fail to obtain any facilities at all.

Nor is there any time to lose. The next four months are distinctly dangerous. Personally I do not think that the Anglo-Saxons could land & stay. Personally I still think they intend to make their main thrust through Turkey or the Balkans. Italy will be bombed & subject to many 'butcher & bolt' raids. Pantelleria will be attacked & Lampedusa, & probably taken. Sardinia & Corsica may be made the objective of serious operations. But I don't think Italy will be made the prime objective and, in the event of the British plans succeeding, Germany might well crack first & Italy be spared an occupation.

But this is all surmise. I must be prepared for the worst, even though this time next year we may find ourselves once more in a [*word deleted*] favourable position, and all our fears dissipated.[133]

15 May evening

Today I have seen the Spanish ambassador Cuesta and my old friend the Ambassador Lojacono.[134]

Cuesta is a man after my own heart – quite one of the most sympathetic personalities that I have ever met – keen, intelligent, strong and highly principled. That is how he struck me. The best type of Spaniard of the Franco class. I told him all my story.

He said he would be glad to refer to Madrid (with every prospect of success) to allow us entry into Spain, if the Vatican asked for facilities to be given us. Of course we should need also the permission of the Germans to pass through France and an exit permit from the Italian Authorities.

All this would probably not be so difficult if I got my Italian citizenship. Obtaining it would by no means be easy.

Hence the reason for seeing Lojacono in the afternoon, with a view to getting Bastianini to receive me and hear my story. He sees Mussolini every day. Of course I have no intention of leaving except in the event of collapse of Italy and I shall prefer to go first to Germany to carry on the fight.

Well, Lojacono promises to arrange a meeting. I have now got the Vatican, Ciano and, potentially, Bastianini on the war path, not to speak of Polverelli.

But things must be pushed forward now with all expedition.

Time may run short. The British will doubtless, I should say, make an attempt to seize Sardinia or take Corsica. They have already started bombing with a view to isolating Sardinia or tamper with communications along the west coast of Italy to attack the aerodromes.[135]

Then I believe they will move heaven & earth and act to get Turkey in with them by October, where they should have a million men massed in Syria.[136] I am still confident that this is their plan, determined with pumping supplies into Russia via Persia, [illegible] and bold raids everywhere and a gradual attempt to snap up the islands along the western coast of Turkey. They may also attempt some landings in Normandy or northern France. Sicily or Puglia are also places which may be threatened.

Churchill probably aims at putting the Axis in the dilemma of having to choose between being massacred by Russia or unconditional surrender to Britain after which, with the disappointment of Hitler and Mussolini, he might be prepared to discuss fairly generous terms of peace on the basis of saving European civilisation from a Russian invasion beyond the 1940 frontiers. Finally he probably contemplates blackmailing the USA, by refusing to help the latter against Japan unless Britain is given a position of equality with the States in the division of the spoils and is remitted her debts.

A very ambitious and hazardous programme. But will England stand the pace? There is the submarine campaign to be reckoned with and the tremendous cost in human lives, as well as the prospect of a bankrupt exchequer if the war turns out to last much longer. People in England fear Russia and the idea of a merger with America, whereby Britain would be reduced to a minor partner of the Anglo-Saxon empire. Churchill, it is feared, is only gambling on his chances of turning the tables on his allies. People in England also dread the causality lists and are more concerned with decision to bring about social reforms than with the war. If we can resist, we may still virtually win – especially if the summer campaign against Russia proves a real success. More than that cannot be said at present. The situation is certainly problematical and dangerous. But it is not hopeless.

On Thursday last I was introduced, by the way, by Pellizzi to Prof Prinzing, the big German SS man here. My [illegible] is to cultivate him too, so that, if all goes well with my Italian citizenship, I shall be able to get the German permission to go through France into Spain, should the enemies arrive – or to Germany.

All this requires great activity on my part, what with my work at the Ministry and my business affairs. e.g the placing of my money in real estate at prices which are not too ruinous & the settlement of my affairs with Auristi, which are becoming profitable but slow to terminate.

In Rome it is damnably difficult to get a move on. That is the difficulty – & things may precipitate before I am ready.

17 May

Last night we had our first taste of an air raid close to Rome. All the guns [popped]. This is the beginning, what with the bombing of Civita Vecchia, in the attempt to isolate [Sardinia].[137]

Messe has surrendered with his troops. It seems to me idiotic that he should not have been recalled; Italians have too much the old [sense] of military honour. Our enemies have none. We need not imitate them in frightfulness, but we cant be expected to fight them with one hand tied behind our back. Besides it is said that Italian generals are jealous of Messe & are not sorry that he has been eliminated!

I have [*illegible*] to see Ciano & especially [*illegible*]. It will be interesting to see Ciano again after all these years. Was he responsible for the [*illegible*] policy of 1939–40? I should not be surprised. But then why did Mussolini give him so much rope? These questions, I suppose, will eventually be answered by the opening of the archives. My instinct has been to defend Ciano, because I hate slander; & prefer to regard a man as innocent, if I have no first hand reasons to regard him as guilty. Besides, I liked & admired him as an airman in East Africa. [*Illegible*] he has shown himself to be a snob (he was always that) – & he <u>was</u> Foreign Minister when we made our great mistakes. He cannot therefore altogether be excluded from responsibility. Maybe he has the profiteering mind & he may have thought the outbreak of war in 1939 was Italy's opportunity to profiteer. A great mistake, which may prove fatal. But how was it that Mussolini, I repeat, allowed him to follow this path to ruin?

Buona was right about Tunisia. But I am always biased against making judgements without positive knowledge. Evidently we never expected to hold out indefinitely & never attempted more than a delaying action. But I always hoped we had the intention and the means to stick it out. Without data to go on, it is better to hope, rather than indulge in fears. The general outlook now, for example, does not look well. But we don't know our enemies' difficulties and we don't know in particular how Russia stands. Why then believe the worst? Let us be prepared by all means; but let us keep a good heart. The man-in-the-street – and I am little more than that – has no data to go on by which to judge the war potential at the disposal of one side or the other in a particular phase of the hostilities. We can really only guess. Intuition, which takes into consideration a thousand imponderables, may help us to guess right – but without knowing a great deal more than we actually do, judgements on the military situation must remain mainly guess work. I feel on firmer ground when it comes to politics; for there I have a life's experience to draw on & a flare which might have been counted as genius, if I had had my opportunity.

22 May

I have seen Dr Egidio Ortona, Segretario di Gabinetto of Bastianini.[138] Lojacono has a_so seen Bastianini and my intervention with him seems assured. Zenone Benini is having me introduced to the new Chief of police, Chierici.

What will be the res lt of the Russian campaign this summer? Still indecisive?

Will the British coerce Turkey to come in?

Will the British succeed in taking Italian islands, small and big?

These are the dangers, which, if, as represented by these questions, come to be answered in the affirmative, might lead to a progressive demoralisation of public opinion, here & in Germany during the next 9 months [illegible] coupled with the bombardments from the air.

If on the other hand the answer turns out to be 'no', then our spirits should [illegible] high. If we, that is, Europe can resist all next year, I should not be surprised if the Allies did not show themselves ready to compromise on all essentials, namely: non interference in Europe and a European [illegible] in Africa & the Middle East.

The Allies went to war as into a speculative business. Their so called ideals are only masks to hide their interests. It is always possible to compromise on interests and it may become their interest in due time to cut losses. They are moreover [illegible] in their [illegible] [line deleted].

Yesterday I saw Dr Prinzing again and Von [illegible] who is leaving for 10 days in Berlin. He is going to try to get me an invitation to visit Germany.

10 June

No great progress yet in anything. But I have passed my university exams and can now give more time to my other pressing affairs. I took 30 points out of 30 in Public Law. So far I have done 5 exams and I [illegible] 5 more next year. Shall I ever do them? The war situation is [illegible]. The test is undoubtedly coming. The Italians will fight magnificently. That much is certain. But I am less certain of the material means at their disposal. Meanwhile the submarine campaign is not doing so well. What is the reason? Are there fewer convoys owing to the [illegible] of ships needed for the plans for attempting the invasion of Europe? Are the submarines [illegible] for the fight in home waters? Who knows?

The rumour also goes that the Germans also intend to keep more or less on the defensive in Russia [illegible] the summer. Maybe this is wise – but it also gives Russia a long breathing space. But how can I [illegible] to [illegible]? I can only wait & hope & pray & be good so as to merit the mercy of God.

I am making a new will & preparing a power of attorney [*illegible*] for Mariano Frasso or A.N.OTHER to use on my behalf in the event of my having to go to a neutral country. What a lot there is to do! But bit by bit I seem to be getting things tidied up. I know [*illegible*] that Bastianini intends to help me about my citizenship, but I have not yet seen him. I cannot say that I am yet worrying over much. I believe in the Star of Italy – and I believe in the justice of God.

Cousin Renzo [Bonetti]'s house has been destroyed in Leghorn.[139] He is therefore not on duty this [word missing] at the Quirinal. This is annoying for me, but I feel most concerned for him and his family. Really, so far, we can consider ourselves very lucky. We have much to thank God for.[140]

Job has failed at his exams & will have to do the whole lot in September. This means hard work for him all the summer holidays. What a trouble he is for us all, including himself! All the same, he is a dear – & he will develop. His failure is not down to any lack of intelligence. But he is lazy & not interested. In some ways he is, unlike me, terribly English; and he just cannot concentrate or control his temper. He can be a plague. But he can also be a perfect darling.

> Oh, I love the gorgeous, golden gorse
> and the points [*illegible*] heather,
> As I pick my way, on the back of a horse,
> in squally weather –
> While the wind comes mourning over the hills,
> blowing fits of rain,
> And my mind, forgetful of human ills,
> of the world in pain,
> Soars like the lark and frees itself in song.
> This seems eternity, and no stage too long.

This was made up for Job, but never published, or, for that matter, finished. He is a good companion on the road –, and, with him, I felt like [*illegible*] our recent most excellent competition.[141]

19 June

Nothing has very much happened these days. I have not yet seen Bastianini, but I hear he has matters in hand. Yesterday on the other hand I saw Albini, under sec. of state for the Interior, and it was a really satisfying interview. I pressed my case and he evidently already knew a lot about it (probably owing to Bastianini). He has promised to speak personally to the Duce; and I got the impression that things are definitely moving towards my getting my citizenship.

The Turks keep on declaring that they intend to remain neutral. But the British are evidently hoping that they may be induced to come in. Violating another neutral country would be just like the British, instead of facing up to the hard task of attempting to invade Europe by their own force.

Life is very busy. We have let the flat for the summer to a German medical officer of the Luftwaffe. B and Job are to go to Florence at the end of the month and I shall stay on till about July 11 at the house of the German Terziari di S. Francesco.[142] By that time I hope to get everything tidy – my business, which is going well, my campaign for Italian citizenship (left to work itself out automatically), my various precautionary measures in case things go adversely. Then I mean to take a good holiday and I shall be surprised if, when October comes, things will have got worse. On the contrary, I am confident that our enemies will be profoundly disappointed with events during the summer.

Today I am resting and writing. B and J. have gone to Camilla Pasolini's tenuta in the Campagna.[143] This and their frequent expeditions to Castel Fusano to bathe make me very envious.[144] But I have no time to share these joys.

2 July

B and Job have left and I am now at the casa di S Francesco, [illegible] [illegible]. They have given me the Marchese Patrizi's suite: bed, bath and sitting room. So I am in real luxury. The food is good and sufficient. Everything spotlessly clean. In fact, it is a great palace and I hope to be able to make use of it again and regularly, once a month, supposing we decide to remain in Florence for the winter. This would in many ways be a good situation, for I could do as does Ezra Pound and come one week in 4 and register a dozen talks. The question can be decided later. Meanwhile, we have concentrated practically all our belongings and stores in Florence, as a precautionary measure.

I regard Nov 1st as the date by which things will have become more or less clear. Four months of suspense. Will the English attack Europe in force with a view to establishing one or more 'second fronts'. Presumably they will. They must, after all the advertisement. Will it be Italy or the Balkans, France or Norway, Portugal or Turkey?

The most probable points are: Sardinia, as a preliminary to invading central Italy. Sicily in order to make the Mediterranean safe for convoys and cut Italy's sea communications from one coast to the other. Puglia, to finish off the heel (Taranto-Brindisi line), bottle the Adriatic and invade Albania (in conjunction with an offensive against the Aegean islands, and in the hope of Turkey joining in).

Otherwise ([illegible]) Norway.

On the whole I am confident. Sometimes I feel bleak. But Gentile is right (reference to his splendid speech the other day) in saying that it is really a sin to try to perceive the future.[145] Our business is to do our duty, take our precautions and leave the rest to God in infinite faith.

I saw the Pellizzis tonight and he promises to phone up Dr Ortona with a view to my getting that talk with Bastianini. The private secretary of the Chief of Police also promises to arrange my talk. I shall not go away satisfied unless I succeed in seeing at least Bastianini or Chierici. I hope to learn on Tuesday 13th and I shall have a very long week getting everything into apple pie order. It seems hopeless to see Ciano. He seems to do nothing but play golf & gamble.

There is a Japanese fascist here at the Casa di S. Francesco called Naga who knows Leo Ward.[146] He also works at the Ministero – an excellent fellow. Our old friend Massimo is also here, but temporarily away. I hope he will be back before I have to leave. What reminiscences we shall have to talk over (India – he represented Italy in certain commercial negotiations when we were there and stayed a long time, one of the few nice people we had to talk to.)

4 July

Alarm between 1 and 2 a.m. Evidently the Yankees intended to celebrate Independence day. Every year the fireworks in the USA account for about 100 lives. A few more women and children in Italy to add to the total may be regarded therefore as a quite natural extension of the festivities, given American mentality.

7 July

Yesterday I saw Chierici, Chief of the Police. I had been informed by the Foreign Office that it was useless for me to see Bastianini at present, because my application for Italian citizenship had stuck hard for [6] six weeks with the Chief of Police. Until that obstacle was surmounted, there was nothing to be done.

Well, I found Chierici a man of parts ~~after my own heart~~. He was a friend of Balbo and is of the same type. A strong man, quick in intelligence and at the same time full of good humour and human. The moment I saw him I felt I had won my battle. He soon cut short further discussions. 'My opinion', he said, 'is that it is up to us either to send you away as a dangerous person or to give you Italian citizenship.' He then laughed and promised I should not have long to wait before getting what I desired.

So that's that. I trust the ambition of my life will soon be fulfilled.

This evening I paid a visit on Emanuela de Bourbon. I am very fond of her, but found her tired and out of sorts. She didn't like the Duce's speech.[147] Thought it vulgar and that he had made a fool of himself with his 22 (!) holes of golf. But she was not defeatist, though I gathered she is in the midst of that dreadful defeatist crowd, who influence her and make her feel it is all to no purpose. The same old leitmotiv of hatred of the Germans cropped up. I reacted. But she's fundamentally all right and a very smart thing – evidently feeling the heat. Don Jaime is in Switzerland with the babies.

11 July

So yesterday, it has begun: the attack on Sicily. We must have faith and pray. Communion this morning. Pray and be worthy of the prayers.

Out with the barbarian!

14 July

Leave Rome for Firenze. Glad to be out of the eternal city to enjoy a little country air.

20 July

And now Rome has had its first bombardment. The Jews and the Freemasons, the Anglicans and the Atheists will be as pleased as Punch.[148] But it is the greatest folly that the Anglo-Saxons have committed to date. It is a crime – that goes without saying. Crimes drop off the back of our enemies like water off the backs of ducks. But as a folly, it is the supreme act. For us Italians, it will rouse hatred to fever pitch. As propaganda on our behalf, nothing better could have been undertaken. It has stirred us to the depths and multiplied indefinitely our wish to resist and win.

It will also rouse the Catholic world. It will set 400 million Catholics, the world over, against the enemies of civilisation. It will finally lose Roosevelt his next election: for the Catholic vote counts. It will weaken the elements, hostile to us, in South America. It will dismay people of good will in every part of the globe. Rome is the symbol of justice and order. The bombing of Rome is the symbol of barbarity. The destruction of S. Lorenzo is a violation of the Pope's neutrality.[149] He has now the proof of this wanton and outrageous method of warfare. British and American intrigues at the Vatican have been nipped in the bud for ever. The most influential person in the world will henceforth be morally on our side without doubts. Lying British propaganda has been exposed.

There never was a clearer case of terrorisation being the object of such raids as this.

The railway installations, which were supposed to be the military objective, were mostly missed – and this proves that bombing from 4000 metres (2 half miles up) is hap-hazard and useless occupation from the military standpoint.[150] Some of the bombs fell as far as 1 mile from the railway (and not so very far from our house, as at Piazza Bologna, where our local post office is situated). Besides, some of the machines flew low with no other object but to indulge in a man hunt with their machine guns. Most of the women and babies were killed in this way, as they ran from the shelters. The use of machine guns against railway lines can hardly be called a military action. For this therefore there is not even a military excuse. President Roosevelt had also only recently told the Pope that the American bombers were highly skilled specialists, whose aim could be regarded accurate, especially in day time. He promised that every care would be taken to spare churches and papal property. The result simply throws into relief the hypocrisy of these assurances and the futility of such raids. The Pope, injured in his person by the bombing of his family tomb in the Verano cemetery, with his neutrality violated, and as an eye witness of the baby killing, will doubtless make the required diplomatic practice. He has already addressed an open letter, which, admirable in its Christian charity, nevertheless makes his scorn and disgust sufficiently plain.[151]

This act of bombing Rome following on the manifesto of Roosevelt and Churchill (in which the hand of serpent-Roosevelt is particularly evident, though it is probably [illegible] up the hand of the Pharisee) has almost galvanized the whole Italian people into a fury.[152] The great psychological mistake of the manifesto has been ensured by the great folly of bombing Rome. Good! And it [illegible] do the 'menefreghisti' Romans any harm.[153] Even they, now, have been galvanized to hate and despise the hypocrites, the usurers and the assassins. For that is what our enemies are: Anglo-Saxons, Jews and Russians – hypocrites, usurers and murderers; and each of them eats a little out of the other's pie. Each of them exhibits some of the criminal propensity of the others in addition to his own particular vice. Together they exhibit the three vices chiefly condemned in the gospel – together with treachery – in their case the betrayal of civilisation.

So the war goes on and the Anglo-Saxons are counting their dead in Sicily. Italy spurns their ridiculous offers of peace. Roosevelt did not even dare descend to details. Italians are not Americans. They are not quite so dumb. They cannot be led astray by vague generalities; and even if they were promised everything they desire, they would not betray their allies anymore than they would put faith in Roosevelt's word. No doubt the bombing of Rome was actuated partly out of spite for the scornful rejection of the manifesto.

If we can resist in Sicily and go on sinking ships at the present rate for 2 months (or even one) the Anglo-Saxons will be done – or they will be, at any rate in bad case. They will be forced to acknowledge failure, if they don't make good quickly – forced to change their plans.

Let us hope & pray & above all fight.[154]

It is a joy to be back in Florence. Here there is a much better spirit than in Rome; and everybody is charming, courteous and clean. The only worry is Sicily. Things are not going well, as I see it. But it is difficult to know the truth – and it is <u>puzzling to hear</u> <u>why</u> things are not going better.[155]

24 July

Palermo has been evacuated. Except for our defence on the sides of Catania, we are now thrown back on the main mountain barrier. From the west, moreover, there is no first class natural line until after Cefalu.[156] So we shall probably be forced back to beyond this town too.

The choice of Sicily, rather than the easier attack on Sardinia, reveals the tremendous strength of the Allied offensive. I expected Sardinia to be their first move, because we were told that Sicily had been so strongly fortified that it might practically be regarded as impregnable.[157] Otherwise, however, Sicily was the obviously most suitable first target from the strategic standpoint. If Sicily falls, the eastern Mediterranean would be severed from the western. The Italian battlefleet which, though strong in battleships, is not sufficiently protected by cruisers and destroyers, would then be [illegible] [illegible] in the eastern Mediterranean. It has not even been able to intervene to help to defend Sicily. It has no bases for fuel supply sufficiently south on the western side, and it would be folly to attempt to pass the Straits of Messina. This all points to the possibility of the Allies' plans being directed, after Sicily, to the Balkans, as I always have believed. If they delivered their main attack against Sardinia next, the Italian fleet might be forced to intervene even to the point of self sacrifice. It could operate in Sardinian waters. Maddalena, Porto Vecchio, Porto Ferraio,[158] & even [illegible] & Spezia would form useful points of support. The fleet could inflict great damage on the enemy's assaulting forces, should they decide to operate against Sardinia or, alternatively, against the Italian mainland – Naples, for example, which could be exposed to attack.

An attack on Puglia, on the other hand, would, with the fall of Sicily, have many advantages. It would be entirely [illegible], while convoys through the Mediterranean would become to a large extent invulnerable. I fear therefore that the Allied plan is scheduled as follows: – 1 month to take Sicily (e.g. to [illegible] 10). A fortnight's delay to reform. 1 month to take Southern Apulia,[159] namely, to establish a line from west of Taranto to north of Brindisi. A fortnight's delay to reform – and, then, the invasion of the Balkans, the entry of the Allied fleet into the Adriatic, the turning of the defences in Greece, the establishment of the 2nd front [illegible] on the

Danube right across at [first] to Salonika. This would mean the revolt of Greeks & Jugoslavs, the [illegible] bombing of the Roumanian oil fields, the possible entry of Turkey into the war against us. The fat would indeed then be in the fire. Italy would become practically a useless limb. From a military point of view the only thing to do would be to evacuate all Italy to the line of the Po. But I doubt if the Italian people would stand this. The sacrifice would be too terrible, the demoralisation too great. The [illegible] might even deem it sufficient this year to establish the old Balkan front from [illegible] to Salonika, together with [illegible] & [illegible] Adriatic ports.

All hope therefore lies in delay, in resistance [illegible] the first stages. There is a limit to the Allied shipping. In a fortnight, [illegible] from the Atlantic & Pacific battles, where not less than 500,000 gross [registered] tons of shipping have been sunk this month, the Allies have certainly lost 300,000 more tons in Sicilian waters. The Germans put it at 600,000 tons. I shall put it [illegible] at 2 1/2 times the tonnage [illegible] in the [illegible] – e.g. 150,000 tons x 2.5 = 375,000 tons. I think this is a safe estimate, because of the large numbers of ships sunk of which the tonnage has not been given.

Now, if we value 3,000,000 tons as the maximum amount of shipping available for the Mediterranean supply system, we have it that in one fortnight, this [illegible] fleet of vessels has been decimated. As much again has been put out of commission by damage. Should therefore these losses continue, 20 per cent of the tonnage available would be disposed of by August 20th – 40 per cent before the Balkans could be invaded and the [illegible] – with as much again damaged. Consequently, resistance beyond the scheduled delay not only means that the invasion of the Balkans would come when the winter rains & snow begins (mid-November) and therefore be hampered by disastrous weather conditions, but the wear & tear on the supply ships might easily become fatal for the Allied plans – probably sufficiently fatal to force them to change their plans, to switch to operating preferably in the western Mediterranean and to [illegible] their bid to [illegible] Europe until the spring. And this might prove too late. That is the hope & the supreme effort must be made to substantiate it – at all costs. Mussolini has been too optimistic. The fall of Palermo has come as a great blow. The country feels M has lost grip. The Scorza efforts to clean the Party & pull the country together have come terribly late. This should have been undertaken months ago – [illegible], years. It should have been undertaken in 1939.

26 July

Last night we were shocked to hear on the wireless of the fall of Mussolini and today the stories of riots in Florence have filled us with alarm. All the subversive elements – all the toads and cowardly vipers took the opportunity to avenge. Fascists have been assaulted and even killed, and fascist emblems torn down and trampled in the dust. It has become unsafe to profess the fascist faith or to wear the fascist badge. People who yesterday cried 'Duce, Duce' are now ready to cry their execration. Banquets have been held to celebrate Peace. At Mosciano the word FINIS has been chalked up on the Blackshirt Afterwork House.[160] Treachery and ingratitude is in the air. Never have I felt so utterly disgusted and humiliated. But it is too early to comment. But surely, the King of Italy and Badoglio are not traitors! And I have still faith in their ability and will to put an end to these disgraceful scenes. The House of Savoy, I believe, will save the situation; and Badoglio, though I do not like him (for he has always been a jealous intriguer) is a magnificent soldier; and now that he has reached the culminating point of his ambition, he will desire to show himself not only master of the situation but to go in history as the saviour of his country. That should be the logic of it anyhow!

As for ourselves we do not know yet what to do. We have resolved to [illegible], to get everything ready to return to Rome, or go North & to leave our things in safe custody. This means sorting & [illegible] & much [illegible]. We must not lose our heads or worry uselessly – just make ourselves ready to face the worst & [ask] for the best, as best may be.

To [capitulate] would mean bolshevism sooner or later. [That is] certain – and the reasons are indifferent. And a British or American occupation, even if it saves us from Bolshevism, will be even worse – because it would mean the [illegible] & death of Italy.

The one crumb of comfort this evening is the B.B.C. which is lying in an [illegible] of excess. That is always a good symptom. Things cannot be as bad as they seem. Badoglio has said that the war continues. The King has said that we shall keep faith.

Yesterday I posted a letter to Mgr. Montini pointing out the lie which the B.B.C. has broadcast with the [illegible] of [illegible] Catholic opinion all the world over. The B.B.C. has in fact announced that the Vatican wireless has denied the published words of the Pope regarding the destruction of the Basilica of S. Lorenzo. It declares that the pope never said that the Basilica had been partly destroyed, but only that it had been damaged. Yet, as I listened in, I had in my hand the Osservatore Romano with the Pope's words officially reproduced. All this is a comfort. It shows that our enemies are afraid.[161]

28 July

Here is my first comment on the situation. It is taken from a talk which I have prepared for my next broadcast.

'The Italian people, in the face of the military events of the past year – the loss of North Africa and the invasion of Sicily – have been feeling a growing disinterest with the conduct of the war. Secondly, many people (for it is easy to be wise after the event) felt that the moment of Italy's intervention had been ill-chosen and that the country had been ill-prepared to face the tremendous military task assumed by Mussolini. Thirdly, there was a widespread conviction that many fascist chiefs had not shown [illegible] worthy of their responsibilities. [had betrayed Fascist idealism] and that the Party machine had not [interpreted], as it was supposed to interpret in [illegible] with the fascist idea, the entire nation. Instead of being, as they were meant to be, a political aristocracy, many had shown themselves to be [moreover], self-seeking and partisan. [The Party had failed to conciliate the necessity for authority and corporative organisation with a right conception of liberty.] For all this, Mussolini was held, as head of the Government, to be at any rate fundamentally responsible; and the demand therefore arose, not necessarily, for a change in leadership, but for a broadening of the basis of the national life [for a greater breath of liberty] [word deleted] a clean sweep of the corrupt and partisan elements and a stronger grip on the whole situation.

In the light of these deeply rooted and openly expressed feelings, Mussolini called the Grand Fascist Council together in consultation. He had just met Hitler with whom he had discussed military plans. What these plans were are of course secret. The imagination of Anglo-Saxon propagandists has speculated on the nature of these plans and it may be said definitely that these speculations have been wide of the mark. Be this as it may, the Grand Fascist Council was called together to discuss the outstanding problems of the day and the outcome of these discussions was the [talking] of a [motion] by Dino Grandi which in broad lines sought to interpret, according to his lights, public opinion. Mussolini did not see fit to agree to the terms of the motion and it was put to the vote. The result left Mussolini in a minority of 19 votes to 7. Consequently, Mussolini had no alternative but to tender his resignation to the King.

These are the facts. The King, making use of the Royal prerogative reserved to him by the constitution, therefore invited Marshal Badoglio to take into his hands the reins of government, and, with the King's wisdom, no better choice could have been made. The result has satisfied public opinion and has brought about the unity of [that] [nation] which was so ardently desired. The military character of the new Government, with Italy's greatest soldier at the top and the King himself in supreme command of Italy's land, sea and air forces, has also provided the required guarantee of a more efficient conduct of the war.

All this is obvious enough. But what has escaped the notice of the Anglo-Saxons is that the Italian Constitution, even in a moment of grave emergency, has worked with a striking smoothness, that Italian institutions are well and solidly founded, and that the voice of the people not only cannot be stifled, as in America and Britain, but that it has proved possible for the Government to maintain with the people of Italy, under the Constitution, that sensitive touch which is the essence of any true democracy.

In plutocratic America and Britain, on the other hand, the power of a President and the power of a Parliament which was elected 8 years ago and has lost all touch with public opinion, can ride roughshod over the people's will. If Churchill were defeated in Parliament, he would be forced to resign. But he has a cast iron majority and he has no intention of obtaining a renewed mandate. The political majority, moreover, of the Italian people has been amply vindicated. This is what has so enraged Mr. Roosevelt and Mr. Churchill [vide their latest speeches]. It is another proof that it is they who [are] the real, ruthless dictators and the real aggressors; and that it is Italy, not America or Britain, who has given proof of her will for freedom, for her love of liberty.

As soon as the new Italian Government was formed, there was a brief period – lasting about 24 hours – of bewilderment. Some fascists, whose personal loyalty to Mussolini came uppermost in their minds, doubted as to the proper attitude they should take up. At the same time, some subversive elements, encouraged by Anglo-Saxon propaganda, imagined in their blindness and folly, that their moment had arrived. But they soon found out their mistake. Marshal Badoglio immediately took all the measures required to [meet] the situation and, in fact, he has had no difficulty, since his Government rests on popular [esteem], in establishing order and discipline throughout the country. The country has indeed responded magnificently to his appeal. It has put aside all thought of partisanship and has rallied to a man round the House of Savoy, symbol of Italian unity, glory and good faith. The war continues. The country is united with a will more firmly expressed than ever to defend its soil from the invader, to face up to the stick, to [illegible] the [illegible] and to win.

The above of course is propaganda. It is not exactly what I think, but what we should endeavour to make our enemies think.

There is of course more to it than all this. It was evident that the greater unity and discipline required to make the emergency was not going to be tolerated by the Italian people at the hands of the Fascist Party. The attempt to clean up things from within had come too late. Mussolini's absence has been felt for a long time. Ever since our return to Italy in 1939 I have been conscious of his loss of grip. His 'tempismo'[162] seemed to have deserted him. His mistakes have been serious and he has paid the consequences. But to say this, is not to desert his memory or to deny his greatness. To turn on him now and on the Fascist regime as initiated and guided by him denying these 20 years would be to forget the wonderful and permanent work which he has accomplished. His name will go down in imperishable fame, as a great and good man, who, more than many other living statesmen or, for that matter, any statesmen of the modern era, has done more for his country and more for the common people. Fascism is not dead. It is, on the contrary, really triumphant. All that Fascism needed was a greater saturation with the Catholic spirit and it is for this which I have always laboured as well as for a broadening of its basis. If this had been done in time, as I urged, the situation might have been saved and Fascism's popularity regained. Fascism has been betrayed by Italians calling themselves Fascists. It is hard to have to say it, but the Italians are an easily corruptible people. They have little civic sense. They are jealous and invidious and each man works too much for his own selfish interests. To blame Fascism for the corruption is not just. There was the same corruption before – Italy has proved unworthy of Fascism. But Italy will go on and grow less corrupt as she grows out, then she will come into her own. Her vitality is unimpaired. Fascism in the ideal sense of the word is moreover indestructible. It will triumph over Bolshevism in the long run and on that equally vile heresy – liberalism. Of that I am sure. Liberalism is dead, in any case. The practical danger is Bolshevism. The changes here in Italy today do not therefore represent the destruction of Fascism, which is the only alternative to Bolshevism, but the purge of the corruptions of Fascism. The penalty has had to be paid. Mussolini of course was personally incorrupt. His faults were rather his jealousy of others and his incomprehension of the Anglo-Saxon world. But he was a great man and it [illegible] my heart to hear the cowards toadies throwing mud on him now. It is disgracefully unjust. History will vindicate him. He will be bracketed with Augustus. As it is, my hope is in the King, my trust in God. We must pray and be infinitely charitable. If we can do that our prayers will be answered.[163]

I remember telling Mariano Frasso (for whom, with Francesca, I feel exceedingly anxious these days) almost 6 months ago, that if I succeeded in seeing Mussolini I would tell him that the only way to regain for Fascism its popularity was not only to take in hand a real and thorough purge, but to declare every Italian member of the Party – in other words to identify Fascism with the nation. A small black list would then be kept of unworthy persons. Having done that, he could renew the ranks in command, selecting people of scrupulous honesty and, especially, prominent Catholics. That was the way out. But I never had a chance to tell him, and, if I had, he would probably not have taken my advice.[164]

It is an criminal fact that Badoglio must do exactly what Mussolini would wish to be done. The only justification for the change, in other words, is that what the people will accept from Badoglio (and the King), they were not ready to accept any more from Mussolini. What would have happened, however, if Grandi had not tabled his motion? Would Mussolini have weathered the storm? Did Grandi and Bottai seek to turn Mussolini out with a view to succeeding him or was their motion more disinterested? These questions are pregnant. Some of them will be answered in due time.

If Badoglio can carry out the task of resistance in Sicily so that the Anglo-Saxon plan for a 2nd front fails to be established by November, the situation may be saved. But if he is overwhelmed by the demands for peace, if he surrenders to the mob or to the British and Americans, then, I fear, all will be lost.[165] Sooner or later Bolshevism would be a certainty. Anyhow, everything would depend on Germany and her task would probably be too heavy.

November 1 is the crucial date. The soil of Italy's mainland must not be violated before then by invasion, nor yet the Balkans. That is the task before us.[166]

I used to say in 1925 that the Fascist Party must be like the Gods of Walhalla. It must work for its own destruction. It must become absorbed in the Nation. It has failed to do this; and in recent years Mussolini became a prisoner of a Party which degenerated into a camorra. Hence the present pass. But a new Catholic, wholly national and European minded Fascism will return. On that I am convinced and Mussolini will lead it. He will come back, greater than ever![167]

31 July

Yesterday & today was like the 'hottest day' in London – damp & terribly oppressive. I hope it is the same & worse in Sicily, for it will try the Allies more than us. We sweated on Friday down to Florence & home again. I saw Niccolò [illegible] and made certain arrangements with him to meet certain hypothetical circumstances. All seems quiet enough in Florence [illegible]. The streets are well patrolled by soldiers and the people have gone back to work as usual. The mottoes from the speeches of Mussolini have the most part been wiped off the houses & many fascist emblems removed. W il Re! W l'Italia! Have taken their place for the most part, though occasionally there is to be seen a few wicked and stupid things scrawled on the walls. Among the stupid ones I saw 'Torneremo dove eravamo – a presto'.[168] Well, history cannot be turned back into a phrase & if there is, when the war is over, an attempt to restore the old liberal institutions, it will end in either farce or disaster. Meantime the Badoglio Government cannot really do anything but do what Mussolini himself would have wished, namely, to get the maximum unity and the maximum discipline among the people with a view the better to repel the invader. Mussolini's motto: 'Credere, obbedire, combattere'[169] is as much today the 'parola d'ordine'[170] as ever; and whether fascist institutions may be [illegible] or taken over by the State, they cannot be dispensed with. The [Maternity] & [Infant] Welfare Association, for example – the After Work Institution, the Trade Unions etc, etc, etc. Their continued existence only shows what is [owed] to the Mussolini regime. There can be no going back to the chaos of individualism. The workers must still be protected & assisted. Cooperation between the classes and conciliation of the interests under the authority of the state, which is the essence of the fascist social ideal must remain the [imperative] of any subsequent regime or we shall slip to Bolshevism. Badoglio's task is to win the war or at least to stop the enemy putting his foot on the terra firma of Italy.[171] If he can do that, his work will be amply justified. If he cannot, he will have done nothing. If he fails & then succeeds in getting better terms for a defeated Italy than what the Anglo-Saxons would have been prepared to concede to Mussolini, so much to the good. But if Mussolini had come face to face with capitulation to the enemy, a change of government would have been inevitable in any case. So it will not be necessary to thank Badoglio for seeking better terms, if we are forced out of the war. Somebody [illegible] [fascist] would have to have done that much in any case. Everything therefore depends on how the war goes. I shall bless Badoglio if he saves our country from humiliation and defeat. If he does not, he [illegible] only [illegible] & be a [illegible].

We have decided to stick together (Buona, Job & I) as far as possible in this crisis – not to separate. It is difficult to know what to do, because it is impossible to foresee events. All we can do is to be prepared as far as possible to [illegible] one move or another according to a plan of alternatives. For the moment, we are packing up everything in the little house, [illegible] only [illegible] strictly necessary for living here should we stay or return. Our present idea is to return with suitcases to Rome for a short period in order to keep in contact; [leave] [illegible] [boxes] [ready for dispatch to Rome] should we decide to stay in Rome (winter clothes and other [illegible] [illegible] here) and leave our other packed things ready to store. All this implies careful selection and '[stiff] work'. Since [illegible] will have [illegible]. We cannot be in two places at once &, if things precipitate, we cannot have everything at hand. Meantime our scheduled date for Rome is in about 15 days time. The military situation should be clearer by then, at any rate. Much depends on the next ten days or so [illegible section].[172]

I should imagine that Badoglio's plan is to stalemate the Anglo-Saxons until [winter comes]. He probably hopes that if by then nothing worse has happened then the loss of Sicily (and all the better if Sicily is not lost) and if no second front in Europe has been established, there might be a good chance of an armistice based on the status quo of the day and of a peace conference. If he fails on the other hand, to carry out this stalemate during the next 3 months & if further military disasters occur, I doubt if he will be able to stop a general stampede for peace. What could happen then, I don't know. It would depend on Germany's ability to save Europe more probably she would eventually surrender too. Pray God that Germany would prove strong enough. But there is also to be envisaged the possibility of the Allies refusing to consider an armistice even if they failed in their objectives between now and November. In that case also, I cannot hazard a guess as to what would happen. There again I can only pray that the Italian people would have the guts to go on. For then we should have a chance of winning the war in the minimum sense.[173]

A Catholicized Fascism is what we must aim at – a Fascism based on unequivocally on the [encyclicals] of the Popes. This will be the great issue when the war is over: a Catholicized Fascism – a march towards Rome as the only alternative to the Devil & [Judaism].[174]

'I have come to [fulfil] not to destroy.' I understand these words of Christ to mean that the old iron law, as revealed to mankind both in Jewish & Pagan civilisations, [*illegible*], the Gospel, however, was to transcend them. But the Gospel without the old iron laws of natural religion is useless. Without the old laws the Gospel degenerates into weakness and sentimentality. Better a Pagan than a worldly Christian. (Thought for the day for the benefit of Italians.)[175]

3 August

I saw my great friend Nello Maraini today. I said to him: [']Se Badoglio ha il buon senso di capire la necessità di voler resistere fino alla metà di novembre (in ogni caso), se esiste la possibilità materiale di resistere fino a quell'epoca, se da militare di grande ingegno [può] escogitare buoni progetti di difesa, e nello stesso tempo, da buon [*illegible*] si dimostra capace di [mareggiare] il popolo italiano, allora ci sarà buona speranza di arrivare ad un compromesso [*illegible*]. Altrimenti tutto sarà perduto, e l'unica speranza per la salvezza del mondo starà nella forza di resistenza della Germania e del Giappone.

Amo l'Italia più che mai; ma gli italiani mi hanno disilluso. Tocca agli italiani adesso di disilludere le mie disillusioni. Nei prossimi mesi, chi vivrà, vedrà.'[176]

Nello agreed with <u>my diagnosis</u> & we were also agreed that the idea of a return to Liberalism was ridiculous except as a means of 'managing' the Italians & as a diplomatic card to play with as far as America & England are concerned. A return to Liberalism might last 2 years. It would inevitably lead to a new form of Catholicized Fascism or else to Bolshevism.

Nello was of the same opinion.

Our Father, lead us not into <u>tribulations</u>.

7 August

I welcome the enquiry which is to be made into the profiteering of persons who have held public office during the last 22 years.[177] The behaviour of some has been scandalous. My prejudice has always been to defend people against calumny, especially in Italy where envy & jealousy is so rife. All the same, I expect Ciano will prove to be one of the chief offenders. But what about Badoglio himself? He has built himself a monster house on a valuable garden site in Rome. If the whole property (unfurnished) cost less than 4 to 6 million lire, I should be surprised; [*deleted word*] Badoglio was reported to be of a family of moderate means. Nor did he marry wealth. Nor did he give many appearances of wealth before 1938.

My prejudice was to defend Ciano in the past. He has many admirable qualities and I fancy <u>Edda</u> is the chief to blame. She has always been an impossible woman, headstrong (like her father) and devastatingly intellectual. [*Words deleted*]. Mussolini adored her & could refuse her nothing. She made Ciano & then corrupted him by her ambition for power, wealth & social position. She turned him into an ape of the worst examples of futile Roman society & is personally responsible for the frivolous foreign policy during our year of non-belligerency. I put the profiteering also down to her, and much of the failure of the fascist Party to reform itself in time. Married to a normal, good woman, Ciano would probably have had in any case quite a brilliant career; but he would not have got spoilt. Married to Edda, his meteoric career has ended in dust.[178]

The great mistakes have been: –

1 The failure of the Party to merge itself in the nation, and make itself nothing more than a National Union Society.

2 The turning of the Party into a regular <u>Camorra</u> (and this is the fault of the Italians.)

3 The failure to democratise the Trade Unions e.g. to allow the completely free elections of their representatives and socialise the big industries.[179]

4 The ghastly complication of the bureaucratic [*illegible*] & multiplication of institutions – all a process of graft. The corporative organisation was admirably economical, but ruined by [superstitions] & red tape.

5 The [*illegible*] policy adopted during our year of non-belligerency & the ill-chosen moment of entering the war (though I doubt if it would have been possible to postpone our coming in beyond the Spring of 1941, because England would assuredly have in any case forced the position in the Balkans & plotted with Russia). But we [would/could] have made ourselves better prepared both morally & militarily by Sept. 1940 (which is the very <u>latest</u> date for us to have entered the war). The country should have been put a year [previously] on a war [*illegible*] footing – and we should never 'have stabbed France in the back'. We should have made war only against England & then only if forced to do so [~~and not if possible until the spring~~].

6 The failure to take full advantage of the conciliation with the Vatican. If Mussolini had been a Franco or a Salazar, in this respect, he [*illegible*] would have shown great wisdom. But just as Italians have generally failed to develop a high civic sense, so they have failed to develop a really deep rooted faith. There are

too many sceptics. Too many [*illegible*] who only go to Church to please their wives, but never confess (except on their death beds) because they cannot bring themselves to repudiate some 'kept' woman around the corner. Too many semi-educated <u>parvenus</u> who think it modern and knowledgeable to declare that all religions are really alike – one as good as another and probably all of them equally wrong, though all, pragmatically speaking, also equally true – Anyhow, nothing much to choose between. Mussolini never really got much beyond grasping the <u>political</u> importance of the [*illegible*] & the po_itical importance of [*illegible*] the growth of a Catholic spirit, as a safeguard against subversive and Jewish conspiracy. He is said to call himself a Catholic & morally perhaps he may be regarded as a sincere convert. But his Catholicism has [*illegible*] in practice a reality easily forgettable while things go well & fear does not grip the heart or [*illegible*] assail the mind. There are countless people like that; and I bet my last bottom dollar that if divorce, for example, were allowed in Italy, 90 per cent of persons declaring themselves to be Catholic, but who happened to contract unhappy marriages, would take advantage of the law. Divorce is indeed a very good test of the presence or absence of a real, deeply rooted faith; & I do not think a high percentage of Italian Catholics would pass the test, though perhaps these would [remain] a high percentage on the other hand of Italians disposed to make their married lives a success as a social unit. In this respect there is still here an excellent, operating tradition. Italians <u>do</u> seem to understand what the English have long forgotten that <u>love</u> is a question of the <u>will</u>.[180]

I see everything drifting towards Bolshevism. The chances of resisting the clamour for peace by the Italian people – peace at any price, here and now, are not great. The chances of not having peace imposed on us by further disasters between now and November (further military defeat and internal collapse) are not great. The chances of Germany thus being able to save Europe are not great. That I fear is the actual situation. All I can say, as far as myself and family are concerned, is that the chances of Badoglio securing conditions for an armistice which could limit the occupation by the enemy to Corsica, Sardinia, Sicily, Calabria, Campania, Lucania, the Puglia, Albania, and [*illegible*], on condition the Germans do not occupy a line south of Spezia-Rimini, are perhaps fairly good (about 50 and 50); and that would at any rate enable us (I speak of myself and my family) to carry on for a bit and take further stock for the morrow. But what then? Central Italy would almost starve.

Unless Britain and America are prepared to garrison Western Europe indefinitely and are prepared, if necessary, to fight Russia, Bolshevism is bound to come within 2 years of the departure of the Anglo-Saxon garrison.

And I regard the chances of the British and Americans being prepared
to defend Europe against the Soviets as practically nil. I doubt also their
capacity, even if the will was there.

What we (myself and family) will be able to do in the circumstances,
God alone knows.

If Bolshevism could be <u>humanized</u>, if it were prepared to tolerate religion
(not only as an inner sentiment, but as an outward expression: to leave the
churches and the ecclesiastical authorities free to minister to their flocks)
and if owners of property were not robbed of their personal possessions,
including their homes, and could receive some moderate compensation for
the loss of their capital (sufficient to keep them in decent conditions over
a 30 year transition period) and, finally, if protection were given to the
small owner and craftsman in some form or another, Bolshevism would
not be so bad and potentially preferable than Capitalism. In other words, a
thoroughgoing form of Socialism, coupled with a wide tolerance of religion
and a human, practical compensation for the dispossessed, would probably
improve the world in many ways and bring that urgently needed unity to
Europe. Italy would live and grow in strength and virility; and nobody need
starve or be persecuted. But is there any hope of Bolshevism being so kind? I
doubt it. I fear the Jews are as much behind it as they are behind Capitalism
and they want to wreck all good life except for themselves.

Capitalism, Liberalism on the other hand would mainly mean the
slavery of the masses and the rotting of Italy and Western Europe – ruin,
unemployment, emigration, and worst of all, social decay and national
ignominy. Really, in such an alternative, I would rather see the Russians
here than the Anglo-Saxons.

If only we could (myself and family) escape from both! But how and
when? No part of the world would be safe from either, the devil or the deep.
Ireland might be the last refuge in Europe; the Argentine and Canada in
the Americas; S. Africa ....[181] or else Japan. But how to get to any of these
places and how to start life again, if we get there?

These are the facts which have got to be faced: and it looks as if only a
miracle could save us.[182]

The reason why I think Badoglio might secure terms allowing for an
'unoccupied' area in central Italy, (including Rome, all Lazio, Tuscany,
Umbria, the Abruzzi and the Marche) is merely because a no man's land
might be to the advantage of the British and the Americans. The Germans
would probably limit themselves to occupying a line from near Spezia to
Parma and along the Po to the Adriatic; and it would probably pay the
British and Americans better to switch their main fighting front to the
Balkans and to control the Adriatic with the fleet. That is the immediate
hope from the personal point of view. It would provide time and a period
of repose during which I could do some business, get everything shipshape
and make new plans as the situation developed. Otherwise, we shall be
hunted refugees.

Or will there be a miracle? Will Badoglio and the King achieve a second Piave?[183]

Talking to people here, they have all, except a tiny minority, turned against Mussolini to a man. They would be ready to cut his throat. They have forgotten all he has done for the working classes and for Italy. They are like wolves against the leader of the pack grown old. Cowards and Liars. All they think of is peace, reckless of the consequences. Next they will be turning on Badoglio and on the King. The only question is whether Badoglio has the force to carry his good intentions through. If he succeeds, then the people, owing to his success, will fawn on him as they fawned on Mussolini. If he fails, they will bury him in mud, as they have buried Mussolini – and set up a new fetish, only to pull _that_ down in turn as things hasten on towards chaos and greater ruin. The truth they will never recognize. In _every_ country the people are beneath contempt. Stalin knows that as well as anybody; and he too would be pulled down and spat upon if it were not for his Chekas and GPUS.[184]

9 August

Someone who knows Badoglio told us yesterday that he had _hopes_ of being able to wrangle a separate peace for Italy by which Italy would be spared invasion or occupation. Of course she would have to consent to being disarmed & [_illegible_] surrender her fleet. Germany, it is said, would consent to this & refrain from occupying any part of Italy, though I should say she would be [_illegible_] take at least also [_illegible_], Fiume, Pola & Trieste & of course [_illegible_].[185] No doubt, in such a case she would also [run] with the Anglo-Saxons for the occupation of the entire Dalmatian coast. Moreover she would probably [_illegible_] the [run] as far as the line [Valona]–Salonika but she might [miss] getting to [_illegible_] first.

Such a solution would be tolerable; for Germany would not be much weakened, if at all. Italy is at present a dead weight to her. This dead weight on the other hand would be set off by a greater burden in the Balkans; and, as I say, Germany would probably not succeed in promoting the establishment of an Anglo-Saxon front from [Valona] to Salonika. It is difficult to say.

From our own personal point of view, this solution would [remove] from us great anxieties. We shall be safe & probably be in a position to do some good business. It would be ideal if Germany then proceeded to win the war and save the world.

Whether Badoglio's _hopes_ have any foundation in reality remains to be seen. I continue to believe that the Anglo-Saxons would be reluctant to give up Italy as a spring board for [penetrating] the Balkans & as a bombing

centre at the present juncture. But if we can resist a few months longer, the chances of getting out of it all, like that, would be [*illegible*] improved.[186]
It is a mistake to plant
Narcissuses in the interstices of the proboscises of rhinocerouses.[187]

13 August

We have packed up all loose objects at the little house, save those strictly needed for daily use, & we are starting back, with many regrets, for Rome – staying at the dear 'Helvetia' two nights en route[.] I am told that Badoglio's monstrosity of a monster house was given him by a grateful Government after the Ethiopian war. So it was <u>not</u> the result of profiteering & I, in suggesting such a thing as possible, have evidently maligned him. I apologise. All the same, I utterly mistrust the man. He is reputed to be a freemason. He is jealous, ambitious and unscrupulous. He let down Graziani in the Ethiopian war in order to keep all the laurels for himself![188]

14 August

8 heavy pieces of luggage were sent off by the C.1.7 to Rome this morning and we have 10 things to take with us – 18 in all. But at 1 o'clock we hear that Rome has again been bombed and that the railway is interrupted somewhere beyond the Central Station. I therefore decide that the best way to keep in touch with our luggage is to register it to Viterbo via Orte by the same train as ours. Blood to the head! For the luggage must first be stopped. I rush to the station and hold it up just in time, subtracting at the same time my bag containing indispensable clothes. After a sweaty day (13th) we get all in order and go to bed early, for we have to leave the hotel at 4.am before the curfew is over. Special arrangements have to be made for a vehicle to take our hand things to the station. But we get off all right in a relatively empty train, as Rome is the last place to which people want to go to now.
We arrive in Orte at 8 o'clock and seek a rest house for the day. The train for Viterbo is not scheduled to leave until 3.35 in the afternoon. After considerable delay we find a primitive little hotel and, after eating the food we brought with us, we go to bed for 3 hours. Then down to the boiling hot station for luncheon at 2 o'clock. The station reminds us of India. Hundreds of people sitting on the platform waiting patiently for trains. After the bombing of Rome and Terni, things are somewhat disorganized. Our train, to be driven by an old steam engine, gives no signs of starting. We sit patiently with the rest of the crowd, sweating from every pore. The train gets away at least an hour and three quarters late. We puff our way through delightful country to Viterbo; but the heat is trying. At 7 we arrive

in Viterbo. The only good hotel is full, but thanks to my old friends at the 'Pergoletta' the situation is saved and we secure a room with 3 beds, the same room as Job, Massimo and I used when we went on our cycling tour at Eastertide. Most of the luggage has to be left at the station as there are no means to carry it. We have to buy the things needed for the night ourselves and it is 8.00 before we reach the hotel. I had to fight my way to unload our 11 packages from the train, for it was literally assaulted on arrival by crowds of refugees from Rome going further north. Rumour has it that also Viterbo is to be bombed. Tired and weary, after a wash down, we wander into the town to get a meal. But there is no food to be had anywhere. The hearty parachutists, who train here – great looking young men, all looking as if they were ready to eat the Anglo-Saxons alive – are allowed to frequent the restaurants and they eat everything, so that there is nothing left for civilians who arrive late. In despair we finally secure a regrettable soup and some bread. Rather hungrily we go to bed.

16 August

Of course when we got back to the Pergoletta last night, there was an alarm. We examined the rifugio used by the hotel – a magnificent cantina hollowed out in the wall beneath a stout looking old home.[189] But we decide to risk it and sleep. The next day starts well. We secure an excellent breakfast. It is the day of the assumption. Mass at 10am at Santa Rosa's. Then a really good luncheon early, an hour's rest and back to the station. Nobody told us, however, that the train we had chosen meant a change at Civita Castellana, so we have to kill time for another 1 and half hours. The heavy luggage is dispatched to Rome to the Trastevere station, while we travel by the little electric railway. The heat is prodigious, but the train more or less empty, thank the Lord.

At Rome there is again no means of transporting our 11 packages. Again we have to trudge with the things necessary for the night all the way to the hotel – the albergo Ludovisi (for our flat is still let). What a haven of peace and comfort at last – for this is a duck of an hotel and we mean to stay in it, regardless of expense, for at least a week.

There was an alarm and an almost total eclipse of the moon or something, however, to the eclipse of our wakening selves in sleep.

Later –
I saw Tesca di Luti and family in the street for a minute. He said that he and Ranieri di S. Faustino were utterly fed up at the Ministry. There was now no propaganda to speak of. [Page], whom we have always called the [illegible] of all good propaganda is in command. Nothing can be said which might give offence to our enemies. Tasca said 'I wish I had never come back to this bloody country. I feel like spitting in everybody's face.' I

said: 'I feel like spitting in the face of most people of most countries. Only the Germans have my respect.' He said: 'Yes, and the Russians.' I said: 'Yes, and the Japanese.'

Rome has been declared an open town. Exactly what this means is not yet clear, anyhow, it may stop further bombardments.[190] Viterbo, it seems, was bombed last night. Well, I [never]! We await details.

18 August

The end has come in Sicily after a 40 days fight. The Anglo-Saxons have paid dearly in men and materials, including at least 1 million tons of shipping. They bargained in doing it within a calendar month and the task will have made them realise what the establishment of a <u>real</u> second front must mean. It is not surprising therefore in the circumstances that they are now talking of forcing Turkey into the war in order to avoid the possible alternative of a landing in Europe and its possible failure.

The Sicilian adventure moreover would not have succeeded had it not been for the treachery of certain Italian Generals & admirals. We heard some of the tragic story from Mariano, whose brother Beppino was down there part of the time. The whole story may not be true, but that there was treachery in certain quarters appears credible. When the Anglo-Saxon assault came, the Duce, Prince [Humbert] & the Duke of Spoleto went down to Palermo, all absolutely confident of victory. In fact there appeared to be no doubt about it. The enemy had little chance of getting a strong footing in the island. But certain Army Chiefs, so it is said, were out to get rid of the Duce even at the cost of betraying Italy. In several places the Italian troops were ordered to give way for no other reason. A whole division, based in [illegible], surrendered. At Augusta, Admiral Leonardi is supposed to have hauled up the white flag after 2 British cruisers had done no more than fire a salvo, though Augusta was the most strongly fortified naval base in all Italy: a lieutenant of the [illegible] got together some of the garrison, did what he could to save the situation, – but of course he could do little – the Admiral having fled.[191] Thus, while the so called fascists by their graft & corruption have betrayed the great fascist idea of Mussolini; while the Italian people, by [withholding] their moral support [to] the army against the enemies of Europe, have betrayed Europe, certain army chiefs it would seem, for part reasons, [illegible] betrayed Italy. That is the horrible truth and whatever Italy now gets she thoroughly deserves. Yet I still love Italy & trust in her resurrection. My hope, however, is in Germany. She may yet save Europe &, with Europe, Italy – and Italy, if she still continues to fight & suffer, may redeem herself.

Mariano's description, first of the disgusting demonstrations in Rome during the 24 hours following the fall of the Duce and before that of the

panic spread by rumours that a train of munitions was about to explode
near the Littorio station laid bare the vile characteristics of the mob. It only
shows what would happen if things got out of control. Not even the gentle
Italian people would refrain from the most appalling actions of revenge
& class hatred. If the war is lost, Italy will not be spared the horrors of
Bolshevism.

On the night after the bombing of Rome (the first time) the panic about
the train spread to numerous quartiers of the city and 50 thousand howling
people rushed into the centre. Mariano had been despatched to warn the
local ~~people~~ inhabitants, but was stopped by the police. There was no
co-ordination in fact between the police & the fascist authorities. Orders
& counter orders were given; & meantime the panic spread. Our own
quarter was one of those affected & we can therefore be thankful we were
not there. When Mussolini, in Sicily, realized the betrayal, he was overcome
with grief. He was recognized by a militia group & his car was surrounded
by cheering fascists. But he could hardly speak from emotion. He said: 'I
may go, fascism may fall, but Italy must live & fight.'

He then went to meet Hitler at Verona; & when Hitler told him Germany
was prepared to stand by Italy to the end, Mussolini would only say: I too
am prepared to stand by you, but the Italian people are not, I fear.[192] But
he did his best; & Badoglio has not been able or willing to do better [five
lines deleted]. Individual groups fought well, though most of the credit is
deserved by the Germans. The Army Chiefs, however, are [clearly] disappointed: because they have since discovered that the Anglo-Saxon's pretence
of fighting fascism rather than Italy was no more than a propaganda device.
They have discovered that the Anglo-Saxons only fought fascism in so far
as fascism meant resistance to their aim of dominating Europe & [*illegible*]
the peoples of Europe to the money power. They realise that resistance must
go on, because the aggression remains the same. They can do no more than
follow where Mussolini has led.

How far Badoglio knew about the plot to betray Italy in order to get rid
of fascism, it is impossible yet to say. He certainly knew that large sections
of the army were at any rate no longer prepared to take orders from a
fascist government & so he planned his coup d'etat. To save Italy – so at
least we hope – that is, we <u>hope</u> his motives were pure & that he himself
was not [*illegible*] in the plot. Today he made an excellent little speech on
the radio to the Sicilians. It was followed by a deplorable speech by [old]
[*word deleted*] Orlando, who could not refrain from indulging in recriminations.[193] He is the last man to point the finger at Mussolini & Fascism.
After all, <u>he</u> was head of the Government at the time of [Caporetto] &
was therefore as much responsible for the disastrous conduct of the war in
1917 as Mussolini was responsible for the disastrous conduct of this war.
True, Orlando subsequently did much by his eloquence to revive the Italian
fighting spirit, but he let the country down again after Vittorio Veneto by
his [*illegible*] to keep the army in being. He allowed the Italians to give way

to a peace stampede & so he threw away all his best cards for the Peace Conference, where Italy in consequence was done down. It would have been better if he had kept silence at this moment. What we need now is unity & a [*illegible*] facing up to the situation – not [*illegible*] recriminations & tearful bleatings by octogenarians who have [*illegible*] [*illegible*] ever since 1922. His speech was also marred by his reference to [*illegible*]. He said 'We were [*illegible*] to [retreat] to Sicily, if necessary & to fight to the end.' But he [*illegible*] ought <u>not</u> to say [that <u>now</u>] we were prepared to retreat to the [Trentino] & fight to the end.

Buona says: There is one comfort. The mere fact that Italy has fought England will in the end turn out to be her title to a renewed glory. Well said!

San Faustino made a good broadcast last night & I hope this means that the new Minister, Galli, realises that if we are to get tolerable terms from the Anglo-Saxons we must <u>fight</u> & [<u>bluff</u>] & not lie down to be trampled on. Until now (since the fall of Mussolini) our propaganda has been absolutely miserable – in short, we have been doing our best to encourage the Anglo-Saxons to open their mouths wider & wider. But I now hope things will go better & I expect to be back on the air myself next week. <u>I have made it a condition that I shall not say anything against Fascism or Mussolini.</u>

The weather is oppressively hot. Even I, who am a veritable salamander, feel it just too much of a good thing. But it should try the Anglo-Saxons badly & so don't let us complain. It remains to be seen what they will attempt now. It looks as if there may be, as a result of the conference at Quebec & Soviet pressure, a change of plan.[194] Perhaps the barbarians will be forced to switch back to the original plan of invading Europe through Turkey instead of Italy. That would be a relief to us personally; and they may also attempt action in the north of Europe. Only time will show. I doubt if they will have any success against the Germans; but they may, I fear, succeed in [invading] Turkey – and this might prove serious.

19 August

Today I had further talks with Msg. Montini. We discussed inter alia the possibility in certain circumstances of our taking refuge in a nunnery. I also asked for a letter of introduction to Guariglia.[195] Montini has promised to refer to the Cardinal – [Maglione] presumably.

I also saw Auristi and discussed my affairs. He assures me I shall not lose a penny in the various business transactions which I have helped him to finance. But there is a lot to straighten out in consequence of recent events and until this is done I shall not be able to avoid anxiety. Auristi was right in the middle of the first bombing of Rome, superintending the unloading of trucks at the S. Lorenzo station. He got away by a minute by running for his life after the first bomb. But his companions were blown to bits. The scenes of destruction were terrible. The bombing raids on Naples, Rome,

Turin, Milan and other places have been ghastly and it is quite clear that terrorisation, as much as military objectives, has been the object.[196] They have certainly caused great disorganisation, especially as the Italians have a congenital incapacity to organise.

The wireless today at 5 o'clock has praised the resistance put up by Commanders & men of all areas in Sicily & mentions Admiral Leonardi. Are then the stories about his treachery at Augusta inventions? Who knows! Perhaps we shall not know the truth until after the war is well over. But that some treachery did occur seems certain. On the other hand, I should hate to malign any particular [illegible] without proof. What I have written is what I have been told. It is interesting as a sample of what countless people are saying in good faith – and all that need be [illegible] is that there is no smoke without fire.[197]

20 August

We go back to the Flat in Via S. Marino 36. We have no servant, but will lunch out until we find one.

(Insert here the King's address to Sicilians, numbered A in red).

22 August

We [illegible] out together to inspect some of the ruins caused by the bombardment. The exquisite little Basilica of S. Lorenzo is an awful state of ruins – the portico completely ruined, the fine roof a skeleton, quantities of the lovely [illegible] works destroyed. But some of the beautifully painted [beams] of the roof remain, others might be restored. The outside is not so badly damaged. The mosaics should be saved & the beautiful stalls are mostly intact.

At the University there was a whole shower of bombs & a lot of damage was done, including the partial wrecking of my Faculty [illegible] (Political Science). For the rest, no doubt the greater [harm] was done to the military roads & institutions. But a great [illegible] of buildings are in ruins and the cemetery is very badly [illegible] [illegible], with the [illegible] of open graves. It is interesting to note how the lower stories of high buildings survived the shock.[198]

Today I have a [illegible] broadcast talk a copy of which should be inserted here. It is a review of the facts touching the reasons for the hastily convened Quebec conference, which concludes its labours next Tuesday. (marked B in red).

23 August

Visited Herr Prof. Prinzing, the German SS man in Rome and so re-established a useful contact in emergencies. He is extremely nice and we get on very well together. We wagged our heads about Italy. He said, when I told him I had no intention of giving way and was prepared to put my services at the command of Hitler if Italy made a separate peace: 'Well, you see Nordic blood counts'. I used to sneer at this idea; but I am now not sure as far as staunchness and loyalty and action are concerned. Yet, as I went on to tell him, I love this land. It is mine. And what about Spain? I would also willingly serve Spain and Falangism.

My broadcast (marked <u>B</u>) is of course propaganda. It represents the truth, supposing the Italians are really able and willing to put up a heroic and determined resistance to further invasion. I doubt, however, if they are; and I doubt if Churchill & Co think they are. Therefore, since the Mediterranean theatre of war is independent of whatever big scale operations may be now contemplated in the channel, the probability is that an attempt to invade southern Italy will be made – and pretty soon too, and that it will succeed in time to enable the Balkans to be invaded 'before the autumn leaves begin to fall'. The Anglo-Saxons are now bombing out all the communications in southern Italy and this bears out my surmise that the attempt will be made. May my lack of confidence in the Italians' <u>will</u> and <u>capacity</u> to fight hard be betrayed by events. But if my fears prove correct, I expect all Puglia (at least) to be lost by the end of September and all S. Italy finished out by the end of October, including even Naples. Of course Russia does not want to see an Anglo-Saxon army in the Balkans and it is said they have vetoed Churchill's original plan of establishing there a second front. But the possession of Puglia alone would be sufficient to open up the Adriatic to the British and American fleet and therefore the taking of Corfu and Valona would present an easy [*illegible*] preliminary to further operations. However, the possession of the big aerodromes around Foggia, not to speak of the sea-planes bases in the lakes north of the Gargano, puts Trieste and southern Germany within easy bombing distance. Also the Rumanians oil fields.[199] So that's that – or likely to be that; for I have really lost all faith in the Italians will to resist.

As for the big scale operations in the North, my guess is an attack to [*illegible*] [*illegible*] the peninsulas of Brittany & Cherbourg, & then to join up the two fronts across the bay of S. Malo. In fact Cherbourg may very likely be the ~~point of~~ epicentre of the whole attack. I pick out these objectives because they represent from the geographical & topographical standpoint the biggest possible [*illegible*] with the minimum effort and [*illegible*] [*illegible*] landing beaches (near Nantes & on the [*illegible*] side of the Cherbourg Peninsula. Secondly a success in this operation would wreck the German submarine campaign [*illegible*] thoroughly, because most of the best equipped bases are in Brittany & Brittany is also the best point for German offence & British defence (if they took it).

If the British succeed in accomplishing this by Xmas the war will be over by the Spring. The only hope is that they are not yet sufficiently prepared & that the Germans are strengthening to withstand the assault. But things look <u>rotten</u>, it must be expressed.

Today I had a long talk with MacWhite, the Irish minister. It is impossible, he says, to go to Ireland, as all ships have to touch at Holyhead & are gone through with a [*illegible*] comb. The only aeroplane connection is English. Besides, he cannot even give visa to non-Irish subjects. For the rest MacWhite agreed with my diagnosis, only more so – that is to say, he was still more pessimistic over the Italian will & capacity to resist & more pessimistic than I am over Russia's capacity to go on & on indefinitely. He thinks, the [*illegible*] bridgehead will go next & that the German mobile reserves have now been [*illegible*] by the Bolshevik attacks over as wide a front that they can no longer be used with effect. Consequently, though the German line is not likely to break, more ground is likely to be lost progressively & there is no reason to suppose that the Russians wont be able to start a new offensive during the winter. Should therefore the Anglo-Saxon offensives in the Mediterranean and in France make any serious headway, the Germans will be in a very critical position. Turkey may at any time [*illegible*] in on the Allied side & all the Balkans would then be on fire. The only hope, he says, lies in a big [*illegible*] [*illegible*] [*illegible*] of the contemplated British offensive against France. This would lift German moral[e] & stay the flood temporarily in the Balkans. Otherwise Hitler would probably be sent about his business as Mussolini was sent about his; and a military dictatorship established to save [*illegible*] is [*illegible*] from the wreck of Europe.[200]

29 August

MacWhite, the Irish minister, tells me that either Father Cuffe or Father Coleman ([*illegible*] later: Father Coleman, it was)[,] both of whom came last year to stay with us in the 'Little House' near Florence before returning to Ireland (he was not sure which of them it was) was arrested at Holyhead & held in custody 3 weeks because the Police spotted my name in a book (The Life of Christ by Ricciotti) which I had given as a souvenir to one of them. Whoever it was, was interrogated for hours every day about me. If therefore there was needed proof positive that if the British come here, one of the first things they would do, would be to lay their bloody hands on me, this is sufficient.

Anyhow, I am doing my best to avoid any risks. I have alternative plans – escape to Spain, to Switzerland, going in to hiding or going north into Germany. I am trying to get things cut and dried – not so easy either, since everything in Rome takes a lifetime to accomplish.

To go to Switzerland requires passport visas, permits to transfer money, forms to fill up. All is being pushed forward with the utmost urgency. Spain, I fear, is more or less impracticable despite the Spanish ambassador's good will; for it means a journey through France with the luggage and a special German permit into the bargain. The Vatican or friends might help us to hide. Various plans are being discussed, cars held ready. I am also in touch with the Germans. Yesterday I saw Conte Mazzolini, our new 'Chef de Cabinet'.[201]

But <u>will</u> the British come? Nobody knows. They may they may not. They may come soon or they may come later. But it would be wise to lose no time. But it is exhausting work getting things 'cut and dried' in Rome and I must not forget also to leave my business behind as a going concern in safe hands. We shall see what we shall see.[202]

Today we all went to Mass at St Pauls without the Walls[.]

A Jew or some other [*illegible*]
Wanted to give a ball.
He did his best to hire
The Basilica of St Paul.
He said: –
   An [*illegible*] at the altar,
   The devil in place of few
   Would well replace the place
   From either point of view.

Indeed the Basilica would make a marvellous ballroom!

The Atrium is fine, the bronze door of Nello Maraini good work, the old [*illegible*] lovely.

We paid a call on the Abbot, Mgr Vannucci, whom I had met at Farfa, a charming & wise-looking man.[203]

Boris is dead.[204] He has been a capable & wise head – and his loss will be felt. The situation in Bulgaria is by no means altogether healthy, though the vast majority realise that their country's fortune depends on a victory of the Axis. Bulgaria has never been given a fair deal by her more powerful neighbours except under Axis pressure. England has never had a thought of justice. But the Communist & [*illegible*] elements are strong &, in the absence of a strong & wise government, might give trouble even before the general situation in the Balkans gets worse as a consequence of an invasion by the British. Boris's influence was a steadying influence and he was deservedly popular. He had done wonders for the country's public [workers]. I am sorry too for our King, who has enough sorrow [*illegible*] these sad & critical days. Was he really murdered? <u>Probably</u> not, but who knows? Sikorsky was & many others too who happened to be a stumbling block to G.G. or Russia.

Insert broadcast marked C.[205]

1 September

Yesterday, with an introduction from M. De [*illegible*], who is a dear and had accorded me the day before over an hour's talk, I saw M. De Salis of the Swiss legation with regard to the form of my application for entry into Switzerland. Like his English cousins I found him rather pompous. But he told me what to do. He also told me that of his English cousins, my friend John is in Egypt, and that one of the younger brothers, poor boy, is a prisoner of war in Germany with an amputated leg.

I also saw the Rector of the Irish College, Mgr. [McDale], a sweet & charming friend. He explained that it was Father Coleman who had the ordeal of being 'third degreed' on my account at Holyhead. I am so sorry to have been the cause of such trouble.

Finally I saw von [*illegible*] of the German Embassy. This evening I see [Scamacca], the new Inspector of our Radio Service. So, what with having seen yesterday my friend & lawyer Andrea [Malengi], I have made a little progress. Anyhow, when we have all been [photoed] & the forms filled up & a covering letter written to De Salis, the application for Switzerland can be sent in. But it will, I understand, take 6 weeks at least before I can hope to get an answer. Everybody advises us to leave Rome as soon as possible.

Last night we had a messy dinner party: Mariano Frasso, Francesca [*illegible*], & young [*illegible*], to whom we also gave a bed. Prof. Ungaro came in after dinner. Buona & Francesca were the cooks & they turned out an excellent meal. Vin [*illegible*], a bottle of old [*illegible*], & a bottle of Malvasia from [*illegible*], not to speak of real coffee, completed the evening – while I dropped down to see my Japanese friend [*illegible*], who offered me a good cognac. These occasions are rarities now-a-days, so they deserve mention.

(Here insert broadcast marked D).

& Pope's broadcast E.

Also broadcast F.

3 September

Yesterday I had tea with the S. Faustino & we fell of course to talking about the war. I recalled my talk with Ambassador Phillips on Jan. 31st. 1941, a resumé of which I gave to my Ministry for transmission to the Foreign Office. Here is the resumé ([*illegible*] copy marked G). I also recalled that the very same evening on my way home after midnight (I had been giving my usual broadcast), I was waylaid by two young Americans. It was a black

and rainy night. They waylaid me in the Via Porta Pinciana, which is at that time a very solitary road. They seized me by the arms and said:
     'Is your name Barnes?

- 'It is', I answered.
- 'Well, you had better stop your propaganda talks.
- 'Why?'
- 'Because, you are worrying the British Government.'
- 'Well, that's exactly my object. But why should it worry them particularly.'
- 'Because it is known that [*illegible*] is you who are speaking and all the people of fascist organisations listen in. You had better stop, or it will be the worse for you ...'

At that I broke loose and ran. But they did not pursue me. Anyhow I was not going to risk becoming the victim of American gangster methods; and the next day I bought a bicycle.

On reflection I imagine it was just an effort to frighten me off the air. I shouldn't wonder if Phillips had not said to some of his young men in the Embassy something to the effect that what a pity it was that I should do propaganda against my country of origin & that I ought to be stopped – rather like the King of England's famous ejaculation about Becket to his courtiers: 'Who will rid me of this turbulent Priest?'; whereupon they took him at his word and murdered him. These young men in my case must have taken their queue in the same way and tried to scare me.

[*Illegible*] S. Faustino said that she also was a friend of Phillips's & had consulted him about sending her daughter back to America (that is, her daughter '[*illegible*]' by her former husband). This was a few months later than my interview. Phillips told her that he did not think it necessary, Italy would have an anti-fascist revolution and would [*illegible*] fine.

This is interesting because I do not doubt that the American Embassy was even at that time the centre of an anti-fascist plot; & he probably had a number of naval & army officers in with him, who were determined from the outset to [*illegible*] the war.

All the same Phillips's [prediction] was over optimistic. The revolution took 18 months to come & Italy is still at war notwithstanding.

The situation, however, is of course very grave & fluid. Yesterday the British have started their attack on the toe of Italy & doubtless it will be extended. How far shall we fight or will only the Germans fight?

Ranieri S. Faustino thinks that it is not improbable that the Germans may decide to make a coup d'état in Italy and set up a new government like Pétain's in France. The Fascists of course would support such a coup and Farinacci is organising in Germany,[206] where there are still some 400,000 Italian workers, a fascist militia which would be armed by the Germans.[207]

But who knows <u>what</u> is going to happen? Things are drifting towards demagoguery that could only end in civil war. Personally I should welcome a German coup. Only the Germans can save Europe and with it Italy.[208]

All Hail Cock-a-Doodle Do! Wake me at dawn,
When I live as I love on a farm _
Like the lowing of cattle, the cackle of geese
The noise that you make is the Herald of Peace,
Inviting the world to disarm.
But here, down in Rome, (ever since I was born)
In their gardens most people are wont
To keep, beside cats, hens, chickens and cocks,
That made noises louder than [*illegible*] alarm clocks,
So please, Cock-a-Doodle Do, DONT![209]

4 September

I wanted Andrea [Malengi] to look after my affairs in my absence & keep a check on Auristi, my partner in business, who, though an admirable fellow in many ways, is [*illegible*] & inclined to be speculative & to run a bit too close to the wind for my likes. But [Malengi] has been put on the black list by the new government because he was lawyer for 8 years to the Party. Of course, there is nothing against him, especially as he cut with the Party a good 4 years ago & has been thoroughly anti-fascist in the party sense ever since. But in the circumstances he feels he ought not to represent me, as he would control my money & might be made the subject of a searching enquiry.

So I have resorted to another man – an aristocrat & a strong papist, quite a man after my heart. I saw him today & [*illegible*] up preliminaries. I also saw Mgr. [Marchesini] of the Nunziatura Apostolica, who is going to back up my application to go to Switzerland.[210]

All my hopes, personal & political, are in the Pope. He is certainly the man of the moment, though so far no one has the sense to listen to him. I think he will, however, go further – further than good advice or a fine diplomacy or even a saintly example can take him. I think he will have the ability, if his present efforts fail, to stake all, with a view to bringing the present horror to an end, by action such as might well shake the world – fling the representatives of [*illegible*] nations out of the Vatican, excommunicate right & left in true [*illegible*] fashion and stat on a pilgrimage of love right among the people beyond the seas & the oceans. With his authority, his humility, his passion, he might well achieve a miracle. I believe he might do it, if the ground was first well prepared. This blood business <u>must</u> be brought to an end or the world will assuredly crash. The violent men must be tamed & brought to reason – all of them on both sides. The worst of them Roosevelt, however, would, I fear be too much of a [strong/slimy] & slippery serpent to catch.

As for myself, I still hesitate to decide what to do beyond my preparations for various alternatives. If we were certain of a permit to enter Switzerland, we would of course go north. But supposing we did so, but could not get into Switzerland where we wanted [*words deleted*], we should be caught in a trap in the event of a collapse of Germany. We should not be able to get back or forwards. To stay in Rome [*illegible*] just [*illegible*] the [*illegible*] thing to do. At a [pinch] I could (and perhaps all 3 of us) throw ourselves on the mercy of the Vatican; or it is quite on the cards, Rome may never be occupied by the enemy at all. May God guide my judgement, when the time for decision arrives – and that day is not far off.[211]

7 September

My birthday; and I have received the finest birthday present that I have ever had: my Italian citizenship. They told me at the Ministry yesterday that the King had signed the decree. It was that excellent man, [*illegible*] (a Maltese, who like myself, has sacrificed his life for Italy) who gave me the news and told me run and have it confirmed. I literally jumped for joy.

In 1913, Corpus Domini Day, I became a Catholic. In 1943 an Italian. These are the two decisive steps of my life – like crossing the Rubicon.[212]

My birthday is to be celebrated today with Mariano and Francesca to dinner; and we shall drink to the future of Italy. How I have loved and love this land. Now that she is down and out and dishonoured by the corruption and treachery of so many of her sons, I desire all the more to be Italian – to suffer with my country and strive for her resurrection. If only the next four months could show a slither of redeeming heroism, the day of resurrection would be hastened. But though our soldiers will, as ever, show admirable courage, their moral cannot be expected to be high while the people, behind them, continue to appear indifferent to everything but personal profit and revenge. The press has become too ghastly for words – a cesspool of scandal, recrimination and frivolity. Look at the 'Messaggero' today and compare it with what it was under Pavolini. It is a wonder people do not realise that this difference is symptomatic of the essential difference between the present regime and Fascism. The Fascists were corrupt, because Italians are corrupt. But at least they upheld the country's national dignity and they generally made sense. We fascists are accused of having killed thought (NB – Anyhow we have produced the [last/best] book on politics written for a generation: Pagliaro's 'Immagine e Miti' and the last life of Christ (Ricciotti).[213] [*Illegible*] has done some important work too, which will be bound with the fascist era (I-XXII)) and indifferent judgement. But if the newspapers today are to be taken as representative of thought and freedom, then the sooner we get back to Fascism the better. A new paper came out today called 'Fronte Unico'.[214] It is an effort to show some coherence. Let us hope it is the beginning of reaction against demagogy and ineptitude, if nothing else.

Last night after dinner we went to see the [Busini]. [Andrea] B. is the architect of our flat. His wife, [*illegible*] nee Olsuvief is the owner. They were at Fregene the other day when Muti was killed.[215] Some 30 persons raided his house at dead of night, made him dress in front of them so that it could be verified that he was unarmed and then [executed] him outside. Among these persons, it is said there was a policeman, who took him under arrest. But what were the other people doing? Anyhow, as soon as they got outside they led him into the wood instead of the cars waiting for him. Muti soon realized that he was being led to his death. So he broke loose & ran for it, but was immediately shot down.

How far the Police are implicated in this murder, I do not know. Anyhow, it was a murder & with the police, if the police were present there were a number of gangsters. The murder of Matteotti by a gang of fascist thugs in 1924 – against the wishes of Mussolini – was nothing to this.[216] The Matteotti murder did not implicate Fascism. But this one implicates the whole anti-fascist movement. They say he was in a plot to bring about a German coup d'état. But that is no excuse for murder. He could have been given a just & regular trial. He was a national hero, an air 'ace' with a gold medal for military valour, a man against whom no suspicion of corruption has ever been raised. He resigned as Secretary to the Party because he found himself impotent to check the abuses. He failed because he was too forthright & simple. Men like he belong to the minority of Italians who are the salt of the earth. Italy is a land of extremes. If the majority are corrupt & therefore beneath contempt, the minority are saints, heroes & men of genius. That is Italy's title to life & her promise of a glorious future; for in the end the leaven of good will work the whole, because the whole is not decadent but wonderfully vital. [*words deleted*] . That is why I keep my faith in Italy – land of saints & summers and therefore of hope. Only the individuals & communities who are neither good nor bad have no future – like the Swiss, the Swedes & the mass of English.

We made our way home in the dark during an alarm and found the approaches barricaded. Lights were flashed at us. For in this quarter where the [Businis] live, there is Badoglio's house, as well as Villa Savoia where the King lives. Both are guarded today as never was Mussolini. Andrea [Busini] says that parts of the road are even mined. And where is Mussolini? We are told he is somewhere the guest of the King & so under the King's protection.[217]

My friend Carmine Auristi tells me that Col. Marino, who is a good friend to us both and a big Brass Hat on the Staff of General [*illegible*], has the opinion that there is no fight left in the Italian army, and that therefore the situation may precipitate from one day to the next. He gives a fortnight for decisive events to develop. Meanwhile he thinks the Germans will make a steady retreat northwards with the British on their heels – & there is no telling how far north or how fast they will come. On the other hand there are rumours of an imminent armistice by which Central Italy is to be left unoccupied as a unit of buffer state. I must [illegible] things [illegible] with all ahead. I must not count on having more than a [illegible] to spare. But I need every bit of this time to get away with things in order. [sentence deleted] I am [illegible] no time. But there a million formalities to perform in quite a dozen different offices & Govt. departments, & the difficulties to surmount are great.[218]

9 September

Well events <u>have</u> precipitated. Things have moved fast during the last 24 hours and it seems like 24 weeks. Yesterday at 6.30 I was warned at the Ministry that an armistice had been concluded and that it would be advisable for us to escape with all speed. [Illegible], the Radio inspector, took charge of our interests. He gave me a letter signed by the Minister ([Galbi]) to the chief of Police (Senise), whom as a matter of fact I had seen in a most affable way [illegible] and days previously. I was told to go round in the morning, present the letter and obtain passports, without waiting for the formalities to be completed regarding my Italian nationality – formalities which it had been hoped might be completed in a week.

Later I had by telephone counter orders. No good going to Senise. We must all be at the Ministry at 8 o'clock. The Foreign Office would arrange for the passports. I telephoned Aniti to get a camion[219] or car ready for instant departure. But I decided not to attempt to leave until Saturday, since I had my power of attorney to sign on Friday morning – an absolute necessity in order to leave my affairs in good hands.

We packed late into the night to the sound of rolling guns. Who was it who were fighting? Germans against Italians or Germans against British? We had a partly sleepless night, as can well be imagined and up at dawn.

We listened to the wireless and heard from England that Italy had capitulated without conditions on Sept 3. Marshal Badoglio's announced the armistice at 8pm. The conditions, however, were not mentioned.[220] It all looks a disgraceful affair, for the interval between the capitulation and the armistice left the Germans entirely in the air, to be bombed and chivied, while the Italians surrendered and welcomed the British wherever they happened to be. Badoglio in fact has ordered that only the Germans should be resisted in future, if they worried the Italians. It looks as if there had been treachery all along. I weep for my country. The Italians might yet have redeemed themselves by one big final heroic effort. But now they are [illegible].

We went down at the Ministry punctually at 8. Particulars were taken for passports. Sc[*illegible*] had been up all night, working for us like a hero, but the F.O. was still talking. We were told we were to go down there as soon as things were ready. We waited and waited.

At 11.00 we were to have met Aniti outside the Vatican. At 11.30 we had scheduled a talk with Msg. Montini. So I sent Buona and Job ahead. But as soon as they were gone, I was told it was no use waiting further. There was nothing to be done for the present. I must be back at the Ministry at 6. Meanwhile, every kind of rumour was about – that the English had landed at Genova, at Civitavecchia, at Ostia. But it was confirmed that the night fighting had been between Germans and Italians; and desultory booms of guns showed that it was still going on.

I hastened to the Vatican. Met the family and Aniti; decided that it was useless in the circumstances to try to proceed out of Rome for the time being. The railways were not running. I had no purpose. Nobody knows where the English are.

Mgr. Montini telephoned to the Abbot of S. Paolo & asked him to come up. But he was unable to do so. The Abbot had [already] told us that he could not take us in & that to go to [*illegible*] was impossible, as there was a British [*illegible*] corps nearby & many troops. Later. It is interesting to note that though he refused me, a [*illegible*] [*illegible*] hospitably, he afterwards took in a lot of anti-fascist refugees. Dirty dog.[221]

The German Embassy is silent, though our friend B[*illegible*], the night before, telephoned that he was going with the German army – but how he did not know. I expect they will look after him.

At the Vatican we had to wait 1 ¾ hours before we were received. St Peter's was shut. Nobody was allowed to enter except under strict [*illegible*]. Mgr. Montini was continually being called to confer with [*illegible*], the Pope & the Cardinal. At last we saw him, his usual sympathetic self. It [*illegible*] is clear, however, that we could not be taken in by the Vatican. There were hundreds of people in a similar predicament of all nationalities, most of them [Croats] all clamouring for protection. All he could do was to advise us to go north if the opportunity or means presented themselves, [*illegible*] to hide. He made various suggestions & gave us a letter to Mgr. Traglia, who would probably be able to arrange a convent or something.[222]

So we came away rather [*illegible*] & severely hungry. Mgr. comforted us by saying that all the rumours of further British landings north of Rome were false & that the Germans were advancing on Rome. The British however had landed at Salerno & were probably in Naples by now.[223]

I got an hour's nap later in the afternoon & was back at the Ministry at six, only to be told that the government had left Rome & that it was impossible to obtain passports. I was given 6000 lire to help expenses & made an appointment for 7.30 at the Foreign Office. I then rushed & signed my powers of attorney. Buona too. I saw my lawyer & [*illegible*] again. Then the F.O.; but it had been decided to burn all compromising documents &

most of the day had been spent doing this. I was given another 5000 lire
– very handsome. But I could not even be provided with a certificate that I
was Italian now. All the same I still have Galli's letter, which may do in an
emergency.[224]

Buona [*illegible*] an appointment with Mgr. Traglia for the [*illegible*]
& [go/so] back home. The latest news at the F.O. was that the Germans
were entering Rome. I hope they do. All the better for us. Then we might
establish contacts & get away. It is rumoured that a Fascist Government
is to be restored & that this new government has already been declared in
the north. Anyhow, as the Radio announced, Dalmatia has been occupied
by the Croats.[225] That is all Badoglio has brought Italy – the loss of our
Province after [*illegible*] & further dishonour. He may have helped to be
able to stem the tide, once Fascism was overthrown, but as the Italians
refused to fight, his coup d'état has only made matters worse. Italy has been
turned into a little [field] & she has lost in a few weeks what she might have
kept all the winter & perhaps for ever. He has been thoroughly bamboozled
by the British. As I was writing this an aeroplane, flying low over our house,
has dropped a bomb in the Via [Nomentana], close by. We ran down to the
basement, but nothing more occurred; so we ran up again. Probably it was
a German plane disposing of a [barricade]. Let us hope so & that we shall
find them in occupation of the city in the morning.

I have to ring up [*illegible*] early. He is still bent on doing his best for us.
A good man and, rare among Italians, a man of action. It was not his fault
that the passports were unobtainable. Anyhow tonight we hope to have a
good sleep. Whatever else happens, the English cant [*illegible*] us for the
next day or so. But of course they may bomb Rome, if the Germans come
in. We shall see.[226]

11 September

We slept well and I was down at the Ministry again early. Fighting going
on all around and always closer. At the Ministry once again and we were
to get out passports; but after interminable waiting, the Germans were
reported to be entering Rome and so all the Ministries had to shut. So
nothing more could be done and I was told to look out for the Germans,
find out where their headquarters were and to get them to look after us.
I accordingly bicycled about to various places. But there was no sign of
the Germans. Went back to luncheon. Buona meanwhile had heard that
they had reached S. Paolo. so I telephoned to the abbot and he confirmed
the fact; but doubted if I could get through to them. I telephoned to Ezra
Pound and suggested we might make the attempt together. At 4 o'clock he
turned up, dressed as a hiker with a rucksack on his back. But the battle
was raging and it had transpired that to reach the Germans we should have

to pass through no-man's land. It was therefore obvious that our project
was impracticable for the time being. I advised him to go home and wait.
But Ezra had made up his mind to walk out of Rome northwards. I told
him he was mad, but he would not hear of it. Ezra is of course in a similar
position to myself and happened to be in Rome when the armistice came.[227]
I gave him some maps and off he walked along the Via Salaria. He has not
been heard of since. I trust he got through. It is not impossible; but he may
have been taken by the Italians and clapped into a concentration camp.
Who knows?

As a matter of fact, about an hour after his departure, news came
through of a truce. The Italians had surrendered. The Germans agreed
to remain outside the city except that they should occupy the Ardeatina
station, the telephone Exchange and the German Embassy. It is possible
therefore that Ezra reached the German lines at night. (Later: yes he did and
went on undisturbed, sleeping in peasants' houses and eventually reached
the Brenner after which he returned to Rapallo).[228]

The obvious thing to do now for us was to go to the German Embassy
and we started off at 7am this morning walking, for no buses or trains are
running. It is about 2 miles from here. All three of us walked off together.
We reached Porta Pia, when Buona spotted a Swiss Legation car and we
called on the chauffeur to motor us down. By a providential coincidence,
the chauffeur said he himself intended to go the Embassy. So we were
saved a long and trying walk. Meanwhile I had arranged with Aniti for a
camion to be at our disposal in the morning in case there was need to start
immediately.

The Embassy was surrounded with troops. Magnificent looking men.
We were told peremptorily that we could not enter. I persisted however and
in execrable German explained my position, saying that I was not going to
surrender to the enemy but I wanted to continue the fight. This declaration
worked wonders. I also told the officer that I was the Italian 'Lord Haw
Haw', wherefrom he told us to wait half an hour;[229] and then another
providential thing occurred. A friend of ours, [*illegible*] by name (he was a
German-American engaged in broadcasting in English from here) came out
to parley with us. We fell into each other's arms. He gave us good news.
He assured us that all the rumours of a British advance towards Rome
were false. The despicable Romans were already preparing to welcome the
enemy today. The news had even been spread about that they had reached
Cisterna last night.[230] But all this is untrue. The Germans are pouring troops
southwards and are not evacuating central Italy yet. They appear to have
the situation in hand. He said the trains would be running again in a few
days time and that we should be evacuated with other German civilians. I
am to go to see him again tomorrow.

What then? We went to the Pension[231] where our friend [*illegible*] had
been staying. It was closed; but we learnt that poor [*illegible*] had been
arrested by the Italians at the station early on the early morning of the 9th

& clapped into a concentration camp at Monte Sacro.[232] He had managed to get leave to come out for an hour & had returned to the Pension. But since then nothing has been heard of him. Monte Sacro is now in the hands of the Germans, so we hope he has been rescued.

We then went on to the Irish College & had some food, feeling pretty [exhausted].

The German Embassy had had a bad time of it all yesterday. They were sporadically assaulted by Italian troops, but managed to hold their own. Even civilians had sniped at them & civilians also had been [armed] by [disbanding] soldiers. For everything was in confusion. The Germans, however, are not [allowing] any nonsense now & the despicable Romans are [cowed]. Civilians carrying arms are arrested. Franc tireurs[233] are shot (and a jolly good thing too). They are all cowards & traitors. But the worst traitors are Badoglio, the King & the military & naval chiefs. The Führer's speech has given all the [facts] & it is evident that Mussolini & Italy were betrayed from the very beginning. The final betrayal of Germany will, as Hitler says, go down to history as the greatest betrayal on record. All my worst surmises are verified & the documents proving the case are to be duly published. I need therefore add nothing here on the subject. It is sufficient to insert here in full the Führer's speech.

(Insert cutting H)

Meanwhile the collapse of the unloyal Italians in the north & central Italy is rapidly occurring. For the present therefore we are safe & the ~~British~~ Anglo-Americans are not going to have an easy time. Eventually the Germans may decide to retreat to a better line, but they are not going yet.

Tonight we have [moreover] been told that our Italian passports are actually ready under false names. I have to fetch them tomorrow, which will be another heavy day; because I have also received a summons from the Vatican.[234]

I should add that on the 10th ~~I was able to sign my~~ morning Buona went to see Mgr. Traglia & find up [emergency] hiding places.

[It was] confirmed that the Fascist Government of Italy is in full activity in Berlin with Pavolini, Farinacci, Ciano (?) Vittorio Mussolini forming part of it.[235] The entire Italian Embassy staff in Berlin has [sided] with them, so it is [rumoured]; whereupon the Badoglio government arrested all the German diplomats at Ancona, which they had reached on the morning of the 9th. But the German troops are moving southward also along the Adriatic & we hope the diplomats will be rescued. But nobody knows the fate of Mussolini. My heart bleeds for him. Have the [skunks] handed him over? Or has he been murdered like Muti? Or will he be rescued? Any number of Italians are rallying to the Germans. In fact there is virtual civil war.[236]

13 September

Two more hectic days. Yesterday I got my false passports & then went to the German Embassy to get the [visa's], but was told to return in the afternoon when the Consul General would be there, Herr Wüster. I bicycled to the Vatican & saw Mgr. Montini, who showed me a telegram he had received from Mgr. Bernardini, the Apostolic Delegate in Berne, saying that he had interrogated the Federal Authorities and had obtained their consent to our going to Switzerland. This is excellent news. I followed it up today with a visit to the Swiss Legation (de Salis) and asked for a visa to be given us. But of course he refused to take into consideration our false passports & our English passports would have to have an Italian exit visa, which it is impossible to obtain. [Moreover] the Legation, he said, must receive first an authorisation from the Swiss Federal Police. So back I went to the Ministry to ask for genuine passport also to be issued to us. This they have promised to try to obtain and to have the [visa's] for visit to Switzerland. At the same time I telephoned the Vatican asking Mgr. Montini, to wire Bernardini, to request the Swiss Federal Police, to [wire] the Swiss Legation here the required authorisation! In this way I hope to surmount the main difficulties of getting into Switzerland; but it means postponing our departure a few more days. Tomorrow I shall follow up my telephone message & go personally again to the Vatican: We may be able thus to get things straightened out in time to be able to get away on Saturday. There are now 2 trains running regularly to Florence, where we plan to stop off for a few days & then go on to Germany.

All this is only a little part of my strenuous activities. I have been all over the place on my bicycle, arranging this, that & the other – and last night I was literally fagged out.

The German consul was quite a jolly man and stood me an excellent glass of Munich beer. He also gave me the address of a lovely little hotel in the [illegible] where we might go & stay for a holiday.

My ~~desire~~ interest would be to go to Switzerland & to get [out] of all hostilities & further difficulties.

The Germans expect me to go to Berlin & broadcast for them; but I prefer not to do this.

It would only mean compromising myself up to the hilt, if the Germans are eventually beaten. So far I have done my duty towards Italy & have always laboured for a good understanding between Italy & England.[237]

I have never said a word on the wireless which I did not sincerely believe was also in the interests of England. I consider this war was imposed on England against the true interests of the British people by a clique of [interested] vested financial interests & Jewish influence & ambitious politicians. There is nothing that I have said which Tom Mosley, as a patriotic Englishman, would not have wished to advocate if he had been free to do so.[238] At the same time I have always loyally refuted to take [word deleted] service under the British [Crown] or join a British political party; and had it not been for the promise to my father, I should have become Italian 30 years ago. I have therefore a [clear/clean] and coherent case, should ever the British lay hands on me – an honest case. It would therefore be [prudent] for me to leave things at that, however much I may sympathise with the Germans, who I sincerely believe, alone stand between civilisation & chaos. But prudent or no, I feel I ought all the same to go to Germany. Anyhow I intend to stick to Mussolini. What has become of him?

Later This morning we had the news of the Duce's release.[239] We literally jumped for joy & hugged each other. Bless the man! This prompts me to go through to Germany to embrace him & place myself at his service right up to the end.

Th[ose] dirty scoundrels & traitors of Badoglio were about to hand him over to the British. The German coup just saved him in time & the British are grating their teeth on the [wireless] with fury and disappointment. Things are not going too well for them either at Salerno. They have failed so far even to take Naples & De Salis says they have 'missed the bus'.[240]

Here in Rome, order seems now to have been completely restored. A little sniping by franc tireurs is still going on in the outskirts; and the Germans until yesterday were doing a few acts of looting – taking bicycles & wristwatches off individuals & in some cases entering homes. But most of the fault lies with Italians, many of whom have been behaving stupidly by indulging in acts of provocation – whole trains & transport lorries have been sacked by them.

14 September

Went to the German Embassy with Ezra Pound's false passport & asked them to look for him & give it to him. Left a few foodstuffs as a present to the Irish College & Nuns. Called at the Vatican & was told that the wire to Bernardini would be dispatched today. Looked in on Mgr. Traglia at the Vicariato[241] to thank him & tell him we counted on leaving Rome soon by train.

Reading back some of these pages, I realise that I am too inclined to give people the benefit of the doubt & believe the best of them. I do so hate calumny & so mistrust gossip. But all my doubts of Badoglio were justified a thousand fold. What I cannot get over, however, is the behaviour of the King, whom I have always revered. I shall now think of him as the 'Re Schifoso'[242] &, as the [Prime] has followed his [traitorous] example, I regard the House of Savoy as finished. It can surely never [word deleted] survive even as a '[illegible]' under British control. This is the saddest thing of all. Compare the King of the Belgians. He kept his honour & his dignity. He gave up when all was lost. But he betrayed nobody.

The Americans it seems have received a severe reverse at Salerno & the British are getting it hard too. In fact it looks like a real defeat for them;

& this only shows what might have been done if we had had the will to resist & if we had not been betrayed all along. My inclination ~~all along~~ throughout to be optimistic – or rather reasonably hopeful – over the military situation ~~throughout~~ all through its development from Al Alamein onwards now transpires not to have been misplaced – from the strictly military point of view. Buona's intimation of pending disaster was probably due to a more acute interior conviction of the rottenness of the [*word deleted*] country. My logic was right within the limits of our [potentialities]; but did not take sufficient account of the rampant treason, which I refused to believe was so deep seated.

My passports were not made out today because the F.O. was occupied by the Germans, who were exhuming the archives. Hope for tomorrow. For the rest, I had a long talk with my lawyer this evening.[243]

15 September

Today I got my authentic passports, visés for exit into Switzerland up to Nov – 15th. This is satisfactory, for I am hoping ardently to have a good month's rest before deciding what to do [*words deleted*] if possible in some delectable mountain spot. Tomorrow is the turn of the Swiss Legation. Have they or have they not received instructions from Berne to give me their visés. If so, we should be able to start north on Monday or Tuesday.

Mussolini's 'order of the day', his first manifestation on resuming the leadership of the Fascist Party, is disappointing.[244] We only hope it will be followed up by something which will appeal to the heart & the head of all classes. This is no more than the driest & dullest of manifestoes. I fear he is still very unwell & ébrulé, & mediocrity distinguishes most of his [collaborators]. Pavolini as Sec. of the Party is O.K., but he is not a particularly dynamic personality – just a nice, clever, cultured & loyal man. But now would be the opportunity to galvanise public opinion.

Anyhow as I said to Pellizzi yesterday (I saw him for a brief half hour as he had come to Rome for one night) a corrupt & mediocre Fascist Government is better than a corrupt & mediocre other sort of Government. The Italians will always get the Government they deserve & as long as most of them are corrupt & mediocre, no change of regime will bring about a really good government.

18 September, morning

It might well be said that Mussolini's chief mistake [*word deleted*] was the unmerited confidence he placed in his countrymen. I myself have made the same mistake. I saw the [logical] side too much out of proportion – that is to say, their <u>vitality</u>, which is, naturally speaking, certainly in the ascendant & it constitutes Italy's one hope in the future. It is not easy to kill a vigorous plant. Morally, however, the Italians as a whole are deficient – a & that is where Mussolini (and I) have made our mistake. For my part I have judged them by moving too much in honest cultural circles or among peasants, who, as everywhere else, are generally good forthright people (though apt to be cunning & to 'make' out of their landlords if not carefully watched). For honesty is bigger dishonesty is more than petty taking [*word deleted*] advantages of opportunity, like going 2° class when one has been given a 1ˢᵗ class fare & pocketing the difference. Italians as a whole are intellectually honest, which is more than the English can boast of. But they are easily bribed, I fear. They are envious, jealous & unfair to rivals. Their civic sense is small. But what I did not suspect was their capacity for treason in so great a measure. The treason of the Navy is the saddest event of all. For it has a fine navy.

Pavolini's speech on the wireless last night was good, very good. I am glad he made the point that the party would require now new men and that the Republic meant more than the abolition of the monarchy. It meant a really <u>popular</u> regime. It was an inspired speech: honest, sincere & well spoken. It struck the heart as well as the head, as I wished in my last note. Good Pavolini!

I had a disappointing day yesterday. Nothing has come from Switzerland; & Mgr. Montini decided he would not ask Mgr. Bernardini to ask the Swiss Federal Police to wire the authorisation of our visés to the Swiss Legation here. He regarded this suggestion as an interference too direct in Swiss government procedure. De Salis, pompous & unsympathetic, says we must wait patiently for the answer from Berne. But we are practically determined to go on Tuesday come what may & leave our English passports behind to the visés & then sent on to us by private courier. We cannot risk staying on here indefinitely & we are tired out.

Getting Swiss money too is becoming what looks like an insurmountable difficulty. The transfer of money through the clearing, even to the diplomatic accounts of [*word deleted*] diplomats abroad, has been suspended, & my only chance now is to get a little cash. The Ministry is helping me in this & I shall know the best or worst on Monday.[245]

The Germans have stopped telegrams even of the Swiss Legation to Berne. B saw De Salis again & he says they are virtually cut off, & that therefore it is no use waiting for the visés. So the only thing for us to do is to go north & see what can be done at the frontier. At least we know now where we stand & that [writing] will do no good. Tuesday accordingly is the scheduled date for our departure. May God speed us.[246]

I might as well here & now withdraw my [apology] to Badoglio. It is time his hideous monster [*illegible*] was given [*illegible*] by a grateful government. He also got 1.500.000 lire a year as a Marshal d'Italia and [1]5.000 extra a month for some sinecure. Few fascist chiefs, if any, have done as well as this; & all they have been accused of is that they got soft jobs (or nominal jobs in some cases) with high salaries or allowances, & then speculated. Is it to be imagined that Badoglio put his millions into treasury bonds? I don't suppose he possesses even <u>one</u>; & he has certainly turned his money over at a high profit, while he filled his larder on the Black Market. The fascists, corrupt as some of them may have been, did not betray their country by saboting[247] the production of armaments & the war generally, even though they may have taken bribes from contractors & been in bad faith as far as Fascism is concerned. Badoglio has surpassed everyone in corruption, personal ambition & treachery.

(Here insert Pavolini's speech I ['H' *deleted*]).[248]

18 September, evening

It was good to hear the Duce's voice again tonight. It seemed to lack a bit of his old punch; but it was the voice of a man, nevertheless; calm, assured, full of faith & love of country. He told the facts, [fastening] on the treachery of the House of Savoy, which he said had been the centre since the beginning of the war of defection & intrigue. This indictment of the King was the essential point. The new Republic will be inspired by the spirit of Mazzini – and, I can add, may those who will give themselves to continue the fight be inspired by the spirit of Garibaldi.[249]

May God bless our journey north & guide us to decisions of courage & faith.

Today there was a terrific aerial bombardment of Ciampino[250] – and last night of the aerodrome of Littorio. The British armies have joined up s. of Salerno & though their advance is likely to be slow, the sooner we go the better. These last few days will be busy to the end & our first thoughts when we reach our destination will be for a period repose & recuperation. Then back to work.[251]

20 September

So tomorrow, D.V., we go off. It has been a last day of rush & considerable depression. The tearing up of [roots] & the going forward into the unknown. I succeeded in getting 500 Swiss francs at the official exchange, but no more than that – about enough to get to Berne & to last 3 days. The difficulties to complete the formalities for crossing the frontier will also be great. Is it worth going in the circumstances? This we shall have to decide on the spot after getting into touch with the Swiss authorities & the Italian Legation. Meantimes the thing to do is to get some rest & then, with strength renewed, to make up our minds.

In the <u>Osservatore</u>[252] tonight there is a notice of Mrs [*illegible*]'s death. She was always a good friend to me & she was a great personality, as well as an important archaeologist. I avoided meeting her during the war, as I thought it wiser to stay away from all controversial contacts. But I should like to have said goodbye to her. May she rest in peace.

22 September

We have reached Florence safely and it is a comfort to be out of the [surcharged] atmosphere of Rome. The journey was long but uneventful. 3 hours late. A munitions train had been blown up at Poggio Mirteto two days previously & the electric line was still under repair.[253] This caused considerable delay as every train had to be hawled a ~~considerable~~ some distance by steam and, the traffic being heavy, there was a bit of congestion. Dozens of trains we saw pass laden with motor transport, tanks & guns going south. The destruction in the station of Poggio Mirteto was a pitiable sight. We also saw the results of the aerial bombardment at Littorio & Orte,[254] where we had been only a few weeks previously. One of the little hotels where we had tried to get a lodging was a heap of ruins.

Florence is quiet & the weather has at last changed to cloudy skies. In the morning papers today there is a report of Churchill's speech on the great betrayal.[255] It is interesting in that it confirms in every way the account given in the Führer's speech and in the notes published by the German Foreign Office.[256] The treason of the King & Badoglio is set out clearly by the lips of his friends. That such a thing should have been possible seems incredible. But there it is – one of the most shameful facts of all history. I have severely criticized the Italian people for their corruptibility, their m[ediocrity], their lack of guts – taken as a whole. They [can] now be [excused] up to a point. They were tired, for the pace has been forced these past 20 years; & the opportunities for profiteering have been huge among half educated persons. All the same, it is a [sure] fact, and I see it now, that had we not been betrayed <u>since the beginning of the war</u> by the King & the Army chiefs, the people would have done their duty & the war would have been won. The folly & injustice therefore of the betrayal appears even greater than the crime. For look at Italy now – humiliated, ruined, divided & dishonoured – and <u>nothing</u> gained.[257]

(Here insert excerpt of Churchill's speech).

'When that which is Strong in Rome shall cease
We shall have War in the name of Peace'
R.I.P.[258]

23 September

So Graziani, as I hoped & expected, has joined up. May he be the organiser of victory. At any rate he is a man of genius, an inspirer of enthusiasm, a man of faith, honesty & guts. Alalà![259] I should like to be on his staff.

(Here insert his speech marked K).

A day in the country. Our landlord [*illegible*] lost his head when the armistice came & took fright that he would be imprisoned if any trace were found of us in the little House were the English to come. Consequently he [popped] all our carefully packed luggage into the attic over the farm building, [prized] open all our cupboards & made a general sorting of our things. There must have been quite a hullaballoo that day up there. [*illegible*] took an aviation officer with him who took upon himself to lampoon me as an Englishman & set everybody talking.

All this annoyed me not a little; so we [swept] up there today & took possession of all our things, though [*illegible*] had given strict orders that nothing should be touched except our pictures & the things in the attic. But we had a regular [*illegible*] day & on Saturday we shall take everything, lock, stock & barrel into Florence to be stored except for a few things which we have left with our friendly, [fascist] neighbours, the [*illegible*]- Monsani.

Thus [*illegible*] has been discomforted. He evidently thought we should never return & maybe hoped to profit from this. If so, he has now been deceived. The peasants we found somewhat surly & Bolshevik. Time will deceive them too.[260]

25 September

A long, heavy, bad day. We went up to the little House and took all our things away in two drays drawn by big fat horses – 28 pieces in all. We took 'em down to the warehouse, which is well situated on the left bank of the Arno. It was a tiring & trying & sad business; and, in the middle of it, came the war's first raid on Florence.[261] We saw the Vandals come over – 36 of them and drop their bombs – not many of them. We saw the smoke & the dust fly up, and noted that most of their bombs had fallen in the direction of the Campo di Marte – a fact we verified later. The nearest hit to the centre of the town was in Via Venezia, a stone's throw from the Anglican Church. It is reported that another bomb fell in the Protestant cemetery ('fra i mortacci loro', as the Romans would say).[262] Quite a lot of damage has been caused and I fear it is the prelude to something a good deal worse. I am moving Buona & Job, who are staying at Morandi's Pension (where we eat & where we eat very well – the house is kept by an excellent Irish woman), renamed to the Albergo Helvetica, where I have a room. Better stick together & keep right in the centre of the town. The railway was the objective & in fact it was not a Terrorisation raid. All the same, it is not easy to aim straight from a great height & several bombs fell dangerously close to the Piazza SS Annunziata where the Morandi Pension is situated. Via Venezia is exactly 400 yards distant.

Goodness only knows when we shall get away. Probably the trains will again be suspended & in any case we cannot possibly get things straight here until Wednesday 29th.

Many people are blaming the bombing on the Germans. But I take up this challenge with spirit. Why are the Germans here? Because of Badoglio's betrayal. What can be expected but a German occupation in the circumstances.

The hotel has been invaded by refugees from the menaced area. One man's meat is another man's poison. Until now the hotel has been practically empty. We are sad this evening, because a Signora Pieralli was among the victims, one of a dear old couple, who last year gave lessons to Job.

28 September

The anniversary of our wedding day – & a busy one too in the rain. We stored away our luggage & I settled up with [*illegible*], the proprietor of the little House. He promises to relet it to us at the end of the war.

Mussolini is back in Italy & is holding his first cabinet meeting. Badoglio's conspiracy is indeed proving every day more and more a complete fiasco. Though perhaps the majority of the people remain on the fence so as not to commit themselves (the inevitable attitude of cowards), the vast majority of that minority which represents principle and action are rallying to the Fascist Republican Government.[263] It is rare that one finds now a good word for Badoglio or the King, even though there may be a considerable number of people who are pro-English because of their silly hatred of the Germans. We hope to start on Saturday.[264]

3 October

To-day at last we accomplished the first stage of our journey North: Florence-Ravenna. But not without another day's delay owing to a disagreeable <u>contretemps</u>. When I was in Rome during those first days of anger & uncertainty, I wrote to Florence to wire the transfer of both our accounts to Rome, so that I might cash in all my available money. But the day after the Armistice, the posts & telegraphs were stopped & so Aniti said he would try to cash our cheques in Florence at his bank. He had not yet, however, succeeded in doing so, when, ten days later – the day before our departure – my money arrived & I duly cashed it in. Of course I told

Aniti to stop the cheques; but apparently he failed to do so, for they were presented in Florence with my account closed. The Florence bank therefore as part of their routine denounced us to the Procuratore del Re. Luckily I found this out just before we left. It was too late, however, to prevent the case going to the Pretore and I had blood to the head that morning stopping the worst consequences – because in Italy it is a penal case to present dud cheques. I got hold of a lawyer who knew the Pretore & we went down to his office together. Unfortunately he could not withdraw the charge, as the dud cheques were uttered in Rome and all documents had to be forwarded there. But he reassured me. It is only a question of Aniti seeing the Roman Pretor & explaining matters; but this meant writing fully to Aniti with copies to my Roman lawyer; and so we had to put off our departure for the morrow.

The train (6.55 a.m.) was packed. Hundreds of Tuscans go up & down this line getting produce for sale in Florence from the rich agricultural districts of the Romagna. The only places we could find were in the luggage van, where we sat upon our luggage (17 pieces in all) with quite 50 other persons thronged about us. We passed through the lovely Mugello & said a goodbye to Tuscany. At Faenza we missed our connection & had to take a later train which meant changing again at Lugo – a matter of some trouble with 10 pieces of luggage (the heavier luggage was registered through Ravenna).[265]

We reached Ravenna at 4 o' clock, weary & dirty. We went straight to bed for a couple hours & then emerged refreshed & clean. The S. Marco hotel is a very comfortable house. But it is not the place [*word deleted*] for meals.

Ravenna seems far from the war – spick & span, infinitely charming & apparently full of good food.[266] Anyhow we had an excellent & cheap meal this evening, including Adriatic soles (in spite of the fact that it is Sunday, when the law says restaurants can only serve vegetables). Other people, we observed, were eating meat.

Naples has fallen & precious little of the town seems to be left.[267] It is terrible to think of. The Anglo-Saxons will [bring] nothing & the Germans will leave nothing. And so it will be all the way up Italy – the ghastly consequence of treachery. Poor, beloved Italy!

4 October

Ravenna. Camilla Pasolini came in from [Coreolia] & lunched with us. She is O.K., but Guido & Caterina seem to be for the King schifoso. We had a open talk, but there is nothing really more to be added to the dismal facts of the situation. Camilla says, with truth, that the people are completely disorientated. They have lost faith in the leaders of all sides

& in themselves. It is a question of 'sauve qui peut'. [Communism] in the Romagna is the only thing towards which people are drifting as towards the only <u>respectable</u> flag left. This is readily understandable; but it shows to what pitch things have reached.[268]

7 October

<u>Venice</u>. Our train left Ravenna at 7.20 a.m. – not even 20 minutes late. We managed to push our luggage into it and sit on it in the corridor. At 10.30 we reached Ferrara. Job had developed a cold with a touch of fever; and since there was no train in to Venice until 6 p.m., we decided to put him to bed for the day. We had scarcely done so however, when there came an alarm and we judged the station hotel where we had taken a room, was scarcely the place to stay in; for [*word deleted*] around the station there is the new industrial zone. The old town and chief hotels are a mile away. We had therefore to tumble [*word deleted*] out of bed [*word deleted*] and stroll towards the centre. But after an hour we returned sick of it, and risked it – Job in bed again and we killing time eating grapes in the Caffé below. Later we visited the Castle & Cathedral. At 5 p.m. we heard of the big bombardment of Bologna and that consequently there would be no train until midnight.[269] In a way this was a blessing, because Job's fever, though not high, was on the rise. We migrated to a sympathetic little hotel the Annunziata in the centre of the town and went very early to bed.

Ferrara is full of good things to eat. Plenty of milk, for one thing, and cakes made out of flour.

As a result of the bombing of Bologna our journey on the next day was comparatively comfortable ~~because~~ as far as Padova. The train had not been able to be made up at Bologna & so there were few travellers except from intermediate stations. For once we were able to get seats. Job was all right again & our troubles seemed ended. We were 4 miles out of Mestre, however, when we came in for a bomb raid. The depot not far up the line from where our train had stopped was the objective. The 'liberators' came over in 3 waves & we watched the bombs fall. The line was of course interrupted and we were four hours marooned in a country station (Mirano) before we were able to proceed. We had a little bread & butter to eat, and I got some grapes from a farm. At 5 o' clock we reached Venice – just 12 hours since we had got up from our beds in Ferrara. It was a glorious relief to get into a gondola & silently make our way to [the] hotel (the Cavalletto, of ancient fame). We had the band in the Piazza too, while we drank our aperitifs at Florian's – all in the traditional manner. We [ate] at the Colomba, which was up to its reputation, & then to bed by nine.

This I am writing at 9 a.m. having just had my caffe-latte & feeling completely refitted by 10 hours sleep. B & Job also O.K.[270]

To-day we intend to look for a Pension; for we cannot go on spending as we are at present. The problem is to find something reasonably cheap where enough food can be had to keep a big man like me going & a growing boy like Job. I fear there will be nothing so miraculous as Morandi's in Florence, where pension rates were still only 35 lire a day & where one could eat one's fill at every meal. Signora Morandi is able to do this because she is almost the only public house keeper in all Italy who does not seek to profiteer!

11 October

It looks as if we were going to fall on our feet this winter in Venice. We have given up going further North to Merano. I called on the Prefetto Luciano,[271] who used to be Pavolini's ~~Chief~~ Cabinet Chief & he told me the best part of the Ministero della Cultura Popolare were shortly coming up to install themselves here. So I made up my mind to join up again. Later I met advance members of the Ministry, among them the Marchesa [*illegible*], & I discovered that some 900 rooms had been booked for the staff & their families. The Casino [&] the Lido has been taken as offices. So we shall get a suite in a first class hotel on the Grand Canal with all expenses covered by my pay (and maybe Buona will also get a job). Meantime we have [removed] to a Pension (the 'Budapest', kept by Hungarians) where the food is good & abundant. The cost on the other hand is high though less than at the Cavalletto: 60 lire per head per diem; and the rooms small. Besides there is nowhere to sit comfortably and so we shall be thankful to move into more spacious apartments. For the time being, however, it suits us.

We called on the Cardinal & he gave us a letter of recommendation to a College, kept by the Salesians at Mogliano Veneto, which lies between Mestre & Treviso – very accessible. We followed things up yesterday & were pleased with the place. It is simple & democratic & the boys are well fed. The priests have a real vocation for their job & in other respects it fulfils our expectations though of course as usual in Italy, properly organized games, washing facilities & bodily comforts are lacking according to standards reached in English schools.

Job passed his [exams] this morning [moreover] & so there remains only one difficulty left to surmount – the supply of sheets, blankets, towels etc. Which have to be found by us – and all such things as these we have left behind in Rome & Florence.

Venice is looking superbly beautiful – the weather is gorgeous and at night there is a high moon this week. The shops are full and we are busying ourselves getting everything shipshape, including a certain number of [purchases]. But things cost 50 per cent more than at Florence.[272]

Fifteen Fine Fat Fellows Falling Fast.[273]

Dino Grandi has apparently escaped to the Argentine.[274] He has fallen heavily between two stools, despite all his cleverness. Doubtless he expected to be called by the King to succeed Mussolini on July 25th. Evidently he never realized that the King was <u>inside</u> the Badoglio plot. I have always admired Grandi & I am sorry to see him make a fool of himself – for that is what it has come to. It is generally unwise to try to be too clever. The best role in life is to keep straight & loyal to principle & to causes, without [hedging]. Grandi has paid the penalty for not doing this. Too Italian. It is always the same tale: ambition of a mind that brooks no rivals (even to the point of a stab in the back of a colleague or friend) and that relies on cunning as its chief means, rather than on magnanimity.

15 October

<u>Friday</u>. Orders & counter orders. The latest idea is that the Ministry should establish itself on the Lago di Garda. Others say Milan. I should much prefer to remain here; but Garda would offer a good winter climate. ~~But~~ It would mean difficulties however [*word deleted*] about a school for Job. We are just longing to be settled. Living in boxes is an awful bore; and the weather having turned cold, we need to reshuffle our clothes. Moreover it is now my turn to <u>catch</u> cold & I am not missing it. Tomorrow I shall have to keep to my bed, for a cold with me is invariably a regular tornado – aches & pains in every bone of the face and a head like a pumpkin.[275]

17 October

Saw Sammartano last night – the new Wireless Inspector of the Ministry (Cultura Popolare).[276] He confirmed that the section of the ministry which concerns me is to establish itself at Saló on Lake Garda. We accordingly made up our minds to go to Saló on Thursday next. The great advantage of this move is that it will enable me to get easily into touch with the rest of the government.

My cold is better, after staying in bed the greater part of the day, reading a history of Venice. But the good weather has come to an end and with the coming of rain, it is perhaps something to be thankful for that we are leaving this beautiful city – for it is evidently a terribly dank place to live in during the winter.[277]

On Friday last we went to see Corradino Lini, who is in hospital. He was commanding a destroyer when the orders came through to give himself up with his ship to the enemy. Luckily for him, his ship was not ready & this act gave him the opportunity to go out of port & bring in the mine sweepers. Having no objection to this, he took out his ship, but it was torpedoed by a

German MAS boat & broken into 3 parts. He found himself with a crushed knee in a sea covered with nafta and for over an hour had to swim for his life with his broken leg amid the fumes of the oil. Being a tremendous fellow he succeeded in keeping going until rescued by the Germans & is now at the Lido Hospital, encased in plaster of Paris. His brother, Ippolite, is my great friend – a prisoner in India. His other brother was commanding a regiment in Greece when the fatal 'armistice' occurred; and nothing has been heard of him since.[278] It is to be hoped, however, that he is safe in Germany.[279]

4 November

To Brescia again yesterday. Got some good stuff for shirts. Buona found walking about Brescia, which is mostly paved with cobble stones, rather tiring – the pebbles were hard on her puddies.[280] But it is a nice town.

This afternoon Job & I bicycled over to Maderno (Lungo Lago Lucy) to see Pavolini.[281] Had a nice enthusiastic talk with him. I told him that the example of Venice must not be forgotten in the framing of the new constitution and that it should be a constitutional law that only the state should have the right to issue money or its equivalent. He promised to arrange for me to see Mussolini, who is at present at Predappio.[282]

The people in the Ministries who prefer to wait in Rome to welcome the British & Americans ought not to be allowed to do so. They should be sent to plant potatoes in Germany. I forgot to say this to Pavolini, but shall take an early opportunity of doing so.

He gave me the good news that Ezra Pound was safe back at Rapallo. I must write to him & get into touch.[283]

10 November

We have been to Riva and have left Job at his 'Convitto[284] Musialdi', where we believe he will be well looked after. There are only about 20 boys in all and he should therefore soon make friends. The Rettore, Father Rossi, seems to be an excellent man. Each dormitory has 2 to 3 beds in it only & the garden, though unkempt, is lovely, stretching down to the lake. The boys have their lessons in the state school; the Convitto is their home.

We walked out to Arco & back (12 kms) & enjoyed our outing.[285] The weather is now turned misty, with snow on the mountains. But today is gloriously sunny. For the rest there is little to report or comment upon, except the dastardly bombing of the Vatican City. The general opinion here is that the actual deed was perpetrated by Badoglio. But I should say that the British are responsible. The idea that the Germans did it is quite absurd.[286]

It is 2 months since the dreadful show down. I think public opinion is gradually rallying to the New Republic. But I fear it is still uphill work, given the general demonstration. I also fear the government is again being too kind. The murmurers and indifferent ought to be chivvied. It is not enough to put the active traitors & corrupters against the [wall]; and there is a sad dearth of first class men – men of character, leadership & enthusiasm. It is really only the Germans & Japanese who produce the goods in abundance. The Führer's speech yesterday could not have been better, the German fighting spirit is shining magnificent & the Japanese have given the American fleet another really bad knock.[287] Graziani is our one 1st class man in the limelight. I must see him – and the Duce. I need the tonic of their contact.[288]

13 November

Pavolini has telephoned to say he may have a car to take me to Florence on Monday, Tuesday or Wednesday of next week. We have therefore postponed our departure in the hope that we may be spared the scabrous train journey.

Called on & made friends with the Conte & Contessa Bonardi [– she a Torlonia]. They have the Martinengo Cesaresco Villa, a beautiful place most of which has been requisitioned by the Ministero degli Esteri.[289] I had known the old lady Martinengo Cesaresco years & years ago at Rome in the house of Count Ugo Balzani; and I remember how I used to devour her books on the Risorgimento. The Contessa Bonardi had been to Gattaiola & so between us there were many links with the past.[290]

Received a letter from Ezra P. in answer to my p.c. He is to be invited up here for consultation & so we hope to see him soon. (Here insert P.'s amusing letter). He has been writing to the Duce & I happened to see one of his letters on Sammartano's desk (Sammartano is our Director of Wireless Propaganda). The letter ran as follows (or almost exactly so; as far as I was able to memorise it).

'Duce,

Non credo che ~~sia~~ è utile o necessario che la Radio sia il monopolio ~~degli~~ di Londra in lingua inglese. Potrei combattere loro infame propaganda. Non ho bisogno di un Ministero, ma senza un microfono ich Kann nicht senden'.[291]

What a chap is Ezra! Quite priceless & probably more effective than a formal epistle.[292]

18 November

Thursday Back last evening in beloved Florence, Hotel Helvetia, a home from home. We came by car, put at our disposal by Pavolini, and his new Private Secretary drove it down (Cattani). A cold but pleasant journey – thick mist over the plains with some rain, snow on the Futa Pass.[293] We were accompanied by an armed militiaman and we were told on arrival that this had been necessary as there were bands of partisans on the Futa who were holding up cars.

At the Helvetia we found my father-in-law, the General – back in service, earning 10.000 lire a month, but disgruntled &, as usual, introspective, self-pitying & plunged in gloom. He is assisting the General in command here, but his lack of enthusiasm (despite his pro-German tendencies) is not encouraging. He says that the people here are all apathetic, but he does not seem to realise that since everything has to be rebuilt from the bottom, galvanisation must start from the top with a ring of confidence. He had stayed behind in Firenze when the others fled & he is lucky not to have been eaten alive by the Communists during the interregnum. My brother in law, Emiliano, has returned to Rome, [hoping] to be there to welcome the English – blast him. May he be bitterly disappointed. He ought to be carried off with a good many other officials to Germany, there to plant potatoes. It would do them all a world of good.

The purpose of our journey is to fetch more things, chiefly linen & blankets; & I may make a trip to Rome to get the other boxes left behind there. It looks as if the English were going to fail to reach Rome this winter. Anyhow their progress is slow & costly. Their intentions have gone entirely awry & I am hopeful of pleasant surprises in store during the coming year. It is too early yet, however, to form any judgement of the situation & I must not allow my vital optimism to be more than a purely subjective asset.

The Fascist Party manifesto on the main directions of the new consti-tution has made a good impression. I should have liked, however, to have seen some mention of the necessity for the state to control absolutely all money issues and their equivalent – token of real sovereignty.

Cattani says that the man who, among the fascist traitors, most deserves to be shot is Ciano; and that probably he will have that fate.[294] That he has been the veritable Judas of the movement. I am now inclined to think he is right, much as I hate judging people without full knowledge of the facts & despite my original liking of the man. I still think Edda is the chief responsible for his apostasy & ambitious intrigue. He seems to me to have been the weak victim. Italians can be so easily twisted round the thumb of a woman, if she is clever enough or pretty enough or obstinate enough. Look how the English wives have led their husbands into treachery.

19 November

Had tea with the [Marainis] & we were horrified to hear that she (Yoï) had been arrested – she of all people in Italy: the most loyal, unflinching, passionate fascist & Italian. She was allowed to go to a nursing home (with a policeman at her door), because of her bad heart, and after a fortnight was released. Friends on all sides [protested] to the prefect, who was at last convinced of her innocence. But the way things are sometimes done in this country is quite absurd, not to say [illegible] unintelligent. Probably some jealous woman with Jew blood in her, angered by her intransigent attitude on all the questions of the day ([illegible] the Jewish question) went and denounced her with an invented story, [illegible] by the fact that she is English by birth and that the Prefect is a man new to Florence. But that the Prefect (Mar[illegible], reputed to be an able & honest man – he is a friend of N[illegible] Danielli) should listen to such rot without first [illegible] a thorough investigation passes understanding. Considering that every Italian is always [ready] to libel his rival, denunciations should never be given any attention to; and, if made out subsequently not substantiated, the denouncer should be severely punished. I remember seeing Mussolini in 1926 just after he took over the Ministry of the Interior from Federzoni[295] so that he himself might make himself responsible for his own security – for there had been a number of attempts on his life. Federzoni had ordered a list to be drawn up of all suspect characters – that is, of people who might be [illegible] in a widespread anti-fascist plot. The list was compiled by the various local fascist chiefs; but Mussolini told me he had put it in the waste paper basket. 'Why?' I asked him. 'Because', he said, 'I noticed that if the local fascist chief was a baker, the rival baker was on the list; if a lawyer, the rival lawyer & and so on. All the rivals, [word deleted] all the people towards which personal grudges were [owed] were on the list without discrimination.'

This characteristic of envy, jealousy, vindictiveness & absence of all loyalty to colleagues is the great Italian defect. It accounts for half the trouble in which we now find ourselves. There is no sphere of local [cooperation] anywhere and until this spirit can be created, whatever form of government Italy gets will be a failure.

20 November

There was a glorious concert at Teatro Comunale & as we are not likely to hear such 1ˢᵗ class music for some time, we took full advantage: – The overture to [illegible] of great charm, Brahm's Concerto for violin and the incomparable V Symphony, the most all-of-a-piece of the lot, the most perfectly constructed <u>as a whole</u>, for there is no theme nor variation that does not offer [*illegible*] so that it is impossible to have any preferences. Nor do I ever remember having a better interpretation. [*Illegible*] is a great conductor, with a wonderful [*illegible*] and a striking ability to bring out the contrasts [without] at the same time overdoing it or sentimentalisations. As for the Brahms, the violinist [*illegible*] had not the requisite [*illegible*] bow & passion for the part. But his technique was excellent, as well as his musical sense. I love this concerto – the kind of thing I should compose were I a great musician. In other words I feel it, like the Overture to the Meistersinger, [*word deleted*] something personal to me, apart from its superlative merits. I first heard it I think in 1909, played by Misha [*illegible*], who in his youth played gloriously. (He has since [*illegible*] himself) I [*illegible*] heard it played by Kreisler (great) and [*illegible*] D'Arranzi (even better still), but best of all by Adolf Busch in this same theatre about 10 years ago. I also heard it here played by [Ciompi], a lovely artist, but too delicate for this particular job.

In the morning we unpacked & [packed] boxes. It was a good thing done and therefore it has been a satisfactory day, particularly as the war news is satisfactory on all fronts. The English have lost the Aegean islands, together with a lot of prisoners, ships & materiel. The Japanese victories in the Pacific seem more & more of a really crushing character as far as the American fleet is concerned; while the Anglo-Saxons are at a standstill in Southern Italy. On the Russian front, the Germans have counter attacked with success, retaking [*illegible*] with quantities of [*illegible*] & [munitions], and they have shot down [*word deleted*] more than 40 bombers over Germany. The British Press is fuming about the loss of Leros,[296] for it has certainly chastened Turkey into caution again after [*word deleted*] snapping at Eden's bait at Cairo last week. Of course the Russian advance all through the summer has given us cause to fear; but, if it is true, as the Germans say, that territory in this vast theatre of the war is of no account, that the Russian losses are [*illegible*], while their own reserves remain strong to strike when the psychological moment is judged to be at hand, we may have here also good cause for hoping that Stalin's rope is running out. The Moscow conference, now that all the Delegates have returned home, can hardly be regarded as a success from the British & American angle, and it has had a very bad Press among the neutrals, who have been made to realise more than ever the Bolshevik menace and the vanity of British & American promises, when they entered the war, to stand by the small nations. The [net] result amounts to little more than a successful Russian blackmail: a second front (other than Italy) <u>before</u> next spring or ....?[297] Well, we shall see what we shall see; and by then at any rate Republican Italy should have a quarter of a million [first rate and] [*six illegible words*].

My friend Duff Cooper, I see, has resigned; but what he has resigned <u>from</u>, I have little notion. He seems to have [*illegible*] a complete [sinecura] since he returned from the East after Japan's entry into the war. What, I wonder, will he be <u>up</u> to now? Good or no good? Probably the latter.

The other English news of the day is the release on a kind of ticket of leave of Tom & Diana Mosley, bless them.[298] I fear it is a question of his health. But he will [illegible] up & be Prime Minister yet. Maybe Duff, as an 18th century [traditionalist], has at last found that Churchill's & Eden's [illegible] in their [illegible] down to Russia of the old [illegible] of [European] balance of power is just a bit too thick. In this respect I give him the benefit of the doubt.

> 17 [illegible]: 'The King of Italy, you know, is a [illegible]atic?
> 17A. 'poor man. Is that why his legs are so short?'[299]

23 November

We have decided to hazard a journey to Rome, given that neither [Auristi] nor Francesca have arrived here, as we had hoped, or even written. The train is only guaranteed as far as Panicale,[300] which is about 1/3 of the way. But we have a letter of recommendation from the German consulate here, which may help us to get further without undue delay. This letter was not too easy to get [either]; but we got it at last through the good offices of Dott. [Maluzzi], who [represents] the Cultura Popolare here at the Prefecture. We all saw the Prefect Manganillo – nice looking man – who spoke to Pavolini about us (P. arrived last night) and the letter has introduced us to the Party Inspector in Roma ([Pizzirami]) who may help us for the return trip.

My father-in-law was interesting yesterday as he was inclined to talk a bit. But one never knows with him what he is really thinking. He says the Italians have never had an army worth speaking about & that is why he finally resigned in disgust. I maintained my faith in the Italian soldier as second to none in the world, but that the system & traditions (such as they are) are rotten & antiquated. The officers a caste, looking upon their career as a means of livelihood only – few feel any vocation – and as a swagger. The men are treated not as comrades but as a herd of underdogs, especially the recruits for whom everything is done to make military life [illegible]. They are 'buggered about', yelled at, given cold & dirty quarters (usually full of bugs) & no effort is made to interest them in the military art. The officers of course [formed] a [illegible] of [camorra] too, with a view to blocking reform – with the result that inefficiency & ill-preparation became endemic, and in the end they betrayed their country for their own caste interests. That is unfortunately the truth; and if the new [enrollments] are to be a success, the [whole] attitude must be changed. Recruits must be welcomed, they must be treated with the utmost [humanity] & made to feel from the outset that the officers are their patres familiarum.[301] Of course there are great difficulties as far as [clothing] them well & [illegible]

them warmly. But everything possible should be done for them & there is
no reason why they should not be thoroughly well fed. My father-in-law
agreed. But he remains pessimistic, though I expect he is doing his best –
and that he is more of a man in his office on duty than he likes to make out
when he talks to his friends like a man in a dream.

24 November

Rome. The train started half an hour late, but we secured comfortable 1st
class corner seats and Chiusi[302] was reached after a crawl of 5 hours. Chiusi
had been bombed two days previously. A connection, however, had been
arranged a mile along the line, whither we tramped with our light packs
through the mud and again installed ourselves in corner seats. We arrived
in Rome at 9.15 – 12 hours after our departure. We went straight to the
Grand Hotel in order to be sure of a room & food – the best hotel in Rome
and close to the station. It was a seventh heaven of luxurious comfort
& cost us nearly 500 lire. Yet it was worth it; and we were rewarded by
finding that Emiliano was able to lend us his little [illegible] in Via Margutta
for the rest of our stay. This and the fact that we were never called upon to
pay our tickets beyond Panicale made up for the initial extravagance. We
have been able to arrange besides, for a free trip back on Monday 31st by
pullmann[303] [illegible] [car] from the Fascio.

30 November

The first day in Rome was occupied in getting out our boxes, which had
been left with the Parish Priest of S. [Agnese]. He had [walled] them up
at the top of a tower and the wall had to be breached, while the heavy
boxes had to be [illegible] down a narrow staircase. [Auristi] provided
the transport and the luggage was dispatched – thanks to an introduction
from Pavolini – with the stuff being sent North (all the way to Lake Garda)
belonging to the Fascio. All very satisfactory.

I then turned my attention to my business and got things on [illegible] at
least a cut & dried basis with [Auristi] and my lawyer [illegible]. I sold [my
old] bicycle for 1500 lire & got 10.000 lire for my lawyer in Florence as a
reserve against possible [illegible] taxation on the flat in Florence. Again,
all very satisfactory.

Rome looks dead. After dark, hardly a soul in the streets. Even the grand
hotel doors shut & barred. People are afraid of food riots. Everybody is
living one way & the other on the black market. We saw Francesca &
Mariano. He will shortly be leaving for Venice or [for] Mogliano Veneto,
& all is being done to enable Francesca to follow him.

Emiliano is as usual [*illegible*] & persistently pro-English. He and all the other renegades, left in Rome, are bitterly disappointed that the Anglo-Saxons have failed to arrive. They now fear they may never arrive.

The only other people, besides our dear friends Francesca [*illegible*] & Mariano Frasso, we have seen are [Godel] (one of my old Ministerial colleagues on the Radio), who is coming north; Gino Villari, who also hopes to come North; and the Pellizzi, who are staying on. I found him distressingly intellectual, arguing round and round on the responsibilities of Mussolini, whom he blames for everything and whom he refuses any longer to follow (though he remains stoutly [*illegible*] & would be prepared to carry on under some other provisional government – an absolutely theoretical attitude, seeing that no other government is possible or practical). We had a [*illegible*] heated argument. It is true of course that Musso lost grip during the past fateful years (after the 1st Munich meeting or at any rate after Sept – 1939) and might, theoretically, have got things [straight] after the Abyssinian War, pulled down the old army system, reformed the Party and sacked the incompetents & self-seeking intriguers. But the fact is he had to deal with the Monarchy and the Monarchy had the Army behind it and its popular prestige was high, while the fascists had grown unpopular on account of the graft and the red tape and the [various camorras]. His hands were therefore tied. He tried to 'manage' the situation and failed. But if he had attempted a coup, the [failure] might have been even more disastrous. The Monarchy is the real factor to [blame]. Surrounded by the [military] clique, it [*illegible*] evidently [been] conspiring for years and waiting its opportunity to rid itself of Fascism at the bidding of the international Freemasons. Mussolini should have [*illegible*] it all [*illegible*], but it is easier said than done. He had Nations to deal with and the mesh of personal intrigue which is characteristic of Italian life is not easily broken or [unmasked]. Oh yes, I saw MacWhite, the Irish Minister, who was as usual full of information & [*word deleted*] amusing gossip. He told me that Badoglio, [*illegible*] (the Court Minister) and the King kept the whole surrender plot to themselves. He had seen [Russo], the second in command at the F.O. at the time and declared himself convinced that [*illegible*] the war [Guariglia], the Foreign Minister, knew [*word deleted*] anything of the 'Armistice'. The declaration made by [Russo] to the German Ambassador, denying the 'Armistice' at 4.30 on September 8th (after the cat had been let out of the bag by an American [lieutenant] from Algiers) was made in good faith.

MacWhite also said that Ciano was in the plot [*six words deleted*] on his own account (a leg in each camp), and had worked against the Axis all along. He had assured Sir Noel Ch[a]rles, the British Counsellor of Embassy, that Italy would never [come] into the war. He never disguised his pro-English attitudes. Charles had orders to keep in the closest touch with Ciano. One evening in his cups he burst out with the statement: 'I am fed up with the man. He always carries off the [prettiest] girl and then leaves me to [pay] the bill.' Ciano had also wished to oust Mussolini & take his place [even] [*illegible*] he had [been] made Foreign Minister.

At the Grand Council Meeting, Mussolini is said to have dubbed [Ciano] as a Judas & accused him first of betraying his family and then his country. [*Word deleted*]. This seems [*illegible*] true [*word deleted*]. I [should say that] Ciano has evidently been the [*illegible*] in the [*illegible*]; & if he gets shot, I now consider he deserves it. I withdraw all I have ever said in his favour in the past. Like the Duce, my instincts have been too generous.

Grandi had his own plot & knew nothing of Badoglio's – according to MacWhite. He expected to be called by the King to take on the succession. But when he presented himself at Villa Savoia on the morning of Sept 9th, he was refused an audience. Grandi probably was prepared to negotiate a separate peace, but not to betray Germany. He wanted to oust Mussolini, but not to destroy Fascism. So MacWhite thinks. Federzoni was working with him. But it is amusing to note that the '[fascist]' Grandi was not [included] by the [still more 'fascist'] Badoglio.

For the rest of the Grand Council, each had his own axe to grind or was too confused to know what he wanted. Most of them [voted] against Mussolini because they thought to get rid of him was the only way out of the crisis. They were not aware of the King's plot to betray the country & its honour. In fact everybody was at sixes and sevens. Plots within plots, personal [*illegible*] lack of vision [*illegible*] each confident of his own cleverness (& got deceived by Grandi's [motion]) to ride the [storm] [and] all [unwise]. Mussolini [really] the only man who saw straight & kept straight, a towering figure to the last, but tangled in the net.

It is absurd in my opinion for Pellizzi to turn on him, though it is true numbers of Italians hold him as the one man responsible for the [crash] & so will not follow him any longer. But history will [vindicate] him and his great work; and as [things are], there is no honourable or practical course but to follow him. He has the confidence of Hitler. [*Three words deleted*] [there] is [no] [alternative] of the State possible. There is no attention to a Republic. There is no attention to Fascism as the ideology of the new state. Therefore people should pass over the ifs and buts of the situation and rally round him for Italy's sake; and fight or help all they can to [*illegible*] victory [*five words deleted*] with Germany's help or, if defeat comes, see their country go down with the flag flying and [consequently] [*word deleted*] ensure its survival as a self-respecting & respected nation. The talk can be reserved for the time when the war is over. To split hairs about what ought to be done in the meanwhile is madness. But, alas, this form of madness is a [*illegible*] decisive; & Pellizzi has caught the malady. [*Word deleted*]. A great pity. In fact the only real [flaw] that can be [*illegible*] on Mussolini is his all too notorious love affairs, which is great harm to his prestige & may be the physical reason of his decline in recent years.

30 November

There has been a [*illegible*] over our car back to Florence, so after all we were forced to travel by train. It was an awful journey. We had to rise at 4.30, tramp with our [*illegible*] to the station (not so few & light as on the outward journey) and take our seats an hour before the train started in a crowded 3rd class coach of antiquated date. It was cold, though not too cold but drafty (the window was broken). We took 9 ½ hours to reach Chiusi and 15 to Florence! We [*illegible*] at Chiusi and at other places in the open country. Short of Orvieto we heard the [*illegible*] of [*word deleted*] a squadron of 'Liberators' over our heads, above the clouds; [but] we could not see [them], and, they, I am thankful to say, could not see us. Chiusi station was in a bad mess – whole trucks blown on to the backs of others and [immense] craters ~~everywhere~~ twisted [*illegible*] & wire everywhere. Luckily we had brought food, but it ran out by the evening, so that all we had to eat for dinner was a little bread, honey & wine. Buona was right, however, in insisting on our starting; for we have gained a day & got home O.K. My wife is a marvellous sport[s]woman. It has been a successful trip against odds and our only mistake was the leaving behind of 2 precious water bottles. I hope Mariano, however, will be able to retrieve them for us.

2 December

We arrived safely in Venice today after a comfortable journey for a change in a sleeping car.

Before leaving Florence I had a talk with Giotto [Dainelli], the famous explorer & academician, about my plan for setting up a small office to produce a detailed plan for the new Europe for propaganda purposes – just to show the world by means of concrete proposals in the form of a 'European Charter' that [*illegible*] peace means a just peace. This in my opinion is the only other [arm] we can forge to win the war with. But it must be used quickly & swiftly; & [if] the solutions must be self-evidently just. Dainelli seemed taken with the idea – [*three words deleted*] and he has authorized me to use his name in support of it. In Venice I saw the Ambassador [Capasso] Torre, whom I have known for many years (since I was Secretary General of the Centre Internationale d'Etudes sur le Fascism). He was a great friend of de Vries & I tackled him on the same subject. He also seemed [*illegible*] by its possibilities & has promised to speak to Mazzolini about it. After I have talked the thing over with Mazzolini myself, I hope to see the Duce & submit it to him – and then we must get to work: Dainelli, myself, Gino Villari, a cartographer, a typist & perhaps two other assistants, a young geographer & a young F.O. man. I really believe we could produce the goods, which, if accepted by Mussolini & Hitler might knock the will to war in the U.S.A. & Great Britain to smithereens.

This time we are staying at the Bella [*illegible*] in Venice, in a room overlooking the Riva degli Schiavoni. The weather is perfect & everything [*illegible*] beautiful.

4 December

Back to Saló, after a night at Desenzano, where we were lucky to find a room in a private house – but it cost 70 lire. To-day the new Ministerial Mess was inaugurated: 35 lire a day per head, which will represent a considerable economy. It appears to be have been well organized by one of our young men, [Franci] by name, who has been to school as an hotel keeper. We certainly ate extremely well. Mezzasoma came to luncheon for the occasion.[304] I saw Sammartano & started establishing my contacts again. We found Ezra here & Nicoletti, who is starting a new Review to which I am to contribute (Ezra, too, on economic reform): 'Volontà Republicana'. But before I can make much headway with my 'great' plan [or with] articles, we shall need a good week getting settled into our new quarters. We found several letters from Job awaiting us (he seems well & happy & more of a man) and one from Manoli Tom[*illegible*], who is with Farinacci, asking me for articles.

9 December

I saw Sammartano about my plan & he appeared to like it. He asked me to put up a memo. on the subject, which I have duly done (<u>Here insert copy of memo</u>). Then we went to Riva to see Job. He seemed well & happy. His reports are not too good (always the same old tale – too much backchat, a mischievous influence & scarce concentration on his work). But the Rector is a good educator & I feel confident he will improve the longer he [*illegible*] there.

We have [*three words deleted*] moved into our new quarters & installed a stove & got in some wood.

The only news of the day is the meeting between Stalin, Roosevelt & Churchill at Teheran. The official communiqué is not likely to arouse much enthusiasm in England or America. It is obviously just a pinning of the Anglo-Saxons down by the Russians to the opening of a western front next spring. If the Anglo-Assassins fail to do so, Russia will cut up nasty. This is about all it comes to. For the rest the official communiqué amounts to little more than a propaganda [stunt]. If I can only get my plan accepted & launched, it would make a most effective reply to those vague utterings which mask the real, [*illegible*] intentions.

9 December

I went all the way to Gargnano to see Dolfini,[305] Mussolini's Private Secretary with a view to firming up a talk with the Duce. Pavolini was good enough to recommend me. All went well to start with. I was promised the talks the following week. But the next day I was informed by Mezzasoma that the Duce was too busy to receive me for the present. This was a great disappointment. But I thereupon spoke to Mezzasoma about my plan. I presented the memo & Mezzasoma expressed himself as very interested. He said he would hand it immediately to the Duce & asked me to write a covering letter in which I should request to be granted an audience. (Here insert copy of covering letter).

On my return from Gargnano, I visited the German Embassy & spoke to Dott. Mollier, the Press attaché, to whom Von Plessus (in Venice) had given me a letter of introduction. He encouraged my idea of a visit to Germany and I told him about Francesca [illegible]'s desire to obtain a permit to go & establish herself either at Venice or Treviso.

Since then I have furnished him with all details & he has promised his best to help her. It would be grand if I could manage to get her away, so that she could stay close to Mariano & be out of danger from the Anglo-assassins!

21 December

Bad news. Mussolini has informed Mezzasoma that he finds my plan interesting, but is of the opinion that for the present its putting into action must be sat upon. That is roughly the literal translation of the letter I received from Mezzasoma's Chef de Cabinet. It is only to be surmised that M. feels that as things stand (no money, [illegible] [justice], constitution unsettled etc.) it is not for him to take such a bold initiative. But I am disappointed, especially as it also means I shall have to wait again before getting a chance of seeing the great man. Damn!

Probably the best thing I can do is to pay a visit to Germany. I have seen [illegible]feld, who is the German wireless propaganda officer at the German Embassy & he says he will gladly arrange for a visit. Maybe as soon as Job's xmas vacation is over, I shall go. Meanwhile I am writing twice a week a [conversation] in English to be transmitted from Milan. It is light work for the [pay] I was promised & so I should not complain. All the same it is maddening not to be able to get a move on with one's ideas – political, economic & [illegible]. My article [on banking] & monetary reform, however, is to appear in the first number of 'Volonta Republicana' & it will probably be read by the Duce & others, since the editor Nicoletti enjoys prestige & government banking.

21 December

Job back from school for the holidays, looking fit & composed. It will be interesting to see if his behaviour has improved.

25 December

A quiet not very Christmassy Christmas[.]

31 December

A tragic year ended. May 1944 prove the turning point! It is all a question, however, of 'ifs' – and therefore it is useless to prophecy. All the same I have confidence that the Anglo-Saxon attempt to [invade] the West will prove a failure. That is the [first] great hope. The second is that the advance up Italy's backbone may never reach Rome – or, even if it does (and I fear it will eventually) will not reach [*word deleted*] beyond the Apennines. By July we should have a considerable, well-equipped army in the Field & a counter offensive against the Anglo-Saxons could be begun with good chances of success. The third hope is a revival of the submarine campaign on a big scale in April. The forth a the terrible punishment of England in reprisal for her terrorisation policy. If these four hopes were verified & if the Germans could develop an offensive against Russia in July, then there would be a fair chance of Stalin making a separate peace & of Roosevelt being hoofed off the Presidential Chair & of Revolution in England ....[306] with a just peace in the spring of 1945. But more than that I cannot say & most of the 'ifs' are improbable! One can only hope & pray & work & love. Things do not look [*illegible*] by any means. But we can [still] hope[.][307]

> When rations grow short, people cease to be fussy –
> So fill up the pot, and pop in the [pussy]![308]
> End of 1943[.][309]

N.B.

We start the New Year with 6 months [*illegible*] of requirements, plus certain services. O.K. In addition, I am earning 8000 p.m., which is the monthly allowance.[310]

Diary 1944

1 January

[*Illegible*] [*illegible*]. Job & a friend go for a gita up a mountain by [themselves]. I am pleased with Job. He has much improved. Big [luncheon] at the Mess.

The only fly in the ointment is that over two losses have [*illegible*] in Rome. The Fascio has not got them up [yet]. But I have written to Pavolini & Pizzirani to put matters right.[1]

Where will the Anglo-Saxons launch their western attacks? Probably it will be Norway to start with and then Brittany – Cherbourg – [unless] Spain has been marked down as yet another victim.[2]

If the so called United Nations win, ~~and I survive~~ there will be stuff enough for half a dozen books for me to write, if I survive to write them: –

1 How we lied our way to victory
2 Through Terror to glory & Ashes
3 How England betrayed Europe.
4 How Churchill [*illegible*] the British Empire
5 Treachery the Trump Card 6. The [Wandering] Jew.

Jewish propaganda, [prodding] by Roosevelt, hatred of Rome, pride & an undervaluing of German strength made war possible. But the real [*illegible*] of it was of course the traditional [*illegible*] of the balance of power. Germany was [growing] too strong. Europe must be kept divided, so as to allow Britain to put the world state further into debt whereby to exploit the world. To this extent England has lost the war. [*Illegible*] of Germany, Europe will be left hopelessly unbalanced & with a more [*illegible*] power than Germany [*illegible*] down the [*illegible*] [*illegible*]; while England herself will be as [much as] as [*illegible*] [*illegible*] any [of] the others – the U.S.A. reaping what England had sown. And European civilisation, which is really the life blood of all that is best & most beautiful in England will be smashed.

Will 1944 see this? Or will God save us in the end? When I say 'us', I mean Europe. I have dreamed, ever since I wrote 'The hour of the wind' as a boy at Eton, of a [*illegible*] & united Europe. Am I to see my dreams turned to a nightmare or shall I turn out to be a prophet [?] Twelve months hence, I should know the answer to these questions. Anyhow, better to have loved & lost, than never to have loved at all; and in any case I can die a good [Italian], which is the same thing as saying a good European, for Italy's spirit transcends the narrow limits of nationality and embraces the whole of this dear continent.[3]

9 January

Job goes back to school. I am very pleased with him. The weather is bitterly cold, but splendid. We suffer much from the cold in the mornings, when we have to do without the stove. But in the evenings we tuck in.

Here insert translations of 2 articles marked thus:[4]
They summarise so perfectly my own point of view, that I might as well allow them to speak for me. I have only to add that undoubtedly the two chief reasons for the widespread discontent with the Fascist Regime are merely two fatal Italian characteristics, namely first, an insufferance[5] of discipline (e.g. of being held responsible towards others rights and those of the collectivity); for the Italian is a terrific individualist, caring little for the interests of anybody beyond those of himself & his family, and while his sense of civic responsibility is still [un]developed. Consequently any regime which insists on discipline in this admirable sense is bound to be unpopular. Secondly, the there is the Italian incapacity of Italians to organise anything without winding themselves up in red tape & [extending] the bureaucratic [machinery] to a point of exasperation. Such incapacity is again partly due to the lack of any great sense of responsibility, so that the bureaucratic machinery has to be swollen in order that every inventive action may be checked and double-checked; and partly to the national tendency of Italians to form 'camorras', that is, self mutual self-helping cliques – to get the best jobs for themselves & make new jobs for their friends. The consequence of this second characteristic was [word deleted] a maddening complication of the corporative organisation & the multiplication of offices & forms to fill up. Many people to save themselves time & trouble resorted to bribery in order to get things [through] quickly & in many cases the bribes were accepted. Nobody likes bribing & those who could not afford to bribe went off their heads by the owing to the interminable delays. [Word deleted] In the circumstances it is not surprising that discontent with the regime grew & grew; but it is absurd to blame Fascism for all this. The Italian must blame himself. Until he learns self-discipline and acquires a sense of responsibility & disinterestedness in the dispatch of [word deleted] public duties, every regime will be unpopular which tries to organise the country in a way necessitated by the conditions of modern social life. We have got to educate ourselves. That is the really great problem. The present disasters will not be suffered in vain, if they we can learn from them our civic lessons.[6]

12 January

This mornings papers (here insert copy) give a long account of the Verona trial, ending in the execution of 5 of the 19 who voted Grandi's order of the day at the meeting of the Grand Council on July 24th last.[7]

The whole thing makes [one/me] feel sick; but it must be conceded that stern measures were necessary – otherwise when the time comes to judge the greater traitors it could be alleged that we were showing a spirit of vendetta & partiality. It is also necessary to [word deleted] give an example to others who may be plotting further acts of treachery. But it is all terrible, especially as we are only at the beginning. Other trials have got to take place, hundreds more will be shot, and it is unbearable to think of the suffering of those left behind – the wives, the mothers, the fathers ...[8] My heart bleeds today especially for the Duce. For him the limit of tragedy – and he so sensitive & partly responsible because of over generosity & too great a clemency in the past.

It is clear that Grandi was the prime mover in the whole bad business. After his brilliant defence of Italy in London at the time of the sanctions and again during the Spanish War, he worked hard to bring about a real rapprochement with England. This was all to his credit. I know he disapproved of the Pact with Germany & he had a perfect right to his opinions. But then he ought to have retired from [word deleted] public life. Instead he accepted office and lay in wait, the better to betray. That he may have become seriously committed that the Anglo-Saxons would win the war, is possible. But he had no right to do more than resign and give the Duce his private advice. He had no right to conspire. That he expected a place in Badoglio's Government & that perhaps he never expected Badoglio to act quite so treacherously as he actually did (deceiving the people about peace & betraying the Germans) may also be true. But this only shows that cunning as he has been, he was not quite cunning enough. I used to have a great esteem for Grandi, though I never doubted he was a dark & intriguing character. But it is a blow to find one's trust in others misplaced, one's original judgement of a man mistaken. He had been good to me and I had been good to him. Now he is as good as hanged as far as I am concerned and I regret that he, the arch-conspirator, has [escaped]. For his treachery was not only [at] the expense of his country, his creed and his leader, but also of his friends. Few, I believe, realized its implications. Ciano and Bottai were of course in the plot up to their necks; and probably also Federzoni.[9] But I believe most of the others were idiots rather than criminals. Cianetti, however, was the only one who got off the death penalty. His letter to the Duce written 10 hours after the event, confessing his mistake & withdrawing his name from the [adverse] vote, saved him. The others have paid the penalty by being [dumb] (in both the English & American senses of the word). All the same, I should have wished the Tribunal to have been more lenient towards them too.

Marinelli broke down, but died shouting 'Viva l'Italia, Viva il Duce.'[10] The others died hard. Pareschi also shouted 'Viva il Duce', & I doubt not he was sincere.[11] Ciano had to be given a double [dose] of shot before dying. These are the gruesome details of the executions, which I had to-day from the photographer who had to be present. Ciano might have saved the others, if he had testified the whole truth. But he had not the heroism to do this, hoping, I suppose, that he might inculpate himself. And where is Bottai? Where are all the other condemned? We only know definitely of Grandi's escape abroad. Then there is De Stefani. How far was <u>he</u> in the plot? In many ways a great man & infinitely charming. All the more terrible. And now the English will make use of the whole wretched business as another means to libel Mussolini, saying that the executions are his personal vendetta – the very contrary of the truth. If it had been a private affair, he would have forgiven them all. History will vindicate of course the great man of his character, but meanwhile it is hateful to think how a [lying] propaganda will make millions believe that he is a monster. Farinacci is perhaps right when he says that Mussolini's great mistake <u>was his</u> attempt to make a revolution without bloodshed & to have compromised with the Liberals and the Monarchy, hoping that time & success would win them over, instead of sweeping the whole opposition away. Now he has paid the penalty for his excessive generosity & leniency.[12]

12 January

The decree of nationalisation of the key industries & the [socialisation] of all, is an ~~good~~ excellent step forward [*two words deleted*] which may have [*illegible*] good consequences, but it remains to be seen whether it will be carried out <u>rigorously</u> & <u>quickly</u>. I trust so; for then the new Republic will ~~which?~~ really show what it is worth. Will the banks be [included]? If not, why not? [Meantime], I [withhold] further comment.[13]

18 January

Job has run away from school! We had an hour of panic, for this morning one of the priests of the school turned up to ask if he had arrived home the evening before – but he had not! He had taken the bus from Riva, after getting the necessary permit from the German Command with the aid of a German acquaintance; and had borrowed enough money to take himself as far as Gardone, where he had walked to the Mess – hungry & tired. Luckily he found our friends the [*illegible*], who fed him & put him up for the night. He has since been sent back, very crestfallen. But I shall have to go to Riva on Saturday to plead with the Rector to prevent his being sent away.

His excuse is that he was being bullied for being a fascist [as most] of the boys (but not the [priests]) are anti-fascists. I told him Fascists don't run away, which braved him somewhat. We gave him a very cold welcome, but on his departure I tried to soften things & give him to understand how much I loved him – but that he must feel greater responsibility towards us and realise the difficulties of our lives & not add to our preoccupations. Of course the whole thing is partly due to his fantastic spirit of adventure, that although this is all very well in a way, it is stupid to engage in adventures which have no sane purpose. He must have known perfectly well that he would only court punishment & if necessary a stricter & more distant college.[14]

24 January

No sign of our Rome boxes yet – and Rome is now threatened by the landing at Nettuno.[15] I bicycled to Maderno to see what might be done again about the [boxes] & I got a telegram request by the Fascio requesting them to be loaded onto one of the lorries of a column which will be shortly leaving <u>Rome</u>. So we hope for the best. We also hope the Anglo-Assassins will find the Germans not so [unready] for them as they fondly imagine.

I cannot believe that the Germans were not strategically prepared for an incursion of the kind. It was an obvious thing to expect sooner or later. But because the landing might have been almost anywhere, it was clearly impossible to spread the defence all along the coast. I therefore surmise that there must be a strong reserve of mobile troops ready in the centre of Italy & that they will soon be counter attacking with vehemence. The Anglo-Saxons risk being drawn into the Pontine Marshes, where a lot of land has been flooded (alas, they are Marshes again).[16] Without knowing what the [*illegible*] amount to, however, it would be ridiculous of me to attempt to foresee the result of the impending battle. We can only hope & put our trust in German efficiency.

30 January

I am pleased with the success my articles are having, especially those which have appeared in the new Catholic Weekly ('Crociata Italica') founded by Farinacci. It was a real inspiration on his part to found this paper, which has already a wider circulation than had the 'Regime Fascista'[17] before July 25th. Don Tullio Calcagno,[18] who runs the paper, has written me an enthusiastic letter in appreciation of my contributions; and now I intend to write a series of articles on monetary reform in a way easily assimilable by the general public.

Today the Germans have invited me to go down to Rome for a few weeks to [speak] on the wireless (talks to Anglo-Saxon soldiers) instead of paying a visit to Berlin. They think I should be more useful just now in Rome, & I feel tempted to accept. It is encouraging too to think that no such invitation would have been extended to me, were the Germans not confident that the Anglo-Saxon march on Rome had no immediate prospect of success.[19]

13 February

The news is better at last. Who knows if this battle for Rome may not turn out to be a battle for Naples![20]

Meanwhile the law nationalizing the key industries & socialising the others has been given its definite [illegible]; and by July 1st it will be a <u>fait accompli</u>. Fascist Italy once more shows the way towards Social Justice & true Democracy.[21] This will be something worth fighting for. It will give the new Army an additional ensign. It will serve to unite our people and confound our enemies.[22]

Here insert article on the Masonic plot (14.2.44).

This explains all. We guessed it; but here we have the proof![23]

31 March

I have allowed quite a time to lapse since I last made any entries into my diary. The reason is that I have been especially busy. I have been transferred to Milan for one thing, to work a new special wireless for the British troops in Italy (though it should also be heard clearly in England and the U.S.A.)

The service is called 'Jerry's Front' and it is transmitted from Rome. It's a good programme as propaganda – mostly composed of Jazz music – directed by my friend Gödell in Rome. My part is a dialogue which [word deleted] I [illegible] and carry out with my friend Burlando, who knows English perfectly. We are supposed to be two Englishmen chatting of an evening in their rooms in London. Burlando & I get a lot of fun out of this, but it takes a deal of invention. [Illegible] of course helps a lot. Our stage names are 'Fat' & 'Jolly'. I'm 'Fat'.

Well, that's that. I hate being separated from B, but I mean to get home for 10 days at Easter; and later B will come & stay here for bits.

As 'Fat & Jolly' we talk as patriotic Englishmen, though '[agin]' the Government & as good Europeans. In fact, my genuine point of view.

The chief events which have occurred since I last put pen to paper are:-

1   Our Rome boxes have arrived – Thank God for that. They had
    somehow found their way to the Isola Garda – the Borghese's place

where the Mussolinis are staying (the Duce's brother's children). There they were discovered & have now been delivered safely at the [*illegible*] Villa.

2   I have paid a visit to Cremona, where, besides seeing [Mandi] Tornaghi,[24] who is now Farinacci's private secretary, I met Farinacci himself (very much on the spot, dynamic & welcoming) and Don Calcagno, the great little priest who inspires <u>Crociata Italica</u>. Also his colleague Father Lantelli.

3   I spent a delightful weekend of [*illegible*] & good talk with Claudio & [*illegible*] [*illegible*] ([Omodeo]'s daughter) at [Meina] on Lago Maggiore. And I have had a talk with Piero Parini, who is an old friend & one of the few men, who in my opinion could take charge of all Italy, if need be.[25]

   I have also met Father Gemelli.[26]

4   The offensive against Cassino has [ruinously] failed.[27] I veritably believe if no more landings take place in Italy before the end of June, we shall have the situation here in hand. The new Army will be in line & will be able to relieve many of those splendid German troops.

The general situation is not so bad. It's improving. The British have had a severe [knock] in India. Chandra Bose's army is in the vanguard of the Japanese & the Indian border has been crossed.[28] The Ides of March have passed & Churchill's prophecy that great events would happen before then has been [negatived]. Churchill's latest speech was a bit of a flop – evidently made to quiet his chief critics (the grumbling masses) and I doubt if it has succeeded. There was little punch in it and the British people are now sceptical of golden promises.

The Russians continue to advance, but they are not succeeding in trapping the Germans, who are fighting with comparatively few covering troops as they fight back bit by bit on their heavily fortified line against which, when the Bolsheviks reach it, I doubt if any impression will be made.[29] The bulk of the German army is being held in reserve.

The 2nd front is still pending & Von Runstedt says 'If it is attempted, it would be too good to be true.'[30]

The next 3 months will be critical, but if the 2nd front fails in the meantime (or is not attempted) & if things go [*word deleted*] more or less as well as at present in Italy, the situation should become much more hopeful.

<u>Easter</u>.

Back at Salò for 10 days well merited rest – not that it will all be rest, as I have a number of things to do. But I need a change after four weeks during which I have had to invent a comedy every evening (and in order to earn the holiday, 2 comedies every day for the past 10 days). We have arranged for Francesca [*illegible*] to be taken on by the Ministry, chiefly as a means to get her away from Rome & be closer to Mariano.

20 April

Back in Milan and a hell of a lot of <u>more</u> work. The new quarters too are emphatically <u>not</u> comfortable. It's like camping out, whereas the Villa Crespi in which we were housed up till now was luxury in some ways, though there was no hot water & the Villa, as so often in Italy, is built for outward appearance rather than for comfort. I saw Mezzasoma in Salò. He wants me to prepare a booklet on monetary & banking reform. That's good. He also said the Duce intends to see me, if possible at Whitsuntide. This is really Buona's good work. She sent a message to the duce via the Contessa Teodorani (Arnaldo's daughter-in-law, who lives now on the Isola Borghese, where our Rome Boxes finished up.[31] That's how she got into touch with her!)

M[u]sso wants me to tell him more about my plan for a 'Carta Europea'. I hope he can be persuaded to go ahead with it. It would be a trump card. But first we must resist on all fronts during the coming <u>shock</u> of the next 3 months.

23 April

Went to Communion today & a number of school children had their First Communion according to the Ambrosian Rite, where <u>both</u> species are given. The wine was given from a tray of little glasses. Very hygienic. It's the first time I've seen this. I prayed for victory, for purity, for faith – for my beloved family & my beloved dead – for Italy – for Europe.

5 May

Life has been hell this last week or so, owing to the Italians' congenital incapacity to think ahead & therefore to organise.

Burlando & I were suddenly called upon to run a [night] programme for America & to train new personnel. This has meant working day & night. Even the new personnel was not forthcoming until to-day & they're not much use. We are consequently already physically exhausted & cant go on for much longer. Blast & damn these bloody fools.

6 May

Bernabei has resigned as chief of the cabinet of my Ministry.[32] He was captured by the rebels a few weeks ago & had to pay 70.000 Lire ransom, so it is said! This is the ostensible reason for his resignation & he says he is retiring to private life. But he will probably be heard of again, as he was one of the very few men at the Ministry who was <u>efficient</u>. He was unpopular probably for this reason – he didn't waste time on being polite; & he knew how to say 'no' (which is a thing few Italians can tolerate. They prefer to say 'yes' & then do nothing).

Almirante is his successor – a hard worker & ambitious.[33] Personally I rather dislike him, because he gives the impression of being a bumptious puppy whose knowledge of the world however is dreadfully limited. A narrow man. But he may expand with time ....[34] Let's hope so. He's intelligent & a real patriot, and this ~~which~~ is in any case a good recommendation. In fact you couldn't have a better one as far as it goes.

12 May

My wonderful wife has seen the Duce. It all came out of the blue with a telegram summoning her to Gargnano, but of course it all came as a result of her having written to him an excellent little letter.

Well, the best thing I can do here is to give her own account of the interview. Oh, what a darling she is, as everybody should see from this letter of hers telling me all about it.

Tomorrow I'm dashing to Saló to see her, as the German assistant to the Consul General[,] a liaison officer with the Embassy[,] is being good enough to give me a lift in his car (Dr Hellmann). What a joy. I'm tired out; but full of plans – and full of battle. When I go to Saló at Whitsuntide I shall be able to suggest a full programme of organisation for our propaganda in English & I bet I get everything I suggest accepted. It will be a battle all the same. Things cannot go on as they are. The new Station at Busto Arsizio[35] should be ready by the end of July & I am resolved to be able to start off there with the best programme for [illegible] in all Europe. It's not an impossible dream, if we can collect a few [illegible] personnel & leave me & Burlandc free to think & supervise & compose & organise. But there must be no more [killing] us by donkey work & improvisations. And then I hope to see the Duce myself, with my scheme for a Carta Europea & an [appunto[36]] on how to cut inflation & the [black] [market]. I shall also tell him about my music, my [wanting] to be taken on by the Ministero degli Esteri (though not to give up my present work for the present) and about my pamphlet which Mezzasoma is having published on my monetary & financial reforms. So that ought to be O.K. Another fortnight of [killing] work – & then, I hope, soon afterwards to be able to go right ahead with [constructive] work.

Meantime the Anglo-Americans have started an offensive on the [*illegible*] front, evidently with the intention of holding the German divisions down & if possible forcing them to send further reinforcements to Italy. I don't think they expect to be able to break through, though of course one never knows if they won't at a given moment try a new landing. I should judge, however, that it is a secondary affair, important, that is, only in conjunction with the bigger show against France. The great attempt seems due to be made very soon now. Will it fail? I am confident it will & if it does, then we can look up towards eventual victory.[37]

28 May

A special [Penitential Communion] for Victory – 'ask & you shall receive'.[38]

29 May

The Anglo-Saxons after nearly 3 weeks of terrific fighting & losses through [many] attacks have succeeded in joining up the [*illegible*] '[death] head', as the tommies have called it, & the southern front. I fear this may mean that Rome sooner rather than later will have to be abandoned. The Romans deserve it; and from a strictly military point of view it is of no grand consequence. But [from a] [moral] point of view it is a blow.

Francesca [*illegible*], who has been taken on by the Ministry on our suggestion, is still in Rome & I am moving heaven & earth to get her away. I hope Gödell has seen to it. But he has already left. Poor thing, she must be in a fearful way. The Ministry (as usual) took weeks before informing her officially of having been taken on & they have done nothing to date to facilitate her journey. But I trust the Germans will have some sympathy.

B. has been here a week & went back this morning. I failed to get away as I hoped for [*illegible*], but am booked to go to Saló next week – & meantime things have been a little easier, as I [start] night work. I just couldn't keep it up any longer.

1 June

That blessed [damozel] Francesca [*illegible*] at last at last has been rescued. And of course it was the good work of the Germans, as a consequence of my urgent appeals to Gödel. She has arrived at Saló & I hope is staying with

B, resting & eating. I've written an express [p.c.] to Mariano Frasso to give him the good news & I hope he will be able to come to Saló also when I go there on Saturday. What a happy reunion it will be.

4 June

Rome has fallen. A moral blow. Important mainly because it will still further depress Italians & make the task of galvanising the home front much harder.

I reached Saló the day before & before leaving Milan had another good talk with Parini, who has given me a letter to the Rector of Pavia University & has promised to help me [get] my degrees. I had asked Rome to send up the documents, but they never did so. Given the exceptional circumstances, I ought to be able to obtain however special facilities & take my final exams up here in October or else be given a degree _ad honorem_. We shall see what can be done. It would be helpful to have an Italian degree, especially if I wish to become a permanent member of the F.O. If I had to go abroad, it would also help me to get work.

The Germans have evidently taken an unexpectedly [hard] knock in southern Italy. We all hoped they would hold out again despite superior odds. But it was too much for them. The chief merit, I gather, is due to the De Gaullist troops. General Juin is worth all the Anglo-Saxon Generals put together & the Moroccan troops proved very clever in stalling the German posts in the mountains.[39] This gave protection to the Americans' right flank & enabled them to advance up the coast (their left flank being covered by the British & American fleets).

Kesselring will now have to [extricate] himself in the [_illegible_], which I am certain he will succeed in doing; but I doubt if he can rally now for long [on] [any] [line] short of the Appenines (~~Spezia~~ Sarzana – Senigallia), which means the loss of our beloved Tuscany. The enemy claim they will be in Florence, Leghorn & Ancona within 6 weeks. I think it will be more like 2 months – but it is only a question of time. Thus we shall _have_ to stand firm. The [first/final] Italian divisions shall be in line by the end of July – & then bit by bit we shall be able, if the offensive line holds, to increase our [effective] during the following 6 months up to some 300,000 men. Italy's fortune depends, whatever the result of the war, on showing capacity to fight. I pray the war may last long enough to allow blood to flow in sufficient quantities with which to redeem her honour. Then she will rise again. Otherwise she will be despised for generations & sink to where she was before 1859.

5 June

The fall of Rome has been swiftly followed by the invasion – at last. I'm glad it's come – the great test. Roosevelt, so the American wireless lets out, seems to [*word deleted*] [*illegible*] that within 5 weeks, it should be possible for the Allies to establish a line from Avranches on the Bay of S. Malo to the mouth of the seine (both banks), with Cherbourg as the American main base & Le Havre as the British, with Rouen & Caen as secondary bases.

Well, we shall see what we shall see.

7 June

My talk with Mussolini has been postponed on account of the big events. But I shall stay here until he sees me. For the moment there is no work for me in Milan. Jerry's front is off for the time being & the English programme, reduced to 10 minutes in the afternoon, can be tackled easily by Burlando & [Messa], who is one of our new young men, shaping very well. He has a perfect cockney accent. Francesca is here, safe & well – but has been told to go to Milan as soon as possible, where she is sure to turn [into] a useful [element]. Unfortunately Mariano has not been able to come here to see her, but will see her before long in Milan. So it is an ill wind that blows nobody any good. The fall of Rome has given me a holiday & its imminent fall resulted in the successful effort to rescue Francesca. The weather, as far as my holiday is concerned, is abominable – still quite cold or stuffy – continuing thunder storms & rain, like a normal April. It's the reaction after the abnormally dry winter & spring.

People, as expected, are feeling very depressed about Rome, though they ought not to be any more depressed than before. The miracle is that the Germans have been able to keep the hordes back all these [4/9] months. The Anglo-Assassins are 9 months late on [schedule]. In fact they expected at the time of the Armistice to be at the foot of the Alps by January 1ˢᵗ & as it is they have only got as far as Rome now. All the same, the Cassino victory had led us all to hope that perhaps Rome might never fall. Now we have got to hold the Appenine Line & delay the enemy's advance up to that line as long as possible. Thus the dangerous flank will be the Adriatic. There are no positions of great strength near the coast & a landing north of Rimini will always have to be reckoned on as a possibility. ~~This constitutes the gravest danger, for This~~ A breakthrough on this flank would result in turning the whole of the Appenine line. No doubt the Germans are aware of this, but whether they have the strength to withstand a resolute attack attack [*sic*] is still problematical. Of course the main decisions will be in France, but the loss of the Po valley would also compromise the position in France, apart from the disastrous effects for Italy, which would cease practically to exist.

Consequently the Appenine Line is of the utmost importance to hold until
the [winter] [snows] [come] to make the task an easier one till [next] spring
– and by then the genera: situation may have turned for the better.

The Russians will soon be attacking again & they are sure to make some
heavy gains. Probably sooner or later the Germans will be forced to give up
the Baltic States. This would greatly shorten their main line of defence &
the hope is that the Russians, once they have taken what they claim to be
theirs by right – the Baltic States, white Russia, Poland east of the [illegible]
Line (or thereabouts), the line of the Carpathians, [illegible] & [illegible],
will pause & see whether their allies are going to do any good at the other
end, before deciding on their next move. In favourable circumstances the
next move might mean a separate peace if we played our political cards well
& agreed in making arrived at an agreement on the basis of a common anti-
capitalist front. The military situation in France & Italy, however must first
be stabilized & all probability possibility of further allied advances [word
deleted] made [to] look improbable.

I remain convinced that the best card we could play is the publication of
my 'European Charter.'

I had a long talk with Mezzasoma on the needs of Milan, if we really
mean to put up a good service. Almirante was present part of the time.
M., who is charming & gracious with the manner of an intellectual priest,
agreed to all my propositions; but the difficulty remains of getting the
personnel. I left him a memo. of our requirements. As far the office in
Milan was concerned, I refrained from giving anybody away, but I made
it plain that if people in Italian offices would only give attention to getting
efficient results instead of cutting a good figure (its a question of reality v.
appearance) and doing down a rival, we might hope to win the war.

8 June

Corpus Domini Communion in comm. of 30 years a Catholic.

9 June

Mussolini has told Mezzasoma he would see me 'soon, but not just these
days.'

16 June

The [Robot] reprisal planes have begun & we feel greatly cheered. At last something has appeared on the horizon which should teach the English that terrorisation doesn't pay. I only hope this VI will be followed up in due course with real war winning [inventions/invasions]. Meanwhile there is little to comment on at the front. The allies are experiencing great losses in France & they have not succeeded in reaching their hoped for objectives according to plan & timetable.[40] But they have got well on to the land & are [illegible] forward – still, however, within range of the naval guns. I imagine the Germans mean to engage these [properly] only after they get out of the navy's range & meantime to [waste] them all they can. In Italy, the allied advance continues as expected, while events in southern Italy become more & more chaotic. The King I'm glad to say, is completely discredited and the monarchy would disappear immediately if it were not temporarily [bolstered] up by the Allies. As for Bad. Dog. Olio,[41] nobody wants him either. Fascism is getting its best possible advertisement, despite the persecution of fascists. Occupied Italy will end by becoming out & out fascist, the more ~~they be~~ it becomes acquainted with the [alternatives] & with the real character of the enemy.

Francesca [illegible] told us that [illegible] had been arrested for going in for large scale black market operations, but that Gödel had got him out. But he spent some days in prison. Probably he will never be arrested again. The people who served Fascism but who deserted in the end, will feel sorry not to have kept straight & faithful. Go straight is the one rule of life. But the Italians just cant. They must zig-zag. They agree to all the best principles & highest ideals, but these things never stop them doing anything they want to do. True, it is better to do the wrong thing from right motives, than the right thing from wrong – & that's why I prefer Italians to English. But I [despise] the Italians for their moral shamelessness. Physically they are [extremely] courageous. One of their few [good/great] virtues, along with [illegible], sobriety & [frugality]. I like them for their strong vitality & for their strongly marked individual personality, for their right values, universal outlook, intelligence & appreciation of ideas, their artistic genius. When I go abroad, I grow terribly homesick very soon I love the Italian land & I feel a physical need to breathe its air & smell its perfumes & eat & drink its produce. But when [I am] in Italy, I am at war with the egoism, the vanity, the venality, the superficiality the lack of discipline & sense of responsibility, the lack of [illegible] sense, the envy & jealousy of the vast majority of the people. But the inhabitants of Rome are the worst of all. I only hope this war will teach them a terrible lesson. The Germans ought to follow the British example & bomb Rome – & for the same [motives] with better reason. But the Germans are too good to us & too decent. As it is the Romans think they have done well in seeing the Germans leave, because they are no longer bombed. It is the one thing promised by the Anglo-Saxons which has been verified, because its verification does not depend on any effort or sacrifice on their part. A good bombing of Rome might also teach the Holy Father a thing or two.

He thanks God for having spared Rome. But he might [first] to thank Kesselring.

22 June

The Russians are now getting [going] strong. So on all main fronts the great [stakes] are being [run].

23 June

Today we went over to the Island of Garda to have tea with the Teodorani – she is Arnaldo's daughter and is a perfectly sweet person. Just what one would wish for as the daughter of Arnaldo, who will go down to history as one of the sub[limest] characters of these times. I was surprised at the growth of the [Teodorani] [heir]. She might be still a flapper by all appearances, instead cf the mother of 2 children (I think) – there were a whole kindergarten of toddlers running wild in the beautiful park.

[Teodorani] had just come back from a 2 months tour of Germany & he said he was greatly impressed. Germans, he said, could <u>never</u> be beaten. He said he had inspected a lot of factories & in spite of all the destructive bombardments, production had only been affected very slightly. The trains still ran punctual & you could telephone from one town to another with almost the same facilities as before the war. Their organisation was outstanding, their moral spirit magnificent. T. had also been with the Duce wh[o/en] inspected the Italian Divisions training in Germany. '[There]' he said 'there was all the spirit of 1935 – enthusiasm and a will to victory, which is an example now to the rest of Italy. They should be in line before so very long.' But there are, it seems, only 3 of these Divisions with some [other] specialist troops. This is not enough. I doubt if those training in Italy are up to standard, [*word deleted*] we need at least 300,000 of [such] troops.

27 June

The fall of Cherbourg & Vitebsk.

Cherbourg gives the Allies one of their main objectives & I fear the fall of Vitebsk will lead to an avalanche.[42]

Cherbourg, I expected to hold out for quite a while, but it remains to be seen if now (or soon) the weight of the invasion can [*word deleted*] made to [reach] down to [*word deleted*] Avranches–Vire-Seine line.[43] Until that time is reached, Montgomery's forces may be regarded as pinned down without any good purposes.

2 July

The weather goes on as bad as ever. I have hardly at all benefitted by my holiday. Hardly any [bathing/boating]. Rain in torrents almost every day.

Went to communion & prayed for don Tullio Calcagno's intentions & that the Duce would see me ~~soon~~. Acting too on the principle that God helps those who help themselves, I have written the Duce a letter via the Teodorani, explaining that my work was in Milan & that I could not wait much longer. The letter contained a few phrases which I hope may strike his interest – for example: 'If we must lose, better to lose to the Russians than to the Anglo-Saxons, because it would be better to have a bolshevized Italy than a servile Italy.' Then I defined victory as 'Stopping the Russians and persuading the Americans to leave Europe, together with her African colonies, in peace to work out their own solutions.'

3 July

God & my letter have done the trick. I am to see the Duce tomorrow.

4 July

Mezzasoma drove me in to Gargnano in the morning to see the Duce, but I was told to return again in the evening at 6. While waiting, I had a talk with [the] Pizzirani, the Vice-President of the Party. In the evening, I waited 2 hours, as Graziani turned up and stayed over an hour. When at last I got in, it was 8.15 o'clock.

The Duce was sitting, as usual, at his desk across the angle of an otherwise practically empty room, like at the Palazzo Venezia. He was dressed in a very simple, well cut fascist uniform. 'Duce', I said as I advanced across the room & saluted 'You have all my understanding, and I am so happy to see you again after all this time.' He said: 'You have not changed.' I said: 'A bit thinner, perhaps. We're both thinner. But that doesn't do us any harm, does it?' The Duce smiled, told me to sit down & apologised for keeping me waiting so long. 'It is so late now,' he said, pressing a bell, 'and I want to have a long talk with you. You must come again.' A Secretary then appeared and after the appointments list was looked at [*illegible*], I was given a fresh date at 7 o'clock for Thursday 6th. [*Words deleted*] ~~Italian~~

citizenship. Buona is quite right. The Duce gives an astonishing impression of controlled magnitism. Yes, he has changed. He is not so dynamic, in a sense, as he used to be. He speaks much more softly and more slowly. It's like meeting with a Sage or a Saint. Goodness & Wisdom are what sums up the whole man. He said Mezzasoma had told him I had 3 things to discuss, but I asked if he would like to read the papers [first] I had prepared first; but, he said, No. Keep them until Thursday. He asked me what I thought of the situation in Normandy. I said: I am not particularly worried about it. It is difficult to judge of course. But so far I should say the Allies had lost more than they bargained for and had gained less. I am more worried about Russia. Whereupon the Duce spoke quite 5 minutes about Russia, while I listened. He spoke of the practical difficulty of laying out a [monster] of the size of Russia. The importance of space in warfare could not be underestimated and Russia could never be ignored in any settlement. He said the Russian generals who had come to the front during the war were proving to be unquestionably brilliant – second to none, and the Russian war potential was in [*illegible*]. The Germans would have to shorten their front & [so] it would be difficult to avoid giving up the Baltic States.

The conversation then switched to my work and I told the Duce a little about the 'Jerry's Front' broadcasts and my dialogues between 'Fat & Jolly' – that American prisoners said they preferred our show to anything of the B.B.C. and debated some of the points we raised, when [resting] behind the lines. I said I thought it good propaganda, because it [*word deleted*] rang true to the listener on account because of my intimate knowledge of the London set up, while at the same time it was good natured fun which did not give offence, though it echoed and emphasised everybody's doubts & fears, and tended to heighten the existing prejudices of the British & Americans against each other.

At that we parted until the day after tomorrow & I was driven home in Mezzasoma's car.

5 July

Note: We are now spending just about 3 times as much on food as we were in Rome 1½ years ago. But we are not spending more than 33% more in all. Actually I am now earning 11,000 lire a month & saving a bit. Formerly my budget stood at 7,500 lire. The economies are in rent & amenities.

6 July

Mezzasoma had promised me his car again (or to be [correct/exact] I had been told by his Guard I could either have it or would be given another) but of course I had forgotten to remind the office – and in Italy, one must always remind people 3 times of an arrangement & then go an hour early to make one's presence felt. I cannot, however, for the life of me get into this habit, though as a consequence I am always being let down. Today I arrived at the ministry punctually at 6.30 – and of course there was no car. I might have foreseen it. Nobody knew what to do. They were only concerned at first in putting the responsibility on each other. It was [*word deleted*] when I [announced] my intention of interrupting the minister himself in conference that at last I got the Chef de Cabinet to move & so at 6.45 a motor bicycle & side car was found for me. Off we rushed. But of course we exceeded the speed limit through the hospital area (I never knew it existed) & I had to pay a fine of 100 lire. At Gargnano there was further delay, as I was not accompanied, & I did not reach the Duce's waiting room till 7.15. I was in time nevertheless, because one always has to wait a bit. At 7.30 I was received. I had taken Job with me on my [*illegible*] & I left him outside. He told me afterwards my talk had lasted 1 ½ hours, but if I am not mistaken it came to exactly 1 hour & 15 minutes.

The first thing I said was to thank the Duce for giving me my citizenship. I added: 'I received the news on my birthday Sept 7th' (Pause). 'Yes, Sept 7th – the [*illegible*] of the day when to be Italian signified being despised by every people on earth.' Then I went on. 'But I can tell you, Duce, I am glad to be Italian – and proud. I want to work to help all I can to make Italy great again. I want to be as close as possible to you – and, whatever happens, to stay with you to the end.' The Duce just looked at me, but made no comment. So I continued: 'Let that be the premise of our talk. Now let's get down to business.' 'Well', said the Duce, 'I did most of the talking last time. Now tell me all you have to say.'

So I started off on my idea of the Carta Europea. I defined victory as 'stopping the Russians & persuading the Americans to leave Europe with Near East & the African colonies in peace to settle her own affairs without outside interference.' England's true interest is identical. But it would be a great mistake to imagine that the British Government will [*words deleted*] necess[arily] aim at promoting British interests. The British Govt. is at the mercy of the strongest winds that happen to blow & the strongest of all the winds (and it is the [prevailing] wind) is the M[oney] Power, representing international interests which do not necessarily coincide with British interests. But all winds at present are blowing in favour of total war, because the mass of the people want to end it at all costs & have been led to believe that [*illegible*] all round offensives will mean a collapse of Germany this year. But if the 2nd front fails & if the [other] fronts get stabilized, the masses in England will be very demoralized. They are tremendously preoccupied with the post war problems & are aware that if the war is indefinitely prolonged, they'll never get their social reforms. England would be – if she is not already – [economically] down & out. Consequently the masses would, if [*word deleted*] things develop as we hope, be on the side of any vocal opinion favourable to peace, provided it were a just peace. But people in favour of a just peace have their tongues tied at present. They have no arguments. It's our business to furnish them with arguments by publishing the principles on which we intend to settle Europe – principles which will strike the imagination of every body as just. And we must declare our readiness to discuss any guarantees of our good faith the enemy might require, as well as one or two other points (Here I showed Mussolini my memo., a copy of which is here attached). We read a few passages of the covering letter. I then referred to other 'winds', such as the filo-Russian[44] wind made of heterogeneous elements ranging from the Communist Party to atheist [intellectuals] & [protestants] who, like the [Duchess] of [*illegible*], back the Reds out of hatred of the Catholic Church – and the filo-American[45] [lot], who are [*illegible*] attached to the idea of the British Commonwealth of Nations above all other groupings & take it for granted that the old country must give way to her grown up son & heir (America). All the same, I said, there exists a strong, cultural body of opinion who feel European, fear Bolshevism, dislike America, [realise] the war was a mistake. If we could furnish this body with a platform of a really just peace, we should be able play a trump card.

During this exposition, ~~Musso asked me what I thought of the situation in France.~~ I asked Musso if he had confidence. 'Yes. I have confidence' he said very quietly. 'I too have great confidence that your work will never perish & that Fascism will triumph,' I said 'but ....'.[46] 'I am still of the opinion', he interrupted 'that Fascism will be the key [note] of the century. 'Yes' I went on, 'but have you confidence in the actual military situation.' 'Yes', he said again quietly 'I have confidence.'

We then went through my memo. clause by clause. At one point Musso said: 'Giusto'.... 'Giustissimo.'[47] There seemed to be no point on which he disagreed. 'I had the idea of publishing something of this kind', he said, '2 years ago after the Salzburg meeting.[48] The report of the meeting hinted at the idea, but it was decided at the time that anything more detailed would be premature.' I said it was a pity. Now it ought to be done quickly. The ideal moment of course would be after the 2° front had failed. But if it didn't fail, then it would be interpreted as a sign of weakness. The Duce agreed; and then he made some very interesting observations. He said: 'What about including Russia in the European Confederation?' I said: 'That would upset the balance of power.' He said: 'The U.S.S.R. totals 180 million people, twice as many as the Reich. In 100 years time, there may well be 500 millions. There is at present an increase of 5 million a year & their birthrate is likely to be maintained for a long time to come. That fact cant be shirked. The idea of a European Confederation without Russia would be interpreted as a challenge to Russia & [could/would] mean another war in 20 years, even if Russia happened to [accept] ~~accepted~~ it now, [*words deleted*], In the long run it would be doubtful if we could stand up to her. Would it not be wiser and face the necessity of co-partnership now?' I said:

'Perhaps.' I should prefer to aim at a European Confederation without her and then develop the European Confederation into a Federation, as a set off to the Russian Federation of Soviet & Socialist Republics; before taking the next step of a Confederation between the two groups. If the process was accomplished in stages, enmity might be avoided & cooperation be established in the end without actually letting in the Slav as a predominant partner inside Europe. I have never feared the 'Yellow Peril' because if it manifests itself, it would do so against America, Australia & New Zealand, not against Europe. But I have always felt that for Europe there was the Slav Peril.

'Yes', said Mussolini, 'but the Russians consider themselves European. They are culturally European – they have greatly contributed to European culture. Racially the Slavs are [not] Asiatic. The other racial groups within Russia would, besides, not necessarily act in unison with the Slavs. There would not necessarily be a lack of balance, if the bigger [*illegible*] were realized['].

I said: 'Very well.' When I wrote to thank the Duce for our talk, I defined out out-&-out victory as above and a victory of a [reduced] but acceptable [nature] as one in which Russia would join forces with the rest of Europe.

[*Word deleted*] I have since been greatly struck by Mussolini's raising of this point, the more I think of it. It displays a marvellous realism & a [*word deleted*] view of the cultural aspects of the whole question which transcends the [*illegible*] view of European culture without betraying it. Probably he will discover the right formula & it may be the only practical way out – the only logical [inducement] for Russia to [*illegible*] out her present alliances.

The next topic we discussed was the galvanisation of public opinion here at home. I had laid emphasis on the need of galvanising public opinion abroad by means of my charter & I said it would also help to galvanise opinion here, for everybody wants a just peace.

<u>Mussolini</u>: Before anything substantial can be done here, we need a victory – even if only a small one.

<u>Myself</u>: But to have a victory we [*illegible*] galvanise the people's morale. It's a vicious circle.

<u>Mussolini</u>: We shall have some Divisions in line before long. If we can give the impression that we can hold indefinitely the Appenine line, that would provide our opportunity.

<u>Myself</u>: Yes, but we must do something dramatic. The best propaganda is your voice & leadership. But I quite understand you cant tour the country & show yourself in every town in present circumstances. [Nor] can a Constituent assembly be summoned with 2/3 [*sign deleted*] of Italy [occupied]. But I suggest a [*illegible*] representative Assembly might be called & through it stage or campaign. [One] would need a good impresario (I said: 'regista'). The assembly would declare the country in danger & itself in permanent session. There would follow a whole series of dramatic orders of the day, with your taking the lead with speech after speech. For

example: <u>First Order of the Day</u>: 'The Italian Social Republic is the continuation of the fascist Revolution'. <u>Second Order of the Day</u>: A clear definition of Fascist ideals & programme, such as would gain easily general consent. <u>Third order of the Day</u>: not the disbandment of the Fascist Party, but its transformation into a 'National Front of Resistance'.[49] <u>Fourth Order of the Day</u>: A recommendation to insert the Lateran Treaty as a fundamental law of the Republic [50] <u>Fifth Order of the Day</u> (by way of dramatic contrast): Denounce the [Concorcat]. <u>Sixth Order of the Day</u> (by way of [subtle] contrast). A recommendation that a new unilateral law to be [*illegible*] also as a fundamental law be passed fully protecting the Catholic character of the country. <u>Seventh Order of the Day</u>. That the Labour Charter be [*illegible*] as a fundamental law of the Republic & that the [*illegible*] of socialisation should be hurried [forward] & a commission appointed immediately to revise [*word deleted*] law.[51] <u>Eighth Order of the Day</u>: the disbandment of 'Catholic Action' and the recognition of the 'Crociata Italica' in its place ...[52]

Here I added in parenthesis that it would be advisable, however, to get an authoritative theologian to revise the statutes of Crociata Italica to make certain there was nothing in them which could be construed as heretical or [*illegible*]. 'We must act with fire, but with cool brains', I said. Mussolini [nodded]. He was taking it all in, as food for thought. But he did not comment. I said: 'If we are to lose, we must be certain to leave a testament behind us'. He said: 'We are [making] a testament.'

Mussolini then turned his attention to my pamphlet on Monetary Reform, a copy of which I had handed to him.[53] He began by asking me if I was in favour of a deflationary or inflationary policy. I [*illegible*] that the subject of my pamphlet was radical reform & only concerned itself indirectly with the question of deflation & inflation. One of things I [aimed] at was price stabilisation. M. asked me to give him an idea of my thesis. I assumed that he had better read the whole thesis. It was difficult to condense. But on being pressed I told him that I started from the recognized fact that the money which circulated did not only consist of the banknotes & coins issued by the State & the State Bank, but also of all the sight accounts. I then described briefly the working of a bank; that it was therefore the private banks who created the greater part of the money in circulation & that they created it out of nothing (by the mere [stroke] of a [pen]) and then tr[afficked] into it as if it were their [private] capital. There was little to distinguish this [practice] from forgery – & it created a power within the State, which [*words deleted*] no sovereign state should permit.

Mussolini's eyes [rolled] in quite his old, characteristic manner as I told him this. Like most cultured persons, political economy was evidently a subject which he had never studied for himself. He was obviously extremely impressed. 'I will read your pamphlet with the greatest interest', he said – 'and then there is this. I have been glancing at it. It [*illegible*] [*illegible*] & I shall also study it with interest.' This was my scheme for the issue of a war [currency] ~~based on~~ coupled with a [fixed] loan based on a progressive proportion of the notes exchanged (in Italy at present there is an immense hoarding of notes & their exchange is the backbone of the black market). My scheme would result in an exact appraisement of the amount of money in circulation in the republic, it would hit the black market hard, tend to lower prices & put out of currency all notes held abroad which were being pumped by the enemy into the country causing inflation & which were being dropped by parachute to finance the rebels.[54]

Well, that I think covers most of our long conversation. I asked the Duce if he would let Job come in and be introduced; & of course he immediately consented. I told him Job had run away from college because the other boys were anti-fascist, but that I had told him he must go back because 'a fascist must never desert his post.' The Duce kissed Job on both cheeks and called him a brave boy. So Job will have something to remember all his life.

In saying goodbye, the Duce said he would call me again. I said he knew where to find me & in any case could always communicate through Buona. He sent his saluti to Buona & ended the interview, which could hardly have been more satisfactory.

It will be interesting now to see if any developments take place along the lines discussed.[55]

10 July

Back to Milan by car with [illegible]. It has been a lovely interlude, though the weather has been abominable & I only got 4 or 5 [illegible] in the lake.

I forgot to say we went over to lunch one day with the [Omodeos], who gave us eggs & honey. We dined one evening with the [illegible] (of the Foreign Office), whom I knew in [America] (he was Consul in Cleveland & gave me a splendid time there). I also saw Mazzolini, Under. Sec. of For. Affairs, to whom I gave a copy of 'European Charter'. I have asked to be taken on by the Foreign Office & I mentioned the fact also to Mussolini who promised to back up my demand. Milan is hot & stuffy; but I'm glad to say there is as yet little work, so that I shall have time to devote myself to my many other activities.

12 July

I forgot to say that I also spoke to Mussolini about my [illegible]. I'm going to send one of my 4 [illegible] [each] to the 4 Italian Divisions which are ready in Germany. I must get them copied & [perhaps] forwarded via the Duce. B is sending him flowers for his birthday.

19 July

Fall of Livorno & Ancona – more or less in accordance with the enemy's schedule. But they will be a little late for their [capture] of Firenze.[56]

The point of the front which preoccupies [me] is the Adriatic sector. Here there are no formidable national defences and if [*word deleted*] the British get as far as Sinigallia, which is more than likely by about August 1st, there are only two more good ridges to defend. The second one is the best, but after that the coastal plain slowly widens. [Our] [Divisions], however, will soon be moving South & they will be absolutely O.K.[57]

20 July

There has been a [bomb] outrage against the Führer from which he has [miraculously] escaped. The Duce was up to meet him the same day. There are the chances that make one tremble. But I trust Providence will protect us. The coup, however, having failed, it will probably do good. It will eliminate the reactionary & self seeking elements & serve to further galvanise the great German effort.[58]

If anything untoward <u>does</u> happen, my only [plans] for the present is to make a bee line for Saló and then to seek out Mussolini & place myself at his orders. One can but die once.

But my spirits remain buoyant. If in 6 months time I am still alive & free & united with the family, we shall have reason for greater optimism. Meantime the best comfort is that it is quite clear that so far the Normandy front is not developing according to Allied plans & expectations. But they are bound to make another huge effort before this month is over.[59]

22 July

I took part today in 'Jerry's Front' with Gödell complete set up – [*illegible*] and all ('Bruno's Tigers') & it was great fun. I [prefer] such parts of the programme, but for the moment am only taking an active part on Sundays.

23 July

Found an old 'Life' with a picture of Tom & Diana Mosley emerging from the Old Inn at Shipton-under-Wishart where they are living since being released from Holloway [*word deleted*] on Nov. 20 last year. Tom looks ill, hobbling on a stick with a bit of a [paunch]. Diana looks as beautiful as ever though sad. The photograph was accompanied by a stinking article of abuse. He was apparently released on the advice of a board of 5 doctors, who said he would otherwise die. He is suffering from Phlebitis, poor man. But he'll get his own back one day.[60]

31 July

Last day of the month. 7 weeks since the capture of Rome & the start of the invasion. Florence is not yet in enemy hands. They are two weeks behind their timetable, which is so much to the good. I feel very anxious about the [illegible]. I don't see how they can move; but they risk a lot staying. Presumably [illegible] Danielli will come North. The Pellizzi, ~~who~~ are now in Florence – so I'm told – will risk a lot staying there too. But they wont have much of a welcome up here, after their dubious 'attendista' attitude. A bit of a falling between two stools. It's fatal to compromise with principle. Bruno Pancini, I expect, will come up & the more committed members of the [illegible] family ([bless] them). Then there is Niccolò [illegible], but I suppose they would be all right. It's difficult to say, because the persecution of fascists is [just] [illegible]. [Gigli] is reported to have been shot – God knows why. If true, it's a monstrous murder. Chaos reigns in the South.[61] As Ezra Pound says: 'Wherever the British & Americans go, they make the best possible propaganda for Fascism.' When the revival comes, as it assuredly will – even if it occurs after our deaths – it will come from the occupied territories who already regret the regime. Mussolini has come back from Germany [tonicked] up by his visit, where he got a taste of all the enthusiasm he so much needed.

The American push in Normandy has been a bit of a set back. But it is set off so far by the [illegible] [and/to] the British and their losses have been very great. So far no great harm done, however. But the battle is by no means over. The British are preparing for a new big effort & the Germans don't yet seem to be able to take the initiative. I wish to God the new secret army would soon come into play. The V No. I is quite a success, but by itself it cant change the situation.[62] It only brings home to roost a [litter] of the terror tactics which the other side started – and they [certainly] deserve all they get. In Russia [illegible] the enemy's sweeping advance continues & if it is not checked soon, it might provoke a serious situation. But from all accounts the Führer remains calm, serene & confident. That much seems certain, so it looks as if he must have something important up his sleeve.

There remains the question of Turkey's attitude. What is going to be decided on August 2, when the National assembly meets. Our hands are full enough already & though Bulgaria, who has an excellent army, would violently oppose the Turks, if they moved, the advantage would be all on the other side.

I've bought a bicycle for B. 8000 lire. Devilish price. But she needs one [*illegible*]. The problem is now to get it to her.[63]

2 August

So Turkey, under pressure from London & Washington, has broken off diplomatic & economic relations with Germany. This may [well] be the prelude for worse. But it comes 5 months later than the British originally expected & that means 5 months gained. It would have been much worse if Turkey had entered the war last March & she shall [*illegible*] 'wait & see' a bit. Churchill & [*illegible*] are banking on a decisive victory in France during the next two months. Otherwise they fear the new German weapons may come into play and – at least temporarily – turn the tables. Turkey may decide to wait & see if this happens before actually going into action. We can only pray that the new German weapons are nearly ready & that the American advance meanwhile to Avranches & St Malo will contained & [not] followed up by a general [retirement] of the Germans & a straight line from the Bay of St Malo to the north of the Seine. The next few days will show.

Meantime Florence is being bombarded & the fighting must now be close to our little house. But it is gratifying [*illegible*] [*illegible*] know the Germans are delaying the advance; for every day lost to the Allies is a day won for us. We must hold tight for the next 2 or 3 months on all fronts now.

4 August

We had a [bomb] [blown] into our garden to-day, [preceded] by a bottle of petrol on fire. Evidently it was intended to set 5 cans on fire which were perched close together under a large, spreading tree. The porter rushed out when he saw the flaming petrol & turned on the hose. But his promptness nearly cost him his life. The bomb exploded 5 yards from where he was standing & he got splinters in his leg & face. All the windows of course were smashed on one side of the house & also the windows of one car. Otherwise no damage. It happened during the [luncheon] interval (Via [*illegible*] 6, where I work on 'Jerry's Front'[)].

But I had been out since 11 am as I had an appointment to see Piero Parini. I told him about my talk with Musso & pressed him to get us bicycles. I who wanted him to come & see 'Jerry's Front' [produced]; & he promises to come along on Tuesday next[.]

6 August

So beloved Florence has at last fallen and not without considerable damage to its beauties. All the bridges, they say, are down except the Ponte Vecchio.[64] The S. Trinitá bridge is the most beautiful in the world, but it can be rebuilt, without too great expense & design. There must have been a lot of houses hit too. I only hope our things are safe. The warehouse is not very far from the Ponte Vittoria, where the shelling was worse.

My heart bleeds for Yoi & [illegible]. Now we shall see if any of our friends come up. I do hope the Monsani do, our neighbours (the old woman in [illegible]) at the little house. It was the New Zealanders who took Pian de' Cervi & worked down towards Florence via [illegible] & [illegible]. I can hardly bear to think of it. But our Divisions are marching into line & Graziani is to command an army of 4 Italian & 4 German Divisions. More will be ready soon. Meantime things look a little better in Russia, but worse in France. The American breakthrough into Brittany is disquieting. But the Germans appear amazingly confident & they have blocked all [illegible] to the [East]. They know what that are doing & there seems to be no doubt that they have accumulated colossal stores of war material, especially aircraft, tanks & guns & petrol for the big counter offensive. And I don't think they are bluffing about the new army. The V No. I certainly <u>not</u> proved a bluff, as Churchill had to admit in his last speech. 800,000 houses damaged in London within 50 days is a colossal assault, even though it may not have any decisive influence on events. But London is not the only town hit & the results, if the shelling can be kept up, will be [accumulative].

16 August

The expected invasion of southern France has begun. Rumours have been afoot for the past 10 days of an attempt to invade the Italian Riviera, but I never thought the attempt would be made there. The country is too mountainous & the strategical objectives limited. The obvious places are on the two sides of Marseilles & I should not be surprised if the present landing is not followed up by another further west.[65] [Illegible] is still all a question of gaining time now. It's a [race] for time. I feel certain the Germans have the remedy for victory up their sleeve, but they are not yet ready. Will they be ready in time?

I've bought a bicycle for Buona; 8000 lire – hell of a price, but is worth it. She needs it & prices are sure to go up further, so it can be regarded as a fair investment.

Poor old Q[illegible] (Colonel Que[illegible]) – the rather incompetent transport officer of the Fascio – has been killed in action against the Rebels,

while Pavolini has been wounded. I'm glad to hear he is getting on well &
his example will be of the greatest value.

27 August

It's odd, but during the first years of the war, when everything on the whole
was going well, my reason told me we were sure to win. But all the time
at the back of my mind I was anxious & felt [intuitive] forebodings. [But/
Now], my reason would say that the war is as good as lost; but my intuitive
premonitions are favourable. In fact never have I felt so calm & assured.
Very odd. Not even [f]oggy King Michael's [*illegible*] has rattled me.

   Gödell saw Musso (with von Rahn, the German Ambassador)[66] & got
him to O.K. our programmes. This means that our new boss Interlandi,
who is an utter [ass], can't interfere [&] [wreck] the good work.[67]

   Gödell was impressed by Musso exactly in the same way Buona &
I were, when we saw him for the first time [since] the fatal crash: a
s[upremely] great, wise & good man – a sage – a saint – thinking in terms
of all the world's good & [*illegible*] [*illegible*] [*illegible*]. I bet he wins the
peace & that Hitler wins the war.

12 September

There is really no comment to be made on account of my [*illegible*]. The
overwhelming predominance of armour and air power has carried the
Allies to Belgium and the very frontiers of Germany. They are [putting]
[forward] all their resources to obtain a [*illegible*] before Germany is able
to [retaliate] with her new weapons & there is nothing to be done but to
take the [*illegible*] & wait for the reaction when it comes all in good time
– and to be prepared for the [course] the resistance on the Italian front has
so far found good. Let us therefore hope that the new army [may] come
into action before the war can be carried towards us here in Milan. But I
doubt if we can hold a month, unless the good news of the new weapons
comes fairly soon. This would mean my returning to Saló & then perhaps
further north. I was over at Saló for a few days last week & gave Buona all
directions for emergencies. 4 boxes are to go off via the German Embassy to
Merano as soon as possible. Passports are to be prepared. Things as far as
possible packed in advance [*illegible*] & other domestic details speeded up.

   All the same, the Germans seem to be full of confidence and they still
[talk] of 'Jerry's Front' going to near Como, where we shall be safer from
air raids.

   This doesn't look like having to quit just yet, anyhow. Meanwhile we
got [*illegible*] the other night (Sunday) when [I] [was] in bed with a chill

& a slight fever. I had taken an [aspirin] & was sweating it out, when the alert sounded. The only wise thing to do was to pull on a sweater & go down. Bombs fell on various railway depots – some not so very far away. However, I'm better this morning, took a purge & stopped the day in bed.

Anniversary of Mussolini's rescue. Te deum.[68]

17 September

If we survive until the middle of November, I think the worst will be over. I'm not too optimistic about our ability to hold the Rimini gap.[69] But if we can block the enemy about there, things will become much easier when the weather [breaks] & the snow falls. [Same in] the Balkans along the Western frontier of Bulgaria & Rumania.[70] The winter will also [suspend] [operations] in Russia for a time & slow them down in any case – & by that time the new weapons ought to be [illegible]. So we have two [weeks/months] of [anxious] [waiting], with every day to be ticked off as one day gained.

23 September

Today I moved to Fino,[71] near Como, where Jerry's Front has been established so as to be out of air raids. I have found lodging in the [illegible] [house] a charming room with access to a [modern] bathroom. Everything beautifully spick & span. The Priest is an old Monsignore & he reads 'Crociata Italica', which is a good sign – & he is a very educated man, who speaks German (having lived at [Innsbrück]) and a little English. So I should be comfortable & have good company in the evenings.

The offices are close by in a fine villa with a lovely Park. The village is pretty & the [fruit] abundant. I shall mess with the Germans & go to Milan for the English service from the Ministero every other day.

Let us hope that we may be able to stay here indefinitely, because that would mean the war going well[.] Meanwhile I have told Buona to get all ready for an emergency move into the Alto Adige[72] – permit to settle there, if need be – clothes & boxes in order – [illegible] 4 heavy boxes have already gone up to Merano with the German Embassy surplus luggage. I shall go to Como one of these days & try to get a [letter] across to Monsignor Bernardini, the Papal Nuncio at Berne, [recalling] what Mgr. Montini tried to do for us last year & asking him to move heaven & earth to obtain permissions for us to cross into Switzerland should he, in the event of an emergency, receive a wire from me. We cant do more than that. I somehow feel in my bones, however, that no grave emergency will arrive. About Oct. 10, I must get a few days off with Buona again at Saló.

26 September

I've been in bed 2 days with one of my devastating colds. But tomorrow I expect to be all right again; and tonight I must write to Buona for the anniversary of our wedding. Bless her, how I miss her – the one prize of [honour] in my life.

10 October

Buona has seen the Great Man again. She gave him Mariano's & Francesca's application to be allowed to marry – and had a nice satisfactory talk. He sent me his saluti.[73] He remains confident that we shall <u>win</u>.

12 October

I was up in Milan yesterday & ~~she~~ Francesca had already received a communication from the Ministry of the Interior registering her marriage. What documents has she & so forth? So it's been quick work.

The Under. Sec. of the War, Signor Basile,[74] said in a speech that in 20 days to a month the Axis would be able to resume the offensive with the new weapons & that the results would be decisive. Well, well ... we'll refer to this again on Nov. 10.

10 November

The V. No 2 has been introduced & no doubt its effects are [*illegible*] devastating. But that is all so far. On the other hand, we have resisted everywhere magnificently except in the Balkans, where the Bolshevik advance continues, with the British in Greece. I feel, however, that we are out of danger for the [*word deleted*] present; and the probability is that I shall be in Fino for the winter. I was wrong in my fears that if the new weapons didn't turn up by the end of October, we might be in the soup. On the contrary the Germans have shown their ability to resist without [any] [*word deleted*] <u>special</u> new weapons & the disappointment in the Allies' camp is tremendous. They were confident that the war could be won by Xmas. Instead they find themselves now up against a stone wall & are incurring tremendous losses – counting their dead, which they particularly hate doing. Discontent in England is growing. But the people are such fools, they always allow themselves to be led on in the hope of victory within the next 6 months. Churchill now talks about victory in the

Spring & the English [*illegible*] [*illegible*] for it. What is needed is a British disaster [&/or] the realisation that there is no hope of victory for at least another year. Then perhaps they might react, because millions of people must be beginning to recognise the fact that it is not the [interest] of the country to go on. The [national] debt has reached the astronomical figure of 20 thousand million pounds, while the debt to America is already over 3 thousand millions! Most of the foreign investments are [*illegible*] up & [*word deleted*] [*illegible*] would only mean Bolshevism throughout Europe or else another war with Russia, which the people would not stand for, even if Churchill wanted it. [*Word deleted*] America would have the rest of the world including England, in her financial clutches – not that it would do the American people any good. Their debt is now 265 billion dollars, the interest on which is [*word deleted*] twice as [high] as the whole volume of their foreign trade in a good year before the war; and they can never [hope] to double it, because they cannot afford to [import] enough to pay for exports without ruining their [production] for home consumption. Thus only the bankers & a few [*illegible*] could benefit by victory; [*word deleted*] it ought to be abundantly clear that England's only hope of [recovery] is through an axis victory, the overthrow of the Money Power and the integration of her interests with those of Europe. All the same it will be difficult to convince the British people of [this] [truth] without giving them first a bad [*illegible*] & force them to face the alternative of at least another year of war, [appalling] [losses] & [*illegible*]. Then they might wake up. Meantime I have had a nice little week; holiday at Saló with Buona, where all is well. I'm thinking how it would be a good thing if she & Job [came] & joined me for the winter at Fino.

12 December

On Sat, Nov. 25 I received the terrible news that Job had run away from home & that Buona wanted me to help find him. The message was telegrammed through by the German Embassy at 1 a.m. & I was informed in the morning. It was almost unbearable to think of what B must have gone through. Besides, I had no details & therefore my mind was speculating on what could have happened. An accident? Captured by rebels? Gone to join up with the Brigate Nere?[75] Probably the latter, I agreed; & that would be not so bad. In time we could doubtless trace him. It was an awful moment of anxiety.

I [rushed] by the first train to Milan – but there no trains to Brescia. At Via Rossini, however, there was hope for a lift. [*Word deleted*] I spent the whole afternoon writing. No use. I was then given letters to the Platz [commandantur] & after a lot of coming & going, I was promised a place at 5.30 in the morning on the military [*illegible*], & given a room in a neighbouring hotel.

Meanwhile I saw Francesca, who had been joined by Mariano. They are
to be married. Mariano had been in Milan during the first [week] & had
overcome all the obstacles with great energy. Documents of all kinds had
had to be drawn up & signed. The Tribunal had to decide on [waiving] the
[rules] [about] obtaining the British (or Swiss) Consulate's nihil obstat.[76]
The usual inevitable delays of the bureaucracy were miraculously swept
aside & now Francesca is to be received into the Church (bless her) during
the next few days before the marriage which is to take place on Thursday.

I was comforted a bit by their happiness (they would never have got
married by the way, but for us; for it was due to my actions that Francesca
was able to get up from Rome, & it was B who fixed things with the
Duce) .....[77]

I reached Brescia at 8.30 & was lucky to take a train straight away for
Saló – lucky because the train line had been interrupted for over a week
by the explosion of a powder magazine at Tormini, the last station but one
before Saló (the displacement of air had broken hundreds of windows in
Saló & even two in our own home, which is 3 miles away!). I found my
Buona at the Mess & we fell into each others' arms. Job had been missing
ever since Tuesday – 5 whole days & there was no trace of him. The
most atrocious thing that could happen to a mother. But I was somewhat
comforted by the knowledge that he had gone off with another boy (Gino
Dei) of his same age [and] that it was certain he had gone to join up with
some military unit.

Buona had already warned the Police, had telephoned to Pavolini to
[circularise] all Blackshirt units & had had a notice put in the 'Regime
Fascista' with his photograph. I saw B[illegible] of the [illegible] [illegible],
& got the German Command to join in the search – & I took steps to have
his photograph also put in the 'Corriere della Sera'[78] & to get a radio s.o.s
call made.

Then I went to confession in the Franciscan Monastery & prayed as I
have seldom prayed before. Somehow I felt my prayer would be immediately [answered] within 24 hours. I rayed for purity & put my faith in
Christ. That was on Monday.

On Tuesday I went to the Omodeo at [Le Posteghe] where Graziani has
his Headquarters[79] – I got Colonel Melia to [circularise] all the special units
like the X Mas & the S. Marco, for there was some evidence Job might
[have] been aiming at joining the X Mas at [Conegliano], as Dei's [father],
was there. Also another friend, who formed part of the [illegible], [had] run
away a week earlier to join a X Mas unit on Vittorio Veneto, where he had
a [illegible].[80]

From Le Posteghe I went with Omodeo's [father] to Desenzano to see
if I could find some traces – but in vain. The enemy fighter bombers were
about. We had to get out once & some [illegible] ahead of us were machine
gunned. Desenzano had been bombed. The station was deserted & there
was a mass of smashed glass everywhere. Anyhow no trains had been

moving for weeks, so he could only have gone away hitch-hiking. At the junction further up the line towards Verona, a Red Cross train was [on] [fire].

I returned home feeling very tired – but when I got to the house, there was Job! Oh Lord, what a relief. My prayer <u>had</u> been answered. I just hugged the boy & felt so instinctive to be angry or mad. I hugged Buona in my joy and we had a grand dinner to celebrate the return of the Prodigal (not that we had much of a fatted calf to [illegible]!). The next morning I went to Thanksgiving Communion.

Job had been found by Mezzasoma at Padua. We had told him – when Mezzasoma left for [Venice] – not to forget to ring up the Pension Budapest. For Job had made friends with the children there, when we stayed there the year before, and we thought that probably he would look them up, if in Venice. Well, that is what betrayed him. He had telephoned to the Budapest from Padua and Mezzasoma succeeded in tracing the call to the Brigata Nera in Padua. In due time we should have heard anyhow of course, because the Federale[81] of Padua had written to us. But it would have taken weeks, as the ordinary post is very slow – in fact the letter has not arrived yet! Some letters never reach their destination & Job says he sent us a postcard from Brescia the first day, but it never arrived. There are constant bombings all along the road between Saló & Brescia. On Saturday we [illegible] them bomb Tormini again and another ammunition dump was blown up. One [illegible] was caught in the explosion & was [forced] to [land]. It was quite a spectacle show from our balcony. Job had had an exciting journey. He had hitch-hyked to Brescia. Looked up a friend there, but the friend had gone too. This moving away to join up has become a regular epidemic & shows how the young boys at any rate are full of spirit & right thinking.[82] Only most of them are underage, so it is absurd & they don't realise the awful pain & anxiety they give to their parents.

At Brescia Job found there were no trains. He hitch hyked a little way at a [first/final] attempt (3 [illegible]), but the car broke down; so he walked back to Brescia & tried again. But this time he was more successful, but it was already late & he only got to Desenzano at 11pm. He wandered about the streets, got a drink (he had 56 lire on him & had spent part of it on bread & cheese at Brescia) & then knocked at the door of a lighted shop. It was a dressmakers & the kind woman took both the children in, gave them beds & good breakfast in the morning. Thank goodness this is Italy. I doubt if anywhere else in the world, except Ireland, would two stray children <u>always</u> find kind people to house & feed them. Next day after [hours] of waiting Job & Gino hitch-hyked on to Padua, where they again arrived late at night. They saw a village badly bombed en route – Job said he actually saw some of the houses tremble & collapse less than a kilometre away. They were also attacked at night by one of the [planes] which goes by the name of 'Pippo' (or is it Peep'o'?)[83] – at least, it swept down within 30 feet of his lorry, which luckily had no headlights & [dropped] a bomb &

machine gunned a lorry with headlights immediately behind his. The lorry was struck, overturned & burned – ~~with~~ a number of people were [killed] & wounded, all civilians of course. It must have been a [*illegible*] experience & I bet the little fellow had some moments of terror.

At Padua he picked up a blackshirt militiaman who took him & his friend to the barracks, where they happily stayed until found.

So that is the end of <u>that</u> story, except that we decided to let me take Job to Fino for a bit – & there he is. Very nice it is too to be [*illegible*] alone with him. [*Illegible*], he is going to be [taken] [on] [by] Jerry's Front. We tried out his voice yesterday & Gödell was awfully pleased with it – & he reads admirably. So this will be a new interest for him & he will earn money for himself at 50 lire every time he speaks. I don't think he will try to run away again.

The journey back was quite exciting, as Tre Ponti[84] on the Brescia-Saló road was bombed & machine gunned just ahead of us. [*Illegible*] were [*illegible*] & when we ran through the place we found one car in flames & several lorries overturned.

~~The day~~ Two days before the private residence of the German Ambassador at Fasano had been bombed & burnt to the ground = fighter bombers again, which are now very frequent on the roads. Poor M. Von Rahn lost all her [jewellery] & they were both left with nothing but what they were wearing.[85]

But about the worst shock of my life happened the night before. It was 7.30 p.m. Job had been to the cinema & was then eating at the Ministry Mess in Saló. Buona and I, on the other hand, were eating at home. We heard a plane come over, so we put out the lights & went on to our balcony. The plane came flying over Saló & then, to our horror, with a huge flame, followed by an explosion, a bomb fell on the Mess – or so it seemed.

I shall never forget Buona's piteous cries: 'They've hit the Mess. Oh, they've hit he Mess ...' I did my best to reassure her, but my own heart was in my boots. I argued that it was not a big bomb, that no fire had broken out & that if there had been a slaughter of innocents (at least 20 children & their mothers were dining) we should have seen lights & heard cars & a great many more shouts & cries than we actually did.

We dashed to the 'Can[*illegible*]' and got hold of bicycles & hurried to Saló, which is a good two miles away from our house, which is exactly opposite the Mess on the other side of the gulf.

Well, of course we found that all was well. The bomb had fallen on the bank at the back of the courtyard. Job was in the air raid shelter & nobody had been hurt. But windows were smashed & blown out. Job said even a table was overturned inside the Mess & bottles & plates [*illegible*] quite a nasty panic. What a dirty war![86]

No one can [*illegible*] the Germans or Italians for dehumanising warfare. This is entirely the responsibility of the Allies. Russia set the example of persecution & torture. England is mostly responsible for the violation of every law of nations: blockades which mostly hit the women & children, indiscriminate air bombing of [open] towns from 20,000 feet & disregard of neutral rights (Persia is the most flagrant example, that & the regular [traversing] of Switzerland by bombing planes en route for Italy. The other direct violation[s] may have had some cause due to fear of being anticipated by enemy action, though it was England who planned to invade [Norway] & use Greek ports as bases against Italy. But there was the [*illegible*] of a certain degree of tacit collaboration from Norwegian & Greek authorities). Besides, economic sanctions have been used since the beginning against weak nations to force them into either joining in the war on the allies' side or at least to toe the line. In this America has been equally guilty, & it was America who began the [*illegible*] hunts – machine gunning along the roads, bombing isolated farm houses, shooting up passenger vehicles etc. Also dropping explosive toys, [*illegible*] & fountain pens for the innocent to pick up.[87] Then came the deliberate terrorist raids like the one which destroyed the centre of Milan, where there [were] no factories or military installations. It was carefully aimed bombing too, because the Cathedral was spared, though every house in a narrow circle around it was hit. And this sort of thing has been done everywhere without any possible justification. The German retaliation is consequently thoroughly deserved & I hope they'll get a double dose of their own medicine. England's [honour] is shamed for all time. Persecution & P[*illegible*] have also been her weapons; & the deliberate teaching of gangster methods of fighting has even been issued to soldiers ('when you get your man down, stamp on his head etc.')

Talk of war criminals!

And these are the people who claim to be defending civilisation & to be able to create a new world order of sweetness & light. My hat!

Wherever they have gone, anarchy, civil war, famine, unemployment & inflation have followed – in North Africa, in Italy, in France, in Belgium, in Greece – not to speak of India, Upper Egypt & Iran. The bringing of India into the war too was a flagrant abuse of trusteeship – for India like [Ireland] might have remained neutral & there was no doubt about this being the overwhelming wish of the people. And God knows what advantage bringing India into the war has brought Britain. She has now got to defend Britain & it is a drain on her resources, greater, I should think, than any war contribution given by India.

Now the Greek situation has turned into a tragic farce. The British find themselves fighting the ELLAS Communist [bands], whom Churchill a few months ago was calling 'noble patriots', but which he now calls 'communists' & 'terrorists'.[88] Stalin, who is a great statesman (however much of a villain he may be) must be amused. At Moscow Churchill insisted on Greece, Holland & Belgium – & Italy (for purely strategical reasons) being given [*word deleted*] Britain's happy hunting grounds. But Stalin knows he can afford to give most of Europe away on paper, because if the allies win, he knows he will be in a position to sweep the board. The agreements would count for nothing in the face of the facts; because either the British army would have to be employed for an indefinite period in occupation of western Europe & in fighting the Communists (& Russia too maybe) or it would have to be withdrawn to allow things to take their natural course, which would have only one [*illegible*]: communism everywhere – at least until the next [*illegible*] war broke out. There is no getting out of this cleft stick – & I'm sure the British people wouldn't stand for a second war against Russia. Nor would the Americans. Therefore it is becoming more & more obvious that only an Axis victory can save Europe from (a) Communism & terrible persecution (b) fresh civil wars & upheaval, which might last 40 years. And England's own chance of rehabilitation also depends on an Axis victory. As part of a well ordered & united Europe, with Russia held back & American dollar imperialism kept out & the Money Power broken, England could secure her prosperity & maintain a position of weight in the councils of the world. Otherwise she will be ruined & sink to the position of a 2nd class [Power], the poor relation of America & with problems of unemployed on the dole provided by new loans from Wall Street. That is what Churchill is really fighting to achieve. 'Poor old England' as he himself said the other day in the House. Poor old Winston! What a fool he has made of himself![89]

18 December

The German counter offensive started on Saturday.[90]
    [Sie] [wiz] .....[91]

27 December

The Germans with their usual generosity & thoroughness gave us a very jolly Xmas – a tree, a [*illegible*] & a bag of [eatables] each. Gödell distributed presents also to Jerry's Front – Job getting a magnificent bow and arrows. It was sad Buona not being here, but we hope to have her for the Befana.[92]

    [*Illegible*] the offensive is going well & are full of hope.

    Job has made his debut at the microphone with instant success. He is delighted. He earns 50 lire each time he appears & is therefore proud of earning, so to speak, his own living and of serving the country in work of national importance.[93]

Diary 1945

3 January

We had another grand party on New Year's Eve & let us hope & pray 1945 will see peace <u>& victory</u> – peace with justice, which means the Russians thrown back into their own lands & the Americans thrown out of Europe (including Africa & the Near East).

My best present was the news that Buona was arriving to-day & I [went] to meet her in Milan. In consequence of the machine gunning of the trains round about here (only the other day 30 people were killed), trains only run in the early mornings & after dark. So it meant getting up [catch] the 6 a.m. Buona arrived at the German Consulate at 9.40 without misadventure, but in the middle of an air raid. They went on machine gunning most of the morning; & in the evening when we were [escorted] in our train, they [were] again over Milan. We saw them diving down close to the station & machine gunning people in the streets. Absolute shits! We didn't like leave our luggage or lose our seats (the trains are appallingly crowded), so we stuck it out. But it was an unpleasant half hour. A station is not exactly the best place to be in during an air raid! But machine gunning people in the streets is a dirty game & it constitutes nothing whatever towards winning the war, except to make people here want <u>to</u> fight to the last.

24 January

Once [*illegible*] I feel down in the dumps. The Russian winter offensive [has] at last come & it's proving more formidable than I expected. True, von [*illegible*] upset the attack plan of a [*illegible*] offensive & that may save our bacon for the present. But I'm very nervous about Silesia.[1] Germany cannot afford afford [*sic*] to lose that industrial zone & the Bolsheviks are absolutely right on the border of it. I was nervous too about my sister in law [*illegible*] who lives in Upper Silesia. It would be dreadful if she became a fugitive.

All the same, I still have confidence in those wonderful Germans. I think the present critical situation will be surmounted. But unless by May, we can resume our offensive with the new weapons, I cant see what can resist the joint [*illegible*] of our [enemies] in the early summer. That means we have 3 months only left of grace in which we've <u>got</u> to [*illegible*] the [*illegible*]. Anyhow, that looks like logic.

Meanwhile B & Job are going over to Saló & this also makes me anxious. I hate the thought of journeys now-a-days. My friend [*illegible*] went to Genoa the other day & [his] train was bombed & machine gunned. He & his wife got out & lay for an hour in the [snow]. But a lot of people were trapped & 60 were killed. Of course B & Job will be going by car, but it's always a risk. Besides, we ought to be together these critical days. The plan is to pack up what remains of our surplus belongings & send them to Merano where our other things are. Then she & Job – in about a months' time – will rejoin me here. But its all very complicated, because now all our summer things are in Merano & we shall have to go there in April or May to fetch them & exchange them for our winter things – and it will not be an easy task. But sufficient for the day is an end thereof.

Mussolini has been [doing] [some] excellent things lately in the way of breaking the Black Market – the turning of all [*illegible*] into public [*illegible*], the requirement of all wholesale dealers & food factories, the creation of a Ministry of Labour & the placing of all the administration of the new laws, as well as the [*illegible*] organisation in the hands of the Labour Union (Conf. di lavoro, arte e tecnica).[2] Mussolini is at his best again. That's obvious & whatever happens, he'll leave a wonderful legacy behind him of social legislation, corresponding to the desires of the working classes all the world over. Copartnerships & collaboration. Conciliation & cooperation – Universal values & individual personality.

What a tragic pity he lost grip of the situation in 1939–40. It becomes more & more apparent that Ciano & Edda are the chief culprits of our woes. I never guessed it at the time, though I [spotted] the mistakes. But Musso should never have allowed them the necessary [*illegible*]. I cant understand it. However, its no use crying over spilt milk. Musso is now back in his old form & we can thank God for that. Now he ought to put into force my plan for the issue of a new currency in order to force people to cough up the millions of hoarded notes & at the same time [retain] a progressive portion of the hoard in the form of a forced loan, while those who cannot explain how they obtained the money would at the same time have to pay [income] tax on their gains, which at present they have evaded. I've written to Nicoletti[3] about this & I think something may be done [was in about it all in good time]. This [*illegible*] in hope of what has already been done would effectively stop the inflation tendency for a long while.

Meanwhile the second Teheran Conference (will it be Teheran?) is in preparation & Stalin will be able to present the western allies with a lot of <u>faits accomplis</u> – Poland & Yugoslavia in particular.[4] Churchill's policy of force has triumphed in Greece, but that's a poor set off to what Stalin has been able to do & in the same time it's a proof that only British & American [*illegible*] in occupation of western Europe can prevent all Europe going Communist. De Gaulle has completely [*illegible*] the last hope of some [*illegible*] of balance of power in Europe.[5] By aligning himself with Russia, the western block [*illegible*] the F.O. thought it would be possible to operate to counterbalance the Eastern block under Russian influence [*word deleted*] has now become a chimera. This means England has definitely lost the war. Its the last of her war aims gone west & for the rest she is [*illegible*]. Only an Axis victory now can save England, for a united Europe capable of withstanding Russia & America in all fields (particularly in the economic field) would now be England's only decent chance of recovery.[6]

26 January

B & Job went back to Saló to-day [*illegible*] the 5.35 a.m. train, rising at 4.15. To our astonishment it had been snowing all night & there was a foot on the round. But I took this as providential, because it will make their journey safer. I only trust that the places reserved for them in the German [courier] will be kept. I expect them back in a month's time, so that henceforth we shall remain united. Took the opportunity of the early rise to go to confession & communion.

1 February

Too much work & not enough sleep – & not enough information to base one's work on.

I hear Suffolk & [Wokingham] are both dead. I wonder who is alive.

Oh what fools these English have been. I would [like] to save the damned country. And I could, if I ever had the chance!

15 February

The Conference at Yalta is ended: 1 master-criminal & 2 madmen. The manifesto issued is a more honest document than anything the allies have issued so far. Anyhow, it dots the i's & crosses the 't' of their intention to destroy European civilisation, to repeats the errors of Versailles on a still longer scale, regard the Atlantic Charter as a scrap of paper and prepare the way for a second world war. Nothing would be better calculated to remove any doubts which might still remain in Germany about the necessity of fighting to the death or victory. So we may regard the results as satisfactory.

It has been an orgy of hatred & [*illegible*]. It shows up the allies for what they really are: the [instruments] of [Jewry].

Churchill of course comes out worse. Nothing is left of the reasons for which Britain entered the war. The ideas have gone, the balance of power has gone, the trade proposals are gone. Debt, unemployment, a falling population, diminished prestige & the certain promise of hundreds of thousands of more young Englishmen sacrificed to make the world safe for Bolshevism & [Jewry] are the things which Churchill has brought away with him in his pocket – together with the prospect of a new world war, a long period during which hundreds of thousands of men will not be able to return home & a [generation] of [illegible] & [illegible] in the heart of Europe. And no good will come to the American people either. But Stalin rakes in all the advantages.

Does he mean to attack Japan on April 26th?

Roosevelt has actually done his best to persuade him & has offered him a bribe of a 6,000,000, [illegible] [illegible] credit, which will [word deleted] insure ~~about~~ the unemployment of ~~about~~ [illegible] [illegible] 18 million Americans as soon as the immediate postwar boom is over.[7]

24 February

The [West] Front (Eisenhower-Montgomery) offensive started on Tuesday last 20th I was sent to Saló for a special service with the German ambassador – to listen to the B.B.C. & comment. [Interlenghi] and I are glad to be joined up again with the family in these days of crisis. We have had to leave the [Lambretti]'s house owing to Mussolini's sister (Signora Mancini)[8] who had already installed herself there, wanting all the rooms. But we have a new & more convenient place now at Barbarano[9] (near Gardone), so all is for the best. Job [meanwhile] is being put up by Sig. [Franci], as there is no room for him in our new quarters (a small sitting room, small hall, separate entrance, kitchenette, bathroom & w.c.)

The war situation <u>looks</u> desperate. The English talk of [the] German collapse by the end of March, Eisenhower says 60 days (e.g. [illegible] April 26th, date of the meeting of the S. Francisco Conference).[10] More cautious people say by July 1st. My own opinion is that unless we can resist with the new arms by early in May, we are done – but we ought certainly to be able to resist until the [period].

As for the war news, [rumour] goes that <u>the</u> special new [arms] which [illegible] the [origin] in the [air] & can destroy all life within a radius of 2 miles cannot be used until air supremacy be established, otherwise the British would retaliate with gas. And as for establishing superiority in the air, the difficulty now is the training of pilots. It is said 40 per cent of the Germans chosen are rejected because their reflexes are not quite enough for the new machines. Italians are better (only 5 per cent rejections) – but that [4] months of training are needed for their training & training only began in December on a large scale. This would mean we should not be ready until the middle of April. But [meanwhile] the machines are in full production, although doubtless the loss of territory (especially the Silesian industrial zone, the suffering of the German people, the refugee problem etc. [*Illegible*] are hampering to a certain extent & may be [hindering] or delaying production.[11] All this may be mere rumour, but if it corresponds with the truth, we shall have in any case a very small margin of time. The only comfort in the situation is the Führer's continued confidence & assertion that we shall win if we stick it out these months. My admiration for the Germans increases every day & I must say they are a most likeable people to deal with – more so than any other I have met. It is a monstrous crime this attempt to [ruin] a great people like that.

1 March

The Yalta Conference & its determination to destroy Germany is helpful in that it removes any last doubt about the allies['] intentions. So it will only stimulate still further the German will to resist. Further [comment] is unnecessary, except that it was a clear surrender to Russia, & the only [thing] that can be said of Churchill's [work] [there] is that he made the best of a bad job.[12]

19 March

St. Joseph's Day – a prayer for the safety of my family. The situation could hardly look worse. But in to-day's German papers a statement has been made, which gives one cause for hope. The statement is to the effect that the great joint allied offensive is not yet in full swing, it is only in its preliminary phases. The Germans must expect more [*illegible*] during this preliminary phase of the critical offensive & steel themselves to receive them. Then the full [brunt] of what the allies expect to be the knock out blow will have to be [faced], and the war will enter its decisive moment. The signal will thus be given for the great German counter strike (presumably the new and terrible weapon or weapons, which the Germans have hesitated to use except as a last and desperate remedy).

The Germans are certainly justified in resorting to any weapon, however terrible, for the other side have not stuck at anything. Now we shall see what we shall see. In any case we are likely to witness within the next 6 weeks decisive, terrible, apocalyptic events.

I have decided to [stay] by Mussolini in all events and share his fate. I think that is the only brave and honest thing to do. I have done my duty. [My] life has been constant, my intentions honourable. I have accordingly prepared a statement to be handed to the British authorities should they become masters of the situation, of Mussolini & of myself. And in the interview I hope to have with Mussolini shortly – perhaps before Easter – I shall inform him of my decision.

Meanwhile I have made certain suggestions to him regarding the [conduct] of foreign [politics] and a special line of propaganda with a view to preparing the ground for a just peace if we are in a position to impose or negotiate it. I have prepared two special broadcasts which would be delivered as from a 'Foreign Office Spokesman of the Italian Social Republic' on a large number of wavelengths beamed [in] England & the U.S.A. They have been prepared as a test for approval by the Duce & [by] the German authorities – and Mellini,[13] who has taken up the work of Mazzolini, the Under-Secretary for Foreign Affairs, who recently died (a charming and honest gentleman), has the matter in hand for the time being. But, as I say, I hope to see Mussolini before long and also the German Ambassador, von Rahn, who is credited with being an able man of wide, liberal views.

My reports to him on the internal situation in England have been judged useful. I have emphasized that it would be foolish of us if we banked on the possibility of a rift between the allies or an any movement in England in favour of a negotiated conference peace. Such a movement of opinion has no chance whatever of making itself felt unless it becomes clear that all the hopes of ending the war this summer are dashed & that victory is not in sight for at least another year & even then by no means certain. Secondly I am convinced that Stalin has no intention of [*illegible*] matters beyond the endurance of the British or American governments. He will act with his customary calculation just up to the point of what Churchill & Roosevelt can be depended on swallowing. If Germany is beaten, we will probably join in the war against Japan & play the same game in China as we have played in Europe. Even there he could push things to extremes – but bide his time until the post war boom in England & America begins to peter out, while the continent becomes more & more chaotic. Then he would resume his active support of communism everywhere – that is, when it is too late for England or America to do anything about it, unless they mean to fight Russia, which is the last thing public opinion would probably in such circumstances support.

There is nothing else to do now but to wait on events. Apart from the betrayal of Italy, we have made great mistakes – political & military. I have already written of the mistakes we made during the years 1938 & especially 1939. Mussolini missed a great opportunity after the Abyssinian triumph both in the foreign & home fields. Hitler also has made great political mistakes especially in his handling of the Russians & in his refusal at an early stage to come out clearly on the principles of a just peace. Turkey should have been attacked after the British debacle in Greece instead of Russia. She would have been overrun in a month – and then we should have held a strategical situation both against Russia & Britain which would have been probably decisive.

As for the fascists as distinct from Fascism, [there] is thought worth nothing. It was important that the rise of Fascism coincided with the rise to consciousness of the lower middle classes in Italy (the result of the last war) of the opportunities of advancement & riches. The war had [poten-tialized] Italian industrial possibilities, the development of electrical power was making still further industrial development possible & so suddenly, unprepared & only half educated, a new class saw the possibility of [*word deleted*] itself going up in the world. The profiteers & speculators had also [given] a bad example of get-rich-quick [*illegible*]. Consequently it was this class of upstarts which came up along into the Revolution & they are responsible for its failures (despite its astounding successes), its discredit among many men of good will & for many of the betrayals (people like Grandi etc.)

This point is an important one from the historical point of view. It accounts for a lot of what has happened. It does not touch Fascism as a doctrine or as a movement in the right direction. But it accounts very largely for the shortcomings which its opponents have tried to fasten on the responsibility of Mussolini & have tried to put in relief in contrast to the [comparatively] [uncorrupt] public life of Italy previous to Fascism. Not that public life <u>was</u> [uncorrupt] before Fascism. One has only to read Salvemini's 'Il Governo della malavita'[14] and [*illegible*]. But things grew worse because of greater opportunities & the [pressure] of a new class of considerable interests coming to the fore.[15]

Mussolini's mistakes:-
Not to have used the moment of triumph after Abyssinia to 'liberalise' Fascism, initiate the policy of co-partnerships & appointed a commission to examine the whole question of banking & currency reform – & to have pushed England to settle the Suez Canal question on the lines proposed by Sir Arnold Wilson,[16] and the question of [*illegible*] [*word deleted*] Italian language in Malta & to have come also to a satisfactory settlement with France regarding Tunisia or Jibouti (a good bargain one way or another) – offering in return an alliance with England & France.

Not to have adopted a clear policy during 1939 – putting the country on an armed [*illegible*] footing, controlling [exports/imports] & private foreign trade more effectively, preparing public opinion for a world crisis, starting rationing – or at least organising it.

Never to have declared war on France – but to have flattered her & obtained the military occupation of Tunisia without prejudice to French political rights.

Not to have gone in for the Greek campaign at that season of the year – to have temporized. And previously to have properly [*illegible*] with Greece & Jugoslavia friendship, won at the cost of concessions.

He should have appointed Balbo in 1939 Minister of War.

To have insisted on German help in North Africa not later than September 1940, if war had become by then inevitable with England.

Not to have declared war on Russia & to have [abstained] from taking part in any campaign outside the Mediterranean & Red Sea.

Hitler's mistakes:-

He should have arrived at a generous understanding with the Vatican before the outbreak of war.

[*Word deleted*] He should have seen that the way to beat England after the collapse of France was to concentrate on Africa without a moment's delay.

He should have attacked Turkey after Crete, instead of Russia & pushed on to the Gulf & to the Levant.

He should have [adopted] a sympathetic policy towards the Slavs from the outset.

He should have published a clearly [just] European Charter as embodying his war aims when he was at the height of his success.

He should not have allowed any Jew [baiting] & been humane towards political prisoners.[17]

All these points were obvious to me ~~at the time~~ all along.[18]

27 March

Things look pretty hopeless. Unless a miracle occurs (the new arms) I put April 21st (the birthday of Rome) as about the last day of hope. I keep on hoping, but since [*illegible*] [*illegible*] proved successful, I have nourished no illusions (Fede & speranza, [*illegible*] [*illegible*] [*illegible*]).[19]

2 April

Communion for the intentions of Buona, for it is her birthday. The military situation looks very very bad. All the same one hopes. One mustn't take British & American propaganda at its face value. They have indulged in the same orgasms of coming victory before & have been disappointed. And this time it is natural that the orgasm should reach its height, for the [*illegible*] for victory would be the final one. Besides, part of the campaign of proclaiming victory is aimed at stampeding the neutrals into war with Germany as far as possible & in order to whip up as many so called 'United Nations' to the [quest] at S. Francisco.

Nevertheless things look bad & we cannot be far off from midnight now.

5 April

At long last I had my talk today with the German Ambassador, Rahn. The purpose of my talk was to convince him of the importance of developing a foreign policy, which would also form the basis of [our] propaganda, to make it plain that our war or rather peace aims were just, moderate, generous, that we mean to [construct] a European Confederation capable of holding its own against the infection of Soviet Russia & the U.S.A. & so maintaining its constitution intact & that we should look forward to seeing Britain take part in its constitution. Such a prospect would be all to the benefit of Britain, who would otherwise have to take a back seat as regards the U.S.A. & Soviet Russia. As for the allied plan, it would not bring peace, but a generation of upheaval & strife – political, economic al & military, not to speak of [illegible]. The organisation of the world on the other hand in large international groups of nations [naturally] bound together by ties of geography & traditions would, as we propose, put [power] politics at a discount, make trade rivalry & the ~~conquest of~~ urge to conquer much less dangerous in that each international group would be easy to defend, difficult to attack & largely self-sufficient economically & having plenty of room for expansion & development – & it would make world security a simpler problem, with each group [illegible] towards the other a [illegible] doctrine of non-political or economic interference. Very briefly that is what I want to see [announced] & a beginning should be made as soon as possible. Of course if the military situation did not improve, I said it would be a plan still-born, but if on the other hand the military did improve & especially if it improved sufficiently to make it apparent that the war could not be won by the allies without another winter campaign, conditions would arise in which vast numbers of people in allied countries would turn towards the idea of a peace by negotiating provided they were persuaded to discuss the question of guarantees of our good faith.

Rahn agreed with me & praised my efforts. The whole difficulty, he said, lay in the character of Ribbentrop, who was jealous of Rahn & difficult ~~with regard to~~ to persuade as to the utility of such a plan, not because he was necessarily against the kind of peace we wanted, but because he was fearful it could be interpreted as a weakness & might raise points which it would be wiser at present to leave alone. Ribbentrop had also been criticised by Mussolini & they were not on too good terms.[20] However, Rahn was going to Berlin in a few days time & my plan would be discussed. He would do his best to get it approved – or at any rate to get us here in Italy to have a free hand to do what we could without [actually] committing the Axis.

Rahn expects to be back about April 17th. He said Germany had been surprised by the rapidity of the allied advance in the West & had timed the counter offensive for May 1st, which might be too late. There would be two offensive armies ready by that date. The question [remained] if the signal could now be given earlier without jeopardising the preparations. As for the new arms Rahn said the Germans did not wish to resort to them except as a desperate strike, because this might lead to [unrestricted] chemical warfare with terrible results.[21] Anyhow, we will expect a very strong German reaction before long – and there was no need to despair yet.

Rahn [appeared] to me a very humane & reasonable man, with an excellent psychological sense. I feel he is right about Ribbentrop, who is evidently no good diplomat. But Rahn is on excellent terms with Hitler. He was very frank with me, & criticized the Germans, who he said were sentimental & at the same time brutally frank. They did not know how to direct foreign policy with any subtlety & were apt to put people's backs up by calling a spade a spade & then, if things didn't go well, by showing their [illegible] by their sentimental [illegible].

I told him that Churchill would no doubt respect the Germans for their stout fighting qualities, but that, being by temperament a bully, he was apt to squeeze [illegible] [illegible] anybody who showed signs of weakness or fear like us Italians. I pointed out that the British were tenacious & proud, but the Government of England did not represent the people except in that subject. They represented international [financial] forces & Jewish [influence] more than British. But British public opinion was still a potent force & if we [could] [combine] such key successes with a really reasonable declared policy public opinion in England, which [wanted] a [joint/good] peace & a solid peace, feared Bolshevism & was apprehensive about England's political & economic future [illegible] the arrangements which were being elaborated by Roosevelt & Stalin, might well react against the Government.

The conversation, in French, lasted just over half an hour – and I am to see him again after his return from Germany.[22]

9 April

To-day I had a short talk with Mussolini (just ¼ hour). Graziani turned up just as I hoped to be received & stayed 1 hour & 40 minutes. Altogether I had to wait 3 hours & 35 minutes. The Duce, who was in a vivacious mood, started by apologising for keeping me waiting for such a monstrously long time. He had particularly wished to see me because he wanted me to reply on the air to [illegible]'s recent letter to the 'Times', where he had pleaded that Italy should be admitted to the S. Francisco Conference. The letter, the Duce said, contained a lot of inaccuracies & [illegible] insinuations, which he ~~could~~ was in a position to refute with documentary evidence. But the documents [were/are] in Milan. They were on their way here & he wished to see me again as soon as they arrived. In any case, he said, he wished to see me again tomorrow, as the evening time was short for a good heart to heart talk. He then abruptly changed the subject, saying: 'And, by the way, arrangements have been made for you to accompany me wherever I may go. Are you pleased?' I said: 'I am overjoyed. That is my wish. I want to stick with you to the end – and if things go badly, to share your [exile]. I hope they wont kill me. But if they do – well, that's that. There is a precedent of an English school teacher – I think he was in Paris, who wrote wireless script & talked on the air for the Germans, and he got 12 years hard labour. But I have a better case. My life has been all of a piece. I always wanted to be Italian & if I had not kept my word to my father – not to ask for Italian citizenship until after his death – I should have become Italian 35 years ago. Consequently, if they punish me they will be punishing me [merely] because I kept my word. If I had broken my word, they would have no jurisdiction over me. Besides, I have always considered myself Italian & to have consistently refused to serve the British Crown or profit by my possessing a British passport. I have stuck to my principles throughout [illegible] to my national disadvantages. If my British judges are honourable men, they ought to respect a man of honour. Anyhow, I am not going to run away. I want to stay by you and I don't think they'll kill you either. More likely, your fate will be St Helena or Mauritius. If so, I want to go with you. We'll [write] our memoirs & our philosophy – & a good many things will happen in the next 10 years. We shall still be young in 10 years time – younger anyhow than Churchill is now, and he's going strong enough, isn't he? We may still have a chance of reconstructing Italy & constructing European unity!' But, I said, are things going to go badly? What do you think of the situation. Have you still [faith] in victory?

The Duce, who laughed at my idea of us writing our memoirs & our philosophy in exile, immediately said: 'Yes, I have. Indeed I have'. I said: 'I know our ideas will triumph, but do you think we shall win a military victory?' And the Duce said: 'I think we may still do so. We are by no means beaten yet. The Germans have been yielding space in order to gain time. As the "News Chronicle" said the other day, "however, if you go on yielding space indefinitely, there comes a moment when you lose time too". The reaction therefore, if it is to come and I believe it will – must come soon.'

I told him what Rahn had said & the Duce confirmed [this/him]. The Germans had the men & the [means]. And it was to be hoped & expected that the Allied hopes of a victory this summer would be dashed.

I then said we must not miss the chance to develop our foreign policy on the lines I had suggested. He agreed. He said he had given instructions for my [first] article to be published in the Corriere della Sera & that the others would follow, as soon as he had passed them. As for their being broadcast in English, I could have them registered[23] when I went to Milan to give the reply to [illegible]'s letter & then they too could be given at regular intervals. He seemed to think there was no reason why we should not go ahead even [without] German consent. They represented the views of the Italian Social Republic in favour of a scrupulously just peace & if the Germans thought that the moment for speaking out was inopportune – well, we could take our own responsibilities & he didn't think, put like that, the Germans would object. We had the same ends in view and we had the [illegible] [illegible] intention.

10 April

This time my talk with Mussolini lasted 35 minutes & we touched on a large variety of subjects. He again assured me that I and my family would follow him, if a move were required. He said transport [would/should] be provided & that we should go to the [*illegible*], where we should find [*illegible*] in a fortress, so to speak. We should be in touch with Merano over the Stelvio Pass[24] & therefore I need not worry about my boxes which were in the German Embassy depot at Merano.

Mussolini [*illegible*] to the German's lack of political sense. He said he had written during the last 2 years a huge pile of letters to the Führer, which were presumably archived somewhere or other, & thought one day be found & published. He had urged one suggestion after another with a view to a policy aimed at convincing the world that what we were out for was justice & no [more than] positive. But he had had very little response. The answer was always that the moment was inopportune. The Germans had no psychology. They had the fatal gift of getting themselves disliked. If they wanted to enter a house where people were eager to receive them, they would break down the door & somehow manage to make the people inside regret their coming after all.

I said they had been particularly stupid in their handling of the Slav peoples. Mussolini agreed. He said Hitler should have proclaimed an independent Ukraine when the Germans entered [Kiev]. They should have created an independent Poland & not the meaningless 'General [*illegible*]'.

Rosenberg was now, in his advances to the Ukrainian pressures, acting 2 years too late.[25] Look at the English by way of contrast, he said. They have psychology. They are masters in the art. Churchill had been extremely intelligent in getting other peoples to fight & bleed for England. What's more, they fought & bled voluntarily. Even the Indians.

I explained that the Indians were well clothed, fed & treated with respect by the British officers. They had no feelings of loyalty to the Empire, but they had a tradition of [*illegible*] to the Government, whatever it was, & they developed an affectionate regard & respect for their officers, who were generally excellent fellows, just & human in their relations with their men.

Mussolini asked me about Ernie Bevin's speech attacking Churchill.[26] I explained that everybody in England took it for granted that the war in Germany would be soon over & that that would be the signal for Churchill to reform his Cabinet without the Labour & Liberal members, so that the parties could be free to prepare for the battle of the general election. Meantime the sparring had already begun perhaps a little too soon. But this was due to the feeling that victory was so close that they might as well begin to think of the election now.

The Duce: 'What sort of a man is Bevin?'

Myself: 'One of the more intellectual leaders of the Labour Party. I believe he first had the [intention] of [becoming] a Protestant Pastor

(Minister). He studied theology. Quite an able man, but like all the others, not an outstanding figure If Labour [get/got] in, [Attlee] would be Prime Minister. Quite a mediocre individual, though a good speaker. The [ablest] man which the Labour Party possessed was probably Morrison, but he was not too popular with the rank & file.[27] Was looked upon as too much of an imperialist – too near the Tories in outlook to be altogether trusted as a Labour leader'.

The Duce: And Greenwood?[28]

Myself: Nice, but also very mediocre. Except for Churchill, there was really nobody to look to & Churchill himself would be a failure as Prime Minister in peace time. There were plenty of clever men, but there was no one who was a real leader, no one with a big idea or moral weight. They were all the same. All in the general [rank]. I had hopes of Sir Sam [Hoare] once, though I always knew him to be a weak man.[29] Well, he has succumbed to the usual game. When he looked as if he might take up an independent, European attitude (on his return from Spain), a Press campaign was set in motion against him. It was stopped when he accepted a peerage. The usual British game, which succeeds so well, of the 'stick & the carrot'. Now he has accommodated himself to the policy of national suicide & European murder, which the international brokers, interests vested in war and the Jews have designed for England.

We reverted for a moment to the admirable psychological sense of the British and the deplorable absence of it among Germans. Mussolini gave as an example the recent citing in the order of the day of the small contingent of Italian troops, fighting on the side of the Allies, which had gained a small success on the Southern front. But the Germans hardly ever troubled to do the same for many & more important actions successfully carried out by the republican troops. This, he said, was a great psychological error.

Mussolini then asked me what standing [Gillingham] had – and Stokes & Shinwell, who all asked the British Government so frequently I said they counted for very little.[30] The same could be said of the Duke of Bedford, Rhys Davies & [illegible].[31] They were [illegible] symptomatic of what a lot of people felt. But that large body of public opinion in favour of a really just peace could do nothing now. Only if the present hopes of a finish to the German war this summer was definitely disappointed, and if we then set out to prove that our [peace] was to be first a responsible one, was there any chance of powerful voices being raised in favour of peace by negotiation.

Mussolini asked me about the position of Jews in England. Were they received in society etc. I said: 'Oh yes, it's [just] like in America. The White Chapel Jews – the low-class Jews of recent immigration in the East End of London were very much disliked by the masses who lived alongside them, but the gentleman Jew was received everywhere & even married into the British aristocracy. Many of them were [camouflaged] Jews, who became Protestants or Agnostics & took other names. These especially were regarded as assimilated.[']

Mussolini asked if, as a rule, they had an accent. I said 'no' – not the upper class Jews. The mark of a gentleman in England was his accent. The public schools were the factories where gentlemen were manufactured. The new rich sent their sons to these schools & they were turned out indistinguishable from the true blue blooded gentlemen & they then mixed with them. I gave the Rothermeres as an example. Old Lord Rothermere was a rough diamond.[32] He was received in society, just because he was rich. But he was looked upon as a boor & a vulgarian. His sons, however, were perfect gentlemen & nobody felt there was any difference between them & the sons of an old aristocratic family. This system brought new blood into the aristocracy & kept it from decay. It had much to recommend it. But crossing with the Jews was another matter. The Jewish mentality persisted & undermined the British character. The impoverishment of the aristocracy and [class] had a bad effect on the governing class. They had since Edwardian times taken to money making and had acquired the mentality of the upper bourgeoisie. The best aristocracy in England was still the untitled country gentleman. The titled aristocracy was mostly composed of new rich, who had bought their titles and there were a large number of Jews in the House of Lords. Jewish influence was [enormous]. It was a mistake to think the Government sought the interests of the people of England. They represented only a small class now-a-days, whose interests were not necessarily British – people who were as at home in New York as in London & who put their money [profits] before their country. This & certain time-[lag] traditions of the Foreign Office & [Admiralty] accounted for the folly of having landed England into the present war, which spelt the end of England as a first class power & would [tear] up the last of her cultural roots on the continent of Europe, without which [England's] culture would wither.

As an illustration of how the way an Englishman spoke English counted more than anything else as the mark of a gentleman (I said if a Englishman came into this room I could place him immediately) I told Mussolini how the F.O. candidates were vetted and how embarrassed the election Committee had been when Colonials were first [admitted]. They no longer were able to tell whether the candidate was a gentleman or not. I remember the case of Peterson, a Canadian, & now an ambassador.[33] He was the first Colonial admitted to the British diplomatic service & because he spoke with what was considered a low-class accent, the Committee had to refer to Canada to find out if in Canada he was considered to belong to a 'good family'.

We touched on other subjects too. I told M. that both Britain & Australia could look forward to a post-war boom, because of the large cash credits which had accumulated. This boom, however, could not last & could be followed by a terrible slump. Stalin would probably not do anything which he did not accurately calculate Churchill & Roosevelt [word deleted] swallow. It was no use counting on dissentions between the Allies as a way out of our difficulties. Stalin would play the same game in eastern Asia as he had played in Europe. He would declare war on Japan at his chosen moment, [annexe] Manchuria & perhaps Korea certainly Mongolia – & get his zone of occupation in China. Then, while, the post-war boom lasted, he would do nothing to upset the position of Europe & China. But when the slump came, he would sweep the board with Communism – having got his army into fettle again & developed on 4 year plan into his [*illegible*] 6 billion dollar credit his export manufacturers. Dumping his goods on Europe & the Far East, particularly his propaganda & with his refitted armies behind him – with Britain & America suffering from the slump – he calculated on being able to have it all his own way & to move towards his final triumph. England would then wake up to her mistakes. Then but not till then would the trouble arise between the present Allies. Meanwhile only military successes by the Axis, followed by a really [*word deleted*] enlightened foreign policy would save us & Europe.

Mussolini then gave me his instructions about propaganda – these points in particular: i) The folly of the unconditional surrender policy; ii) the folly of the war [criminals] [stand].[34] Both policies only meant the stiffening of axis resistance & the sacrifice of hundreds of thousands of more young lives. He pointed out how the decadence of France was the result of the 'sacrifice' of the Napoleonic Wars.

(iii) The social legislation of the Italian Social republic. Copartnership & Co-operation. The New Socialism: the levelling up of the people to the rank & [liberty] of property owners instead of degrading them to the level of proletariats all. Private Capitalism & State [Socialism] were much the same. There were 3 classes of goods – necessaries, accessories & [luxuries]. The first should be produced on a cooperative basis, eliminating thus the profit element. The second needed to be controlled. The third could be left completely free. But luxuries were things which even the poor not only needed but always insisted on having – even if it were only a bowl of goldfish, a vase, an ornament, embroidery, lace ....[35] Luxuries were not things to be regarded as superfluous. But their production could be left to the free play of supply & demand. The production of accessories on the other hand must be controlled – that is supervised & directed by collective action. Necessaries should be produced by cooperative organisation.

I told Mussolini that [these] three points had already been my chief planks in my propaganda – these & the <u>justice</u> of our peace aims. I regarded a free hand to develop this theme as more important than anything else – and he agreed.

'And you shall accompany me – you & your family – if I have to move. Remember that', he again declared. 'If things go badly, I expect they'll want to [exile] me. If they take me, you shall be my witness'.

At that we shook hands & parted & he said he would be glad to receive Buona next time.[36]

12 April

Had a few minutes talk with Anfuso who has taken up his duties as Under-Secretary of State for Foreign Affairs.[37] I told him a bit about myself & talked a bit about politics & the war. We discussed the western European block which England helped to build up as a counter weight to Russia. I said it was not likely to survive without American support, though the showdown might not come for some years – that is, not till the post-war boom had turned into a slump. But Russia held the long [illegible]. It was only a question of time & she would shatter the western block, unless England & America were prepared to fight for it. They would come to regret their [breaking] of Germany & having torn up their European roots from which their great civilisation drew its [nourishment]. I then asked him to tell me [frankly] about what he knew of the military situation. He said Germany had some terrible gasses, but was frightened of using them as they would [affect] their own people now. They were also frightened of reprisals. I asked about the German aviation. He said the report regarding the [large] [percentage] of [deaths] & accidents among the pilots training in the new machines [being] not true. But he was not confident – that is to say, he could not tell – about Germany being in a position to regain, even temporarily, the mastery of the air.[38] On the other hand he thought Germany, even without using the new weapons, could hold out until the end of June & that guerrilla warfare could continue for a considerable period beyond that. He thought the Germans would hold out all right on the Italian front. For the rest, some [kind] of reaction might be expected before long, but he could not say to what extent it would be effective. He hoped for the best. I said that if it was sufficiently effective to make it obvious to the allies that, to win they would have to face another winter of war, then we could hope – provided our foreign policy was wise & enter-prising – in securing a satisfactory peace. He agreed & complimented me on my initiative.[39]

Rahn is not going to Germany at present after all, but has given his [consent] to my plan of developing our foreign policy by outlining our peace aims on the air. That is a great triumph for me and, whether we win or lose, it will be good work done, which may one day lead to something.[40]

13 April

Roosevelt is dead – the individual, who, more than any other, can be held responsible for this ghastly war* – the man who has played the Jewish [game] to wreck Christian civilisation, who aimed at becoming – megalo-maniac (*more than Stalin, because, he not only did all he could to bring it about, but was in a position to prevent it) that he was – [illegible]

President of half the world, who successfully conspired to [wreck] and [supplant] British supremacy and who will go down to history, in contrast to Washington, as the greatest [liar] who ever resided in the White House – and the greatest, most fraudulent deceiver of his gullible fellow countrymen.

His death, I don't suppose, will now make any difference to America's war effort, but it might tend to result in a better and more sensible peace. His successor has the reputation of being a more honest man and, judging from his first utterances, is more likely to take a less dictatorial line and to govern the country with greater respect for the Constitution & the will of Congress. He is a man of a certain independence of thought, but more than that I don't know very much about him.

Providence has justly cheated ~~him~~ Roosevelt from enjoying a personal triumph. De mortuis nihil nisi bonum?[41] But [millions] of Americans will be secretly, if not openly rejoicing today. Of the three allied dictators, his character is to be most despised![42]

17 April

[*Word deleted*] Today I [travelled] to Milan with Mezzasoma to register my first 5 talks on World [Problems], which have to be [given] [*word deleted*] as the official or, rather semi-official, views of the Republic. On Poland, on my continental grouping of nations plan, on how to go about the unification of Europe, on the responsibilities for the war & on some economic [problems].

Mezzasoma put me up for the night at the 'foresteria' of the E.N.I.T.[43] Cucco[44] came in & others were there & we talked late. Good dinner & breakfast (honey).

18/19 April

Office. Talked my plan over & explained it to Volpe, who is now in charge.[45] Volpe is enthusiastic & shows himself prepared to enlarge my programme by making a special daily broadcast to America of 45 minutes (repeated twice – times 3.30, 4.30 & 6.00 on 2 wavelengths, [one] [*illegible*]). I suggested Gino Villari, who is now in Milan should help. [Malia], the Maltese [patriot], was suggested as another, M. [*illegible*] & [*illegible*], all of whom we co-opted during the day. I chose a lovely Vivaldi as our signal tune (Summer, from the 'Stagioni') & thought out the musical part of the programme. I am to have a free hand as to what to say.

In the evening I [moved] to Fino, packed most of my things & brought them back in the morning. George (Gödell) came back with me for a conversation with Mezzasoma. Lunched with De Rozz[en]i, the commander

& his English wife. A typical [cultivated] diplomat of the old school, & we [discussed] [*illegible*] problems. He said the Germans [had] acted very fairly & impartially in the [*illegible*] Commission of which he had been a member.

Saw Almirante in the evening & our programme [& other] arrangements were given the O.K. I suggested that to wind up our campaign Mussolini should be asked to make a big speech on foreign affairs; & our campaign was [*illegible*] as 'Our S. Francisco Conference'. Justice is to be our theme throughout – and the slogan 'What Italy thinks to-day, the world will think tomorrow.' If only we could have done work like this 2 or 3 years ago just to show our aims are just & reasonable. Up to now all our propaganda has been negative & [*illegible*]. Now it is to be at last (too late [*illegible*]) positive & [creative/concrete].

I only had a 4 hours sleep & went to bed dog tired.

20 April

There was an important Cabinet meeting today.

A hard day. Registered 3 talks at M[*illegible*] & had much [else] to prepare.

21 April

Registered the remaining 2 talks & still a lot to prepare.

22 April

To-night we give the first broadcast. Hard at work all day & I shall probably have to write the whole script for the first programme – an all-night session.

Later. Everything went off with a bang. It took me 7 hours of hard labour [*illegible*] & dictating the script & programme. Got no sleep next morning either. Too much to do.

23 April

Got 2 hours sleep in the afternoon, and then was begged to stay up another night to run the 2nd day's programme, so as to train the others. I consented to another white night. Dead tired. Mussolini was supplied with my first night's script & declared his approval. He came to Milan the day as we did, but is reported to have gone away today.

24 April

Slept 2 hours on my return at dawn to the Principe hotel, where I have been staying. Called in on Claudio Marcello during morning. Arranged to go back in [the] German Embassy [camion] in the evening. Was again called to the office in the evening at 7 p.m., after I had got another short rest, to receive a message from Mezzasoma. [But] when I arrived, Mezzasoma was not to be found in the telephone & I never got his message. Started back to Saló at 10 p m which means a 3rd white night running, more or less, for we shant get there till the early hours of tomorrow.

25 April

We [got] in at 3.30 a.m. & I got to bed at 4.30 for 3 hours. Buona had been very anxious, seeing the enemy was reported to be rapidly advancing. Ferrara & Modena taken.

I called on the German Embassy & was told we must prepare to leave for [*illegible*], where 'Jerry's Front' was going.

Later, we got a message that we must leave this very night – for <u>Merano</u>. The English were near Verona & Peschiera. No possibility of delay. Hell! So spent the afternoon frantically packing. Saw Nicoletti & Manzani before going. Left our heavier luggage with the Perozzi to be sent over & housed by the Contessa [*illegible*] (Martinengo Cesaresco) & packed all we [dared] to take, seeing that we had been told to travel light. [*Illegible*] sent a car to fetch us to Fasano at 7 p.m., but it broke down. I bicycled [*word deleted*] He [got] [*words deleted*] another car, but that also broke down! Blood to the head. Snatched a meal at Fasano later, where Buona & Job joined me after the car had been set right & I had bicycled there & back & we were loaded with our luggage on to a spare camion at 11 p.m.

27 April

Well, here we are at Merano, after a 24 hour journey. Owing to a variety of delays, we didn't actually get away till 2.10 pm & only reached Riva at dawn (5.30). The enemy planes were active all along the route, throwing flares; & as we were in a long column, we risked being spotted all the time. But luck was with us; and again at Riva, when I thought the danger, in the open country & in daylight, could be greater. After we had branched off the road to Madonna del Campiglio,[46] however, [*two words deleted*] our lorry travelled alone & we saw no more enemy aircraft except some heavy bombers. It was a cloudy day, but fortunately it did not rain. We were [plumped] down in the Teater Platz at Meran, left our luggage in the lorry except for 2 light things & trudged up to the German Embassy in Alta Maria. It was difficult to discover, but at last we got there at 1.30 in the morning. I felt dead beat, after no proper sleep for 5 days. Buona & Job were also worn out. Luckily beds were found for us. ~~To-day~~

The good [news] at the [*illegible*] found room for us & we moved in for our first good night's rest.

3 May

Well, these have been awful days. We heard of the murder of Mussolini, Mezzasoma, Pavolini, Bombacci[47] & 14 others at Milan, which fell into the hands of the Communist partisans on the 26th. It is difficult to reconstruct events. I imagine the [Cabinet] meeting on the 19th April decided to defend Milan & then to retire to the Valtellina. Apparently Mussolini had come up to M[eran] on the 23rd with the Japanese Ambassador & Rahn for a consultation. Rahn tried to persuade him not to go back & offered him an [airplane]. But Musso refused & went back to be with his [Ministers] &, as it turned out, to die. I cant understand how it was the partisans were able to get hold of Milan, but I gather only the Muti battalion put up a fight. Treachery & cowardice again, I suppose. Poor Italy! We are overwhelmed with grief & horror. And God knows who of our many friends & acquaintances in Milan & Garda gave escaped. Gödell & Graf got away from Fino were ambushed near the Lago [Iseo], but managed to rush through & reached Merano. The rest of the people at Fino were left behind.

The Führer is also dead. The news was officially announced at Bolzano yesterday, where we spent an awful day in the destroyed [city] in the [rain] trying to get our permit to stay in Meran. We had certificates from the Embassy giving us the necessary permission, but the police formalities had to be subsequently gone through, in order to enable us to exchange our Saló ration cards for new ones. The luggage we sent up 6 months ago here is safe. But it has taken a lot of time & trouble to settle in. We [discovered] our old friend [*illegible*], who we hope will keep us posted with news. An armistice has been signed for the Italian front & so the enemy are likely to be here soon.[48] Tomorrow we hope to get our ration cards just in time. Our thoughts & prayers are [entirely] with Mussolini & his companions. It is the greatest crime since the Crucifiction.[49] All had done no more than their duty. Mussolini had become almost a saint & there never has been a more generous & magnanimous [*word deleted*] statesman. History will avenge him. His ideas will live & triumph. May I live to be the healer of all this ghastly sore of hatred & persecution. I forgive my enemies. And, now, God protect us, especially my darlings.[50]

I do not feel in the mood to write now. My comments may be added later. My hope now is in England. There we may see the right reaction one day & may I be privileged to help it for her sake, for Europe's sake, for Italy's sake, for the sake of the common people.[51]

NOTES

Introduction

1 'Major Strachey Barnes. A Paladin of Fascism', *The Times*, 29 August 1955, p. 9. James Strachey Barnes should not be confused with J. Sidney Barnes (1881–1952), later Sir Sidney Barnes, who was Deputy Secretary of the Admiralty from 1936 until 1944, and later Director of Greenwich Hospital until 1948. See 'Sir Sidney Barnes', *The Times*, 8 December 1952, p. 10.

2 'Nel quinto anniversario della morte. James Strachey Barnes', *Il Secolo d'Italia*, 25 August 1960, p. 3. Founded as an independent daily of the right in 1953, *Il Secolo d'Italia* became the official newspaper of the neo-Fascist party MSI (Italian Social Movement) in 1963. Villari's article had first appeared in the same newspaper on 27 August 1955, p. 3, with the title 'Jim Barnes, italiano'.

3 See D. Bradshaw, '"Those extraordinary parakeets": Clive Bell and Mary Hutchinson', part 1, *The Charleston Magazine*, Autumn–Winter 1997, 16, 5–12; part 2, *The Charleston Magazine*, Spring–Summer 1998, 17, 5–11.

4 C. M. Mancini, *Le carte del maggiore James Strachey Barnes R. F. C.* (Rome: typescript, 2007; latest edn with CD Rom, 2012); the diary is in Archivio Centrale dello Stato, Rome (ACS), Archivi di famiglie e persone, James Strachey Barnes, b. 4.

5 On 25 July 1943 the Grand Council of Fascism (the supreme institute of the Fascist Party and main body of Mussolini's government) decided to depose Mussolini, who was arrested and replaced by Marshal Pietro Badoglio. After Italy's surrender to the Allies on the following 8 September, Mussolini established with German help a Fascist republic over central and northern Italy, with its centre at Salò on Lake Garda. This republic lasted until the Allies finally liberated the entire peninsula from German forces in April 1945.

6 Dino Grandi was a 'first hour' Fascist and one of the four leaders (*quadrumviri*) of the March on Rome in 1922; Foreign Minister in 1929–32; and Ambassador to London in 1932–9. As Mussolini considered his approach to be too pro-British, he replaced him with Giuseppe Bastianini (see *Diary 1943*, note 60, p. 200) as Ambassador to London, and made Grandi Minister of Justice from 1939. In 1943 Grandi prepared a motion which led to Mussolini's dismissal at the Grand Council of 24 July 1943. He was condemned to death in 1944, but had already fled Italy in

August 1943. The only existing biography of Grandi is by P. Nello, *Dino Grandi* (Bologna: Il Mulino, 2003; first edn 1993).

7 C. Petrie, *Mussolini* (London: The Holme Press, 1931); D. Jerrold, *Jeorgian Adventure* (London: Collins, 1937) and *Britain and Europe, 1900–1940* (London: Collins, 1941); J. F. C. Fuller, *The First of the League Wars: Its Lessons and Omens* (London: Eyre and Spottiswoode, 1936); M. Currey, *A Woman at the Abyssinian War* (London: Hutchinson, 1936) and, with H. Goad, *The Working of a Corporate State* (London: Nicholson and Watson, 1933); E. W. Polson Newman, *The New Ethiopia* (London: Rich and Cowan, 1938); H. Goad, *What is Fascism? An Explanation of its Essential Principles* (Florence: Italian Mail and Tribune, 1929) and *The Making of the Corporate State: A Study of Fascist Development* (London: Christophers, 1932). See C. Baldoli, *Exporting Fascism: Italian Fascists and Britain's Italians in the 1930s* (Oxford and New York: Berg, 2003), chapter 4.

8 The Locarno Treaty of 1925, signed by Germany, France, Britain, Italy and Belgium, confirmed, among other things, the post-war territorial settlement in Western Europe decided at Versailles in 1919.

9 See for example 'The Stresa conference', *Bulletin of International News*, 11 (21), 18 April 1935; 'Italy and Ethiopia', ibid., 12 (2), 27 July 1935; 'Italy's economic position', ibid., 12 (4), 31 August 1935.

10 J. E. Wrench, *Francis Yates-Brown, 1886–1944* (London: Eyre and Spottiswoode, 1948), p. 120.

11 C. Petrie, *Monarchy in the Twentieth Century* (London: Dakers, 1952), and *The Modern British Monarchy* (London: Eyre and Spottiswoode, 1955).

12 J. Pollard, '"Clerical-Fascism": Context, overview and conclusion', *Totalitarian Movements and Political Religions*, 8 (2), 2007, 433–46.

13 For a short but reasoned appraisal of the relationship between the Catholic Church and Fascism, see A. Kelikian, 'The Church and Catholicism', in *Liberal and Fascist Italy*, ed. A. Lyttelton (Oxford: Oxford University Press, 2002), pp. 57–61.

14 J. S. Barnes, *Fascism and the International Centre of Fascist Studies*, CINEF (Centre International d'Études sur le Fascisme), unpublished typescript (Lausanne, 1929), p. 3.

15 On Sir John Strachey see T. H. S. Escott (ed.), *Pillars of the Empire: Sketches of Living Indian and Colonial Statesmen, Celebrities, and Officials* (London: Chapman and Hall, 1879), pp. 308–15.

16 Barnes, *Promemoria*, 1947, in ACS, Archivi di famiglie e persone, James Strachey Barnes, b. 1, fasc. 1: 'Appunti vari su filosofi/filosofie politiche'.

17 Barnes, unpublished manuscript of 'Life Made Whole', p. 2, in ACS, Archivi di famiglie e persone, James Strachey Barnes, b. 4.

18 Ibid., p. 9.

19 D. Bradshaw and J. Smith, 'Ezra Pound, James Strachey Barnes ("The Italian Lord Haw-Haw") and Italian Fascism', *Review of English Studies*, 64 (266), 2013, 672–93.

20   Named the 'suicide club' in Barnes, *Half a Life* (London: Eyre &
      Spottiswoode, 1933), p. 131.

21   Barnes, *Diary of 1913*, in ACS, Archivi di famiglie e persone, James
      Strachey Barnes, b. 4, 13 August 1913, p. 2.

22   Ibid., 5 October 1913 (no page number).

23   Barnes, *Life Made Whole*. See also details of Barnes's life in Mancini, *Le
      carte del maggiore James Strachey Barnes*.

24   ACS, Archivi di famiglie e persone, James Strachey Barnes, b. 2, fasc. A,
      Harold Nicolson to Barnes, 10 September 1931. Having left the Labour
      Party, Oswald Mosley founded the New Party in 1931. The Party's
      participation in the elections at the end of October of that year resulted in
      failure, and in 1932 Mosley founded the British Union of Fascists.

25   See L. Villari, *The Awakening of Italy: The Fascista Regeneration* (London:
      Methuen, 1924) and *The Fascist Experiment* (London: Faber & Gwyer,
      1926). The distinguished professor of history and anti-Fascist activist
      Gaetano Salvemini spent most of his time as an exile in the United States,
      writing extensively on Italian Fascism, and occasionally replied to Villari's
      publications, denouncing the falsehood of many of his allegations and
      producing evidence to the contrary; see, among his many works, *The Fascist
      Dictatorship in Italy* (New York: H. Holt, 1927).

26   Camillo Pellizzi was one of the regime's most prominent intellectuals,
      journalist and author of many books on the doctrine of Fascism. Member
      of the *Fasci* since 1921, he was founder of the London *Fascio* and
      representative of the *Fasci* in Britain and Ireland, 1925–38. From 1920
      to 1938 he was Lecturer of Italian at University College London. From
      1940 until the fall of the regime in 1943 he was president of the National
      Institute of Fascist Culture. On Pellizzi see D. Breschi and G. Longo,
      Camillo Pellizzi. La ricerca delle elites tra politica e sociologia, 1896–1979
      (Soveria Mannelli: Rubbettino, 2003); R. Suzzi Valli, 'Il fascio italiano
      a Londra. L'attività politica di Camillo Pellizzi', *Storia contemporanea*,
      6, 1995, 957–1001; A. J. Gregor, *Mussolini's Intellectuals: Fascist Social
      and Political Thought* (Princeton, NJ: Princeton University Press, 2006),
      pp. 165–90. On his papers and publications, see *L'archivio Pellizzi: il
      percorso di un intellettuale tra fascismo e Repubblica*, (ed.) L. Petese (Rome:
      Fondazione Ugo Spirito, 2003).

27   Throughout the 1930s, it was mainly to Pellizzi that Barnes wrote in order
      to receive help in getting his books published or reviewed in Italy. It is
      evident from Barnes's letters that he held Pellizzi in high esteem. The two
      met regularly both in Italy and in London, whenever Barnes travelled there.
      See Barnes's letters to Pellizzi in Fondazione Ugo Spirito, Rome, Archivio
      Storico, Fondo Pellizzi, Serie V, especially b. 33, fasc. 67, and b. 30, fasc.
      56.

28   See especially Pellizzi, *Problemi e realtà del fascismo* (Florence: Vallecchi,
      1924); Breschi and Longo, *Camillo Pellizzi*, pp. 55–6.

29   Barnes, *The Universal Aspects of Fascism* (London: Williams and Norgate,
      1928), p. 63.

30 On Giovanni Gentile see *Diary 1943*, note 145, p. 206.

31 G. Turi, *Giovanni Gentile. Una biografia* (Florence: Giunti, 1995), p. 408.

32 Barnes, *Fascism and the International Centre of Fascist Studies*, p. 21.

33 E. Pound, 'The Fascist ideal', *The British-Italian Bulletin*, 18 April, 1936, p. 2.

34 Barnes, *Fascism and the International Centre of Fascist Studies*, p. 22. 'Prescinding' is Barnes's version in English of the Italian 'prescindere', which means 'aside from'.

35 Barnes, *The Universal Aspects of Fascism*, pp. 48–56; 63.

36 Barnes, *Promemoria*.

37 See L. Grassi, review of Barnes, *The Universal Aspects of Fascism*, in *Educazione Fascista*, 6 (9), September 1928, 554–9.

38 H. Goad, 'Italy's proud poverty', *The British-Italian Bulletin*, 8 November 1935.

39 E. Pound, 'A keystone of Europe', *The British-Italian Bulletin*, 27 December 1935.

40 O. Sitwell, 'Alma mater', *The British-Italian Bulletin*, 3 January 1936.

41 Barnes, *Promemoria*.

42 On Barnes's articles for *Social Justice* see P. Jackson, 'James Strachey Barnes and the Fascist Revolution: Catholicism, Anti-Semitism and the International New Order', in *Modernism, Christianity, and Apocalypse,* (eds) E. Tonning, M. Feldman and D. Addyman (Leiden: Brill Academic Publishers, 2014).

43 Barnes, *Io amo l'Italia. Memorie di un giornalista inglese,* translation of *Half a Life Left* (1937) by F. Caddeo (Milan: Garzanti, 1939), foreword to the Italian edition. Journalist Mario Bassi wrote a detailed and enthusiastic review in the Italian daily *La Stampa*: 'Un inglese d'eccezione e il suo libro di fede' (1 January 1940, p. 3).

44 ACS, Ministero della Cultura Popolare, 'Reports (1922–45)', n. 75. Head of the First Division to the Inspector of Radio Broadcasting, Ministero della Cultura Popolare, Ispettorato per la Radio Diffusione e per la Televisione, British section, 26 April 1942. On the Ministry of Popular Culture, and more generally on the organization of culture during the Fascist regime, see M. Isnenghi, *Intellettuali militanti e intellettuali funzionari. Appunti sulla cultura fascista* (Turin: Einaudi, 1979); G. Turi, *Lo stato educatore. Politica e intellettuali nell'Italia fascista* (Rome and Bari: Laterza, 2002).

45 Except for the content of one radio programme, reported by Barnes in *Diary 1943*, 28 July, pp. 73–5.

46 The National Archives, Kew (TNA), WO 204/12841. Headquarters Allied Commission, Public Safety Sub Commission, Security Division, to Rome Allied Area Command, 26 January 1945.

47 TNA, WO 204/12841. 'Major Jim Barnes, British Renegade', report by J. Martin, Sgt., 29 September 1944. On Joyce's programmes from Germany, see M. Kenny, *Germany Calling: A Personal Biography of William Joyce,*

'Lord Haw-Haw' (Dublin: New Island, 2003), pp. 151–60; P. Martland, *Lord Haw Haw: The English Voice of Nazi Germany* (Richmond, Surrey: National Archives, 2003), pp. 43–7, 134–5, 172–8.

48   Considering that the average annual salary of an industrial worker was around 4,000 lire, and that of a white-collar worker around 12,000 lire, 33,000 lire was a substantial sum of money. On these aspects of daily life during Fascism, see G. F. Venè, *Mille lire al mese. Vita quotidiana della famiglia nell'Italia fascista* (Milan: Mondadori, 1988).

49   TNA, WO 204/12841. Headquarters Allied Commission, Public Safety Sub Commission, Security Division, to Rome Allied Area Command, 26 January 1945.

50   See S. Colarizi, *L'opinione degli italiani sotto il regime, 1929–1943* (Rome and Bari: Laterza, 1991); G. Rochat, *Le guerre italiane, 1935–1943. Dall'impero d'Etiopia alla disfatta* (Turin: Einaudi, 2005); N. Labanca (ed.), *I bombardamenti aerei e l'Italia nella Seconda Guerra Mondiale* (Bologna: Il Mulino, 2012).

51   M. Fincardi, 'Il fronte interno', in *Gli italiani in guerra. Conflitti, identità, memorie dal Risorgimento ai nostri giorni*, vol. 4, (eds) G. Albanese and M. Isnenghi (Turin: UTET, 2009), pp. 141–8.

52   See, among the files on the bombing of Italy held by the National Archives, 'An appreciation of the employment of bomber forces to carry out heavy scale attacks against objectives in Italy', from Bomber Command to the Chief of the Air Staff, 13 November 1942, TNA, AIR 8–777. See also C. Baldoli and A. Knapp, *Forgotten Blitzes: France and Italy under Allied Air Attack, 1940–1945* (London: Continuum, 2012), pp. 19–22.

53   G. Rochat, *Le guerre italiane*, pp. 239–44; M. Knox, *Hitler's Italian Allies: Royal Armed Forces, Fascist Regime, and the War of 1940–43* (Cambridge: Cambridge University Press, 2000), especially chapter 4; J. Gooch, *Mussolini and His Generals: The Armed Forces and Fascist Foreign Policy, 1922–1940* (Cambridge: Cambridge University Press, 2007), especially chapter 8.

54   Barnes, *Diary 1943*, 1 January, p. 30.

55   Ibid.

56   In October 1922 about 50,000 Fascists marched on Rome from all over Italy, while thousands were simultaneously taking power in a number of provinces, occupying local sites of power, seizing weapons and destroying the headquarters of the anti-Fascist press and parties. Some 50 people were killed during the days that led to the final march on the capital on 28 October. Illegal acts, violence and intimidation were also made possible by the limited intervention by the police. The request to King Victor Emmanuel III from the liberal Prime Minister Luigi Facta to declare a state of siege was rejected; instead, the King declared Mussolini to be the new Prime Minister. Hence the march never turned into a revolution, although it was often described as such by Fascist propaganda during the regime. For a recent assessment of the March on Rome see G. Albanese, *La Marcia su Roma* (Rome and Bari: Laterza, 2006) and 'Reconsidering the March on

Rome', *European History Quarterly*, 42 (3), 2012, 403–21; E. Gentile, *E fu subito regime. Il fascismo e la Marcia su Roma* (Rome and Bari: Laterza, 2012).

57　As he observed as early as 1 January 1943 (*Diary 1943*, p. 31).

58　See especially Pellizzi, *Fascismo-aristocrazia* (Milan: Alpes, 1925). D. D. Roberts, 'Myth, style, substance and the totalitarian dynamic in Fascist Italy', *Contemporary European History*, 16 (1), 2007, 20; R. Griffin, *Modernism and Fascism: The Sense of a Beginning under Mussolini and Hitler* (Basingstoke: Palgrave, 2007), p. 1, p. 4.

59　See, for example, his comparison between Rome and Florence after the first bombing of the capital, *Diary 1943*, 20 July, p. 71.

60　Lojacono was the author, among other books, of a volume on Fascism in the world (*Il Fascismo nel mondo*, Rome: L'Economia Italiana, 1933).

61　*Diary 1943*, 15 May, p. 62. On Franco's Spain see *Diary 1943*, note 106, pp. 203–4.

62　ACS, Archivi di famiglie e persone, James Strachey Barnes, b. 1, fasc. 4/1.

63　The experience of that generation of university students was brilliantly narrated by R. Zangrandi, *Il lungo viaggio attraverso il fascismo. Contributo alla storia di una generazione* (Turin: Einaudi, 1948).

64　E. Gentile, *La grande Italia. Ascesa e declino del mito della nazione nel ventesimo secolo* (Milan: Mondadori, 1997), p. 194.

65　*Diary 1943*, 22 May, p. 65.

66　*Diary 1943*, 4 July, p. 68.

67　N. Gallerano, 'L'arrivo degli alleati', in *I luoghi della memoria: Strutture ed eventi dell'Italia unita*, (ed.) M. Isnenghi (Rome and Bari: Laterza, 1997), p. 459.

68　C. Pavone, *Una guerra civile. Saggio storico sulla moralità nella resistenza* (Turin: Bollati Borighieri, 1991), pp. 190–1.

69　*Diary 1943*, 11 July, p. 69.

70　M. G. Pasqualini, 'I bombardamenti sulle città italiane', in *L'Italia in guerra. Il quarto anno – 1943*, (ed.) R. H. Rainero (Gaeta: Stabilimento Grafico Militare, 1994), p. 267; see also P. Monelli, *Roma 1943* (Rome: Miglioresi, 1943).

71　ACS, Ministero dell'Interno, Direzione Generale Pubblica Sicurezza, IIGM, A5G, b. 62, 'Pro Memoria da parte del commissariato di Borgo', 22 October 1940.

72　M. Carli and U. Gentiloni Silveri, *Bombardare Roma. Gli Alleati e la 'città aperta' (1940–1944)* (Bologna: Il Mulino, 2007), pp. 9–17; C. Baldoli, 'Bombing the eternal city: The Allies and Rome in the Second World War', *History Today*, May 2012, 10–15.

73　*Diary 1943*, 20 July, p. 69.

74　On the meaning of that event in Italian history, see M. Franzinelli, 'Il 25 luglio', in *I Luoghi della memoria: Personaggi e date dell'Italia unita*, (ed.) M. Isnenghi (Rome and Bari: Laterza, 1997), pp. 217–40.

75   Marshal since 1926, Pietro Badoglio was made Governor of Tripolitania
      and Cyrenaica in 1928, with the task of suppressing the long-term Libyan
      resistance to Italian rule there. By 1930, having authorized the deportation
      of 100,000 people from Cyrenaica into concentration camps, which
      caused the death of 40,000 Libyans, he proclaimed to have succeeded in
      his mission (A. Del Boca, *Mohamed Fekini and the Fight to Free Libya*,
      Basingstoke: Palgrave, 2011, p. 134). Commander of the Italian army in the
      Ethiopian campaign, Badoglio was responsible for the use of mustard-gas
      bombs to quell Ethiopian resistance (A. Del Boca, *I gas di Mussolini. Il
      fascismo e la guerra d'Etiopia*, Rome: Editori Riuniti, 1996, pp. 141–2).
      From May 1925 to December 1940 he was Chief of Staff of the Italian
      army. Badoglio was Prime Minister of Italy from the fall of Mussolini until
      the armistice in 1943, and subsequently of the Kingdom of the South (under
      Allied control) until the liberation of Rome in June 1944. After the Second
      World War, Badoglio's name appeared in the League of Nations' list of war
      criminals, but he was never brought to trial. For a biography of Badoglio,
      see G. De Luna, *Badoglio. Un militare al potere* (Milan: Bompiani, 1974).

76   *Diary 1943*, 26 July, p. 73.

77   *Diary 1943*, 28 July, p. 75. On the cult of Mussolini at the time of his
      fall, see C. Duggan, *Fascist Voices: An Intimate History of Mussolini's
      Italy* (Oxford: Oxford University Press, 2013), chapters 12 and 13; A. M.
      Imbriani, *Gli italiani e il Duce. Il mito e l'immagine di Mussolini negli ultimi
      anni del fascismo, 1938–1943* (Naples: Liguori, 1992), chapters 5 and 6.

78   *Diary 1943*, 28 July, pp. 75–6.

79   *Diary 1943*, 7 August, p. 83.

80   In October 1917 the Italian army was defeated at Caporetto (in present-day
      Slovenia) by the Austro-Hungarian forces, which broke into north-eastern
      Italy up to the River Piave. Italian losses were huge, and many soldiers
      deserted in what looked like a military strike. However, in June 1918, the
      Italian army obtained a decisive victory on the River Piave.

81   *Diary 1943*, 19 August, p. 89.

82   *Diary 1943*, 23 August, p. 90.

83   On the armistice see *Diary 1943*, note 220, p. 212.

84   In particular E. Galli Della Loggia, *La morte della patria: la crisi dell'idea di
      nazione tra Resistenza, antifascismo e Repubblica* (first edn, Rome and Bari:
      Laterza, 1996).

85   C. Mazzantini, *A cercar la bella morte* (Venice: Marsilio, 1995), p. 21.

86   *Diary 1943*, 7 September, p. 96.

87   *Diary 1943*, p. 97.

88   *Diary 1943*, 25 and 28 September, p. 110.

89   *Diary 1943*, 11 September, p. 102.

90   The years between the armistice and the liberation of Italy have been
      described by historians (for some time controversially) as a period of civil
      war, as a result of the growth of an organized anti-Fascist partisan resistance
      that pitched Italians against Italians. For a critical discussion of the concept,

see M. Legnani and F. Vendramini (eds), *Guerra, guerra di liberazione e guerra civile* (Milan: Franco Angeli, 1990).

91   R. De Felice, *Rosso e nero* (Milan: Baldini e Castoldi, 1995) and *Mussolini l'alleato, 1940–1945*, vol. 2: *La guerra civile, 1943–1945* (Turin: Einaudi, 1997); for a critical assessment of this historiography see especially E. Collotti and L. Klinkhammer, *Il fascismo e l'Italia in guerra. Una conversazione fra storia e storiografia* (Rome: Ediesse, 1996).

92   Although central Italy had not been attacked until the spring of 1943, in the following 15 months it was the most bombed part of the country (M. Gioannini and G. Massobrio, *Bombardate l'Italia. Storia della guerra di distruzione aerea 1940–1945*, Milan: Rizzoli, 2007, p. 11).

93   Rodolfo Graziani was a general of the Italian army, well known for his murderous repression of both the Libyan (1921–31) and the Ethiopian (1935–7) civilian populations (see G. Rochat, *Guerre italiane in Libia e in Etiopia. Studi militari, 1921–1939*, Treviso: Pagus, 1991; A. Del Boca, *Mohamed Fekini*). While Governor of Libya, he was defeated by the British Commonwealth armies in 1940–1 (Rochat, *Le guerre italiane, 1935–1943*, pp. 294–8). He became War Minister during the Salò Republic, when he promulgated a deposition which condemned to death partisans and deserters (F. Deakin, *Storia della Repubblica di Salò*, Turin: Einaudi, 1963, pp. 670–1). Alessandro Pavolini was Mussolini's Minister of Popular Culture from 1939. During the Salò Republic he became Secretary of the Republican Fascist Party. He was shot with Mussolini on 28 April 1945 and his body hanged upside down in Piazzale Loreto in Milan with the corpses of Mussolini, his mistress Claretta Petacci, the Republic's Minister of Interior Paolo Zerbino, and the former Secretary of the Fascist Party (1931–9) Achille Starace (M. Missori, *Gerarchie e statuti del PNF*, Rome: Bonacci, 1986, p. 254; F. Snowden, 'Pavolini', in *Dizionario del Fascismo*, vol. 2, (eds), V. De Grazia and S. Luzzatto, Turin: Einaudi, 2003, pp. 351–4).

94   *Diary 1944*, 1 January, pp. 129–30.

95   *Diary 1944*, 7 June, p. 140.

96   J. Goebbels, *Diario intimo* (Milan: Mondadori, 1948), p. 547.

97   M. Michaelis, 'Mussolini's unofficial mouthpiece: Telesio Interlandi – Il Tevere and the evolution of Mussolini's anti-semitism', *Journal of Modern Italian Studies*, 3 (3), 1998, 217–40.

98   C. M. Bettin, *Italian Jews from Emancipation to the Racial Laws* (Basingstoke: Palgrave, 2010), pp. 26–7.

99   The victims of the Shoah in Italy were 8,529. See F. Levi, 'The Shoah in Italy: Its History and Characteristics', *Jews in Italy under Fascist and Nazi Rule, 1922–1945*, (ed.) J. D. Zimmerman (Cambridge: Cambridge University Press, 2005), p. 219.

100   See for example R. Farinacci, *Realtà storiche* (Cremona: Cremona Nuova, 1939), p. 8.

101   M. Isnenghi, 'Parole e immagini dell'ultimo fascismo', in *1943–45. L'immagine della Repubblica Sociale Italiana nella propaganda*, (ed.) Fondazione Luigi Micheletti (Milan: Mazzotta, 1985), p. 34.

102 Barnes, *Promemoria*.

103 An anthology of *Crociata Italica* (held in the Cremona civic library) has been published in A. Dordoni, *Crociata Italica: Fascismo e religione nella Repubblica ai Salò* (Milan: Sugarco, 1976).

104 ACS, Archivi di famiglie e persone, James Strachey Barnes, b. 3, fasc. S. Statement by prefect Alessandro Varino, General Secretary of the President of the Republic, Rome, no date.

105 ACS, Archivi di famiglie e persone, James Strachey Barnes, b. 1, fasc. 4/1. Postcard from Sister Annunziata, convent of Adorazione, Rome, to Buona Guidotti Barnes, Meran, 8 November 1945.

106 *Diary 1944*, 12 January, p. 132.

107 *Diary 1945*, 19 March, p. 169.

108 S. Luzzatto, *The Body of Il Duce: Mussolini's Corpse and the Fortunes of Italy* (New York: Metropolitan Books, 2005), pp. 10–11.

109 *Diary 1945*, 3 May, p. 184.

110 Barnes, *Life Made Whole*, p. 127.

111 TNA, FO 371/24965/76904. Foreign Office to Home Office and War Office, 15 June 1940, cited in Mancini, *Le carte del maggiore James Strachey Barnes*, p. 36.

112 TNA, WO 204/12841. Security Report n. 2, typed memo, undated and unsigned, but from Allied Headquarters in Rome in July 1944.

113 Ibid.

114 TNA, WO 204/12841. Allied Headquarters in Rome, 27 November 1944.

115 TNA, WO 204/12841. 'Promemoria', typed memo from the *Questura* of Rome, 17 August 1945, and Allied Force Headquarters to Personnel Section, PWB, 19 August 1945.

116 TNA, WO 204/12841. 'Major "Jim" Barnes', typed letter, unsigned and undated but with reference to February 1946.

117 TNA, WO 204/12841. 'Further interrogation report on Barnes Buona', signed by R. Tattersall, Capt., 30 September 1946.

118 TNA, WO 204/12841. 'Major Barnes J. S.', Rome Area Allied Command to Major P. H. Montague, 24 May and 22 July 1947.

119 Mancini, *Le carte del maggiore James Strachey Barnes*, p. 47.

120 Ibid., p. 48.

121 Barnes, *Giustizia sociale attraverso la riforma monetaria* (Venice: Ministero della Cultura Popolare, 1944).

122 *Introduzione* to Barnes, *Giustizia Sociale* (Società Editrice Barbarossa, http://www.signoraggio.com/signoraggio_libro_giustiziasociale.html, last accessed 29 September 2013), p. 8.

123 As defined in the title of M. Tarchi's book *Esuli in patria. I fascisti nell'Italia repubblicana* (Parma: Guanda, 1995).

124 See the work by F. Germinario, in particular *L'altra memoria. L'estrema destra, Salò e la Resistenza* (Turin: Bollati Boringhieri, 1999) and *Estranei*

alla democrazia. Negazionismo e antisemitismo nella destra radicale (Pisa: Biblioteca Franco Serantini, 2001).

Diary 1943

1 Between June 1941 and October 1943, Turkey delivered raw materials to Germany, but remained neutral. In August 1944 it began to move towards the Allied side, but only in February 1945 did it declare war on Germany and Japan. Romania and Bulgaria were allied with Germany during the Second World War. See also *Diary 1944*, note 70, p. 222.

2 At the beginning of January 1943 the Soviet Army advanced along the line of the Don, from Stalingrad towards Rostov.

3 Japan had occupied the Solomon Islands between January and March 1942. However, after a long campaign, by February 1943 the Allies conquered the strategically important island of Guadalcanal, hindering the Japanese attempt to invade Australia.

4 Chinese politician Wang Jingwei established a Japanese-supported collaborationist government in Nanjing in March 1940, which declared war on the Allies in early January 1943. Hideki Tojo was Japan's Prime Minister between October 1941 and July 1944. Nationalist politician and military leader Chiang Kai-shek led China during the Second World War campaign against Japan.

5 This section is followed by a single line.

6 The advance of the Axis troops in Egypt was halted at El Alamein between October and November 1942. As a reaction to the Allied landings in Morocco and Algeria on 8 November, Germany invaded Vichy France and sent troops to Tunisia. In the meantime, Rommel withdrew the remaining troops in Cyrenaica and Tripolitania. Tripoli was finally abandoned on 23 January 1943, signalling the end of the Italian Fascist empire. G. Rochat, *Le guerre italiane, 1935–1943. Dall'impero d'Etiopia alla disfatta* (Turin: Einaudi, 2005), pp. 335–59.

7 When the Second World War broke out, Italy opted for a status of non-belligerence, due to the knowledge, shared by Mussolini and by the commanders of the three armed forces, that the country was not ready to take part in a long conflict. In April 1940, only two months before Italy's entry into the war, Marshal Badoglio informed Mussolini that Italy's preparation was at 40 per cent – that percentage was not related to any specific hypothesis of conflict, but revealed the state of crisis of the armed forces. See also Introduction, p. 12 and note 53.

8 Italian independence from the Austrian-Hungarian Empire was obtained through three wars, in 1848, in 1859 and in 1866. However, by the time of the outbreak of the First World War, parts of north-east Italy (the areas of the Trentino and Trieste) were still under Austria, and currents of the interventionist movement interpreted the Great War as the fourth war of Italian independence. Barnes's description of the Second World War as the

fifth war of Italian independence was unlikely to be shared by the majority of the population by 1943, also because the 'traditional' enemy of Italian independence (Austria in 1848–66, Germany and Austria in 1914–18) was now officially Italy's ally.

9   Italianized word: *potenziare* means 'to strengthen'.

10 On the March on Rome, see Introduction, note 56, p. 191.

11 This was allegedly a sentence uttered in 1849–52 by Liberal Prime Minister of Piedmont Massimo D'Azeglio, rather than by Camillo Benso Count of Cavour, the Piedmontese Prime Minister and principal architect of the Italian unification between 1852 and 1860.

12 Italianized word: *radicato* means rooted.

13 On Barnes's anti-Semitism, see Introduction, pp. 19–20.

14 Ministry of Popular Culture. On the value of the lira at that time, see Introduction, note 48, p. 191.

15 Italianized word ('registrare'). Here Barnes means 'recorded'.

16 Alessandro Tasca di Cutò was the son of the homonymous Sicilian prince, well known for being a Socialist sympathizer, who died in 1943. Unlike his father, he was a pro-Fascist, and worked with Barnes and Ezra Pound broadcasting anti-Allied programmes on the Italian radio. Prof Giuseppe Morelli was a journalist and a lawyer, later President of the Court during the Salò Republic. Prince Ranieri di San Faustino was a Roman aristocrat who worked for the Ministry of Popular Culture in close contact with Barnes and Pound.

17 'Dowry'.

18 Camilla Pasolini Altieri was a Roman countess, member of a noble family from the Marche with traditional links with the Vatican (*Indice biografico italiano*, (ed.) T. Nappo, Munich: Saur, 2002; 3rd edn, vol. 8, p. 2659).

19 This section is followed by a double line.

20 The *squadristi* were the 'first hour' Fascists, who took part in violent actions against political rivals in the 1919–22 period. For an overview of the movement see M. Franzinelli, *Squadristi. Protagonisti e tecniche della violenza fascista, 1919–1922* (Milan: Mondadori, 2003).

21 Ala Littoria was the state-owned Italian airline company, founded by Mussolini in 1934.

22 The EIAR (*Ente Italiano per le Audizioni Radiofoniche*), created in 1927, was the Italian broadcasting corporation during Fascism. See F. Monteleone, *Storia della radio e della televisione in Italia. Società, politica, strategia, programmi 1922–1992* (Venice: Marsilio, 1992), chapter 2.

23 The Foro Mussolini (now Foro Italico) is an athletic centre in Rome opened in 1932. On its importance, both architectural and in terms of education of the Fascist youth in the 1930s, see S. Martin, *Sport Italia: The Italian Love Affair with Sport* (London: I. B. Tauris, 2011), chapter 3; B. Painter, *Mussolini's Rome: Rebuilding the Eternal City* (Basingstoke: Palgrave, 2005), chapter 3. The G.I.L. (*Gioventù Italiana del Littorio* – 'Italian Youth of the Lictors') was a Fascist Party organization devoted to the education

of young Italians. On the Party organization of youth see T. Koon, *Believe, Obey, Fight: The Political Socialization of Youth in Fascist Italy* (Chapel Hill, NC: University of North Carolina Press, 1985), pp. 90–107.

24   On Camillo Pellizzi, see Introduction, pp. 6, 12–13 and notes 26, 27, 28, 58.

25   On Luigi (nicknamed Gino by Barnes) Villari, see Introduction, pp. 1, 6 and note 25.

26   Marquis Vittorio Spreti, of a noble family from Ravenna, was a historian and literary critic, and the author of a multi-volume encyclopaedia of the Italian nobility published between 1928 and 1936 (*Indice biografico*, vol. 10, p. 3302).

27   The British troops occupied Tripoli on the following day. Italo Balbo (1896–1940) was a pilot, reorganizer of the air forces, Air Minister between 1929 and 1933, and then Governor of Libya. Balbo promoted the idea of modernity of the Italian air forces with his successful transatlantic flights and through clever use of propaganda in the press and schools, and created one of the most popular Fascist myths. His plane was shot down by mistake by Italian anti-aircraft in Tobruk in Libya on 28 June 1940. See his biography by G. Rochat, *Italo Balbo: lo squadrista, l'aviatore, il gerarca* (Turin: Utet, 1986; 2003).

28   By 20 January the Soviet offensive had progressed through the entire front from Voronež to the Caucasus.

29   Privy Chamberlains of Cape and Sword were created in the sixteenth century and chosen among the nobility as lay servants of the Popes. By Barnes's times, they could attend ceremonies of the Papal court.

30   *Ministero dell'Educazione Nazionale*, Ministry of National Education.

31   Giuseppe Bottai was one of the founders of the Fascist movement in 1919, participated in the March on Rome, and founded the Fascist journal *Critica Fascista* in 1923. He was Minister of Corporations in 1929–32, and Minister of National Education in 1936–43. At the Grand Council meeting of 24 July 1943 he voted in favour of Grandi's motion that brought to Mussolini's dismissal. He was consequently condemned to death *in absentia* in January 1944 at the trial of Verona against the members of the Fascist Grand Council who had 'betrayed' Mussolini. See *Giuseppe Bottai e 'Critica Fascista'*, (eds) G. De Rosa and F. Malgeri (S. Giovanni Valdarno: Landi, 1980); A. De Grand, *Bottai e la cultura fascista* (Rome and Bari: Laterza, 1978).

32   In January 1943 the war between Allies and Axis in Africa centred around the mountainous area south of Tunis, which was finally conquered by the Allies on 13 May. Allied bombers (in particular the 9th and 12th USAAF from the end of 1942 to the end of 1943) used North African bases to attack Italy.

33   Alessandro Pavolini was the Minister of Popular Culture from 1939. During the Salò Republic he became Secretary of the Republican Fascist Party. He was shot with Mussolini on 28 April 1945 and his body hanged upside down in Piazzale Loreto in Milan with the corpses of the Duce, his mistress Claretta Petacci, the Republic's Minister of Interior Paolo Zerbino, and the

former Secretary of the Fascist Party (1931–9) Achille Starace (M. Missori, *Gerarchie e statuti del PNF*, Rome: Bonacci, 1986, p. 254; F. Snowden, 'Pavolini', in *Dizionario del Fascismo*, vol. 2, (eds) V. De Grazia and S. Luzzatto, Turin: Einaudi, 2003, pp. 351–4).

34   Ettore Cipolla was a Sicilian magistrate. He contributed to the law journal *Rivista Penale* and was made Senator in 1939.

35   A blue arrow is inserted here, at right hand margin of the page.

36   Nicola De Cesare was Mussolini's private secretary from 1941 to 1943.

37   Barnes's wife, Buona.

38   Names of Italian sweets.

39   Italian soft cheese.

40   Palestrina is a town in the countryside south-west of Rome, near the wine-growing area of the Castelli Romani.

41   'Chess Club'.

42   Carmine Senise was the Head of Italian Police from 1940 until April 1943, when Mussolini, following the strikes in the factories of Turin, replaced him with Lorenzo Chierici. Under the government of Marshal Badoglio he returned to his position until he was arrested by the SS in Rome in September 1943. Senise wrote an autobiography, *Quando ero capo della polizia, 1940–1943* (Rome: Ruffolo, 1946). On the Italian police during the regime see J. Dunnage, *Mussolini's Policemen: Behaviour, Ideology and Institutional Culture in Representation and Practice* (Manchester: Manchester University Press, 2013).

43   This section is followed by a single line.

44   Waiting room.

45   Treasury.

46   *Ministero dell'Educazione Nazionale*, Ministry of National Education.

47   Ministry of Popular Culture.

48   Ministry of National Education.

49   Italianized word: 'iscrizione' means 'enrolment'.

50   Guido Buffarini Guidi was under-secretary of the Ministry of the Interior between 1933 and 1943. At the Grand Council meeting of 24 July 1943 he voted against Grandi's motion, and became Minister of the Interior during the Salò Republic. He was condemned to death by the extraordinary High Court of Milan in May 1945, and in July he was executed (Missori, *Gerarchie*, p. 179). On the vote at the Grand Council, see Introduction, p. 14 and note 5.

51   'Roman step' and 'Lament beyond the sea'.

52   'Axis on the march'.

53   The first name is illegible. It seems to be a female name, perhaps related to Paolo Ignazio Maria Thaon di Ravel, Minister of Finance between January 1935 and February 1943.

54   A Medieval Benedictine abbey in the province of Rieti, north of Rome.

55   'Lucky them'.

56   Cardinal Giovanni Battista Montini was one of the closest collaborators of
      Pope Pius XII. On the Vatican during the Second World War see F. Malgeri,
      La Chiesa italiana e la Guerra (1940–1945) (Rome: Studium, 1980); P. Blet,
      *Pius XII and the Second World War According to the Archives of the
      Vatican* (Hereford: Gracewing, 1999).

57   The Battle of Stalingrad, which had begun in the summer of 1942,
      ended with Soviet victory on 2 February 1943. Following Stalingrad,
      by mid-February the Allies conquered Rostov and Kharkov; however, a
      German counter-attack followed, which brought the Wehrmacht back to
      Kharkov on 12 March.

58   At the Casablanca Conference in January 1943 the Allies planned their
      strategy over the war in the Mediterranean.

59   This section is followed by a single line.

60   Giuseppe Bastianini was Ambassador to London in 1939–40 and foreign
      affairs under-secretary both in 1936–9 and from February to July 1943.
      Giacomo Acerbo was Minister of Agriculture in 1929–35, and Minister of
      Finance between February and July 1943. See Missori, *Gerarchie*, pp. 168,
      158.

61   Galeazzo Ciano was Mussolini's son-in-law, and Foreign Minister between
      June 1936 and February 1943, when, following his attempt at persuading
      Mussolini and the Chiefs of Staff about the need for a negotiated peace,
      he was made Ambassador to the Vatican until the fall of the regime.
      At the meeting of the Fascist Grand Council on 24 July 1943 he voted
      in favour of Grandi's motion for the destitution of Mussolini. He was
      condemned to death and executed at the Verona trial (see *Diary 1944*,
      note 7, p. 218). For a biography of Ciano, see R. Moseley, *Mussolini's
      Shadow: The Double Life of Count Galeazzo Ciano* (New Haven, CT,
      and London: Yale University Press, 1999); *The Ciano Diaries, 1939–1943:
      The Complete, Unabridged Diaries of Count Galeazzo Ciano, Italian
      Minister for Foreign Affairs, 1936–1943*, (ed.) H. Gibson (Garden City,
      NY: Doubleday, 1946).

62   On Dino Grandi, see Introduction, note 6, p. 187.

63   Gaetano Polverelli was the last Minister of Popular Culture of the Fascist
      regime, from February 1943, when he replaced Pavolini, until 25 July 1943.
      Although he voted against Mussolini's dismissal at the Grand Council of
      Fascism, he did not take part in the Salò Republic (Missori, *Gerarchie*,
      p. 261).

64   Ezio Maria Gray was a journalist, a 'first hour' Fascist, a commentator
      at the Italian radio (EIAR), president of the LUCE (film) institute, and a
      member of the Grand Council. He adhered to the Salò Republic as president
      of EIAR (Missori, *Gerarchie*, p. 221).

65   Gabriele Paresce worked for the Ministry of Popular Culture as director
      of radio broadcast and vice-director of foreign press. In 1944 he became
      director of Mussolini's press office.

66   Alberto De Stefani was Mussolini's first Finance Minister (1922–5), an

economic journalist and a member of the Grand Council of Fascism from 1932 (Missori, *Gerarchie*, p. 200).

67 Zenone Benini was Mussolini's Minister of Public Works from February to July 1943. He voted in favour of Grandi's motion at the Grand Council meeting of 24 July, and in November 1943 he gave himself up to the police; consequently, he was arrested and brought to trial at Verona, but was acquitted. He wrote a memoir of his time in prison in Verona, *Vigilia a Verona* (Milan: Garzanti, 1949 – recently republished as *Carcere degli scalzi*, Florence: Ponte alle grazie, 1994).

68 Carlo Alberto Biggini was Mussolini's Minister of National Education between February and July 1943. At the Grand Council meeting of 24 July he voted against Grandi's motion and in October he joined Mussolini at Salò. He continued his role as Minister of National Education during the Fascist Republic (Missori, *Gerarchie*, pp. 172–3).

69 Umberto Albini, after having served as a prefect in a number of Italian cities from 1925, became Undersecretary of the Ministry of the Interior on 6 February 1943 until the fall of the regime on 25 July (Missori, *Gerarchie*, p. 159). Carlo Tiengo was Minister of Corporations between February and April 1943, when he abandoned his political career because of illness (Missori, *Gerarchie*, p. 282).

70 Vittorio Ambrosio was chief of staff of the Italian armed forces between February and November 1943.

71 The papers.

72 Police headquarters.

73 Conservative politician William Maxwell Aitken was granted the title of Lord Beaverbrook by Lloyd George in 1918. In the 1930s he collaborated with the Italian Ambassador to London Dino Grandi towards improving Anglo-Italian relations. During the Second World War he was Minister for Aircraft Production (1940–41), of Supply (1941–2), of War Production (1942), and Lord Privy Seal (1943–5).

74 This section is followed by a single line.

75 This section is followed by a single line.

76 This section is followed by a single line.

77 This section is followed by a single line.

78 This section is followed by a single line.

79 This section is followed by a single line.

80 This section is followed by a single line.

81 On Barnes's sister, Mary Hutchinson, see Introduction, p. 1.

82 A lively and chatty woman.

83 Emilio Salgari was Italy's best-known writer of novels for children. He invented adventurous heroes like Sandokan or the Black Corsair, and set his fantastic stories in exotic countries (most notably Malesia), which he never visited, but the historical context of which he thoroughly studied.

84 A well-known boarding school in North Yorkshire.

85 This section is followed by a single line.

86 This section is followed by a single line.

87 Here Barnes merged a number of incidents together with a certain amount
    of chronological confusion. The Russian campaign in Finland (1939–40)
    resulted in disaster for the Red Army. Despite numerical superiority, the
    Russians lost 126,875 men in four months. By March 1940, Finland sued
    for armistice and surrendered some its territories to the USSR, but the
    Russian army was too exhausted to continue the war and conquer the
    whole country. Barnes is also making reference to the war on the Russian
    south-western front launched by Operation Barbarossa between June and
    September 1941. On the German counter-offensive at Kharkov, see above,
    note 57. The Far Eastern armies were important only in the defence of
    Moscow in December 1941 (R. Overy, *Russia's War*, London: Penguin,
    1998, pp. 55–7, 187).

88 The war in Africa was finally lost in May 1943, when, after the fall of
    Tunis and Biserta, the Axis surrendered. This provoked a harsh blow on
    Mussolini's prestige within Italy. After defeat in Africa, only a minority of
    Italians continued to believe in victory, as the Fascist police made evident
    in their reports to Mussolini from all over the country. See S. Colarizi,
    L'opinione degli italiani sotto il regime, 1929–1943 (Rome-Bari: Laterza,
    1991), chapter 7.

89 This section is followed by a single line.

90 Kharkov and Belgorod were on the south-western front, on one of the most
    disputed frontlines between June and November 1942, and again between
    March and July 1943. Orel was in the central front, where the Soviet army
    launched an offensive in July 1943. Kharkov, one of Russia's largest cities
    and capital of eastern Ukraine, was first conquered by Germany in October
    1941, and then lost on 16 February 1943, but recaptured on 15 March.
    Taganrog is near Rostov, on the southern front. Rostov on the Don was
    taken by the Germans in July 1942 and recaptured by the Russians at the
    beginning of February 1943.

91 On 12 March the British Foreign Secretary Anthony Eden arrived in
    Washington to discuss war and post-war problems, including the role of
    the United Nations after the war. He returned rather pessimistic from his
    meeting with Roosevelt, as issues of post-war foreign policy emphasized
    a clash between the aims of the two Allies when areas such as Russia
    and China were discussed. A. Eden, *The Reckoning: The Eden Memoirs*
    (London: Cassell, 1965), pp. 371–9.

92 This section is followed by a single line.

93 Barnes is referring to Churchill's speech broadcast on 21 March, which
    dealt with post-war plans and expressed the Prime Minister's conviction
    of the need for social reform, particularly in agriculture, public health,
    education, and unemployment. W. S. Churchill, *Onwards to Victory: War
    Speeches of the Right Hon. Winston S. Churchill, 1943* (London: Cassell,
    1944), pp. 32–45.

94 This section is followed by a single line.

95 Giovanni Messe was a general of the Italian army during the conquest of Ethiopia and of Albania. In February 1943 he was commander of the 1st army in Tunisia and distinguished himself by delaying the defeat of the Axis troops. For that reason, he was promoted to marshal in May 1943, shortly before he was made a prisoner. After the armistice he was liberated and became Chief of Staff of the Italian army, a position he kept until May 1945. Historian Giorgio Rochat described him as the only successful Italian commander in 1940–3 (Rochat, *L'esercito italiano in pace e in guerra. Studi di storia militare*, Milan: RARA, 1991, p. 255).

96 The Mareth line in southern Tunisia had been built as a safeguard against Italian aggression by the French before 1939. On 20–27 March 1943 it became theatre of a battle which ended in defeat for the German commander Erwin Rommel.

97 After the armistice of June 1940, Italy occupied the area of Nice, Mentone and the Alpine frontier. Following the German decision to extend the occupation of France to the whole country in November 1942, Italy occupied a larger area, from Toulon in the South to the region east of Lyon. By this time, Italy was also involved in the occupation of the Balkans, with military presence in most of Greece, Albania, Montenegro, Kosovo and parts of Croatia and Slovenia. See D. Rodogno, *Fascism's European Empire: Italian Occupation during the Second World War* (Cambridge: Cambridge University Press, 2006).

98 Careggi is a neighbourhood north of Florence.

99 This section is followed by a single line.

100 This section is followed by a single line.

101 Founded by Pope Pius IX in 1852, this was a college for English clergymen converted to Catholicism.

102 In April 1943 the Wehrmacht found the corpses of thousands of Polish war prisoners who had been murdered by the Soviet army after the invasion of Poland, between April and May 1940. Immediately Berlin radio turned this discovery into anti-Soviet, and consequently, anti-Allied propaganda. Only in 1990 did the Russian government admit the mass execution, which did not involve the shooting of 10,000 officers, as Barnes reported, but of more than 20,000 officers and civilians who had been taken as war prisoners into different camps. On this massacre see G. Sanford, *Katyn and the Soviet Massacre of 1940: Truth, Justice and Memory* (New York: Routledge, 2005).

103 Polish general Władisław Sikorsky was Prime Minister of the exiled Polish government following the German invasion of 1939. He collaborated with the Allies but was weary of Stalin's plans over Poland. He died in July 1943.

104 This section is followed by a single line.

105 This sentence is followed by a single line.

106 Although historians have long debated the extent to which Franco's Spain and Salazar's Portugal can be defined 'fascist regimes', Francisco Franco in Spain and Antonio Oliveira Salazar in Portugal gave rise to dictatorships that shared aspects with Italian Fascism. Influenced by Italian Fascism from

the start, these two regimes developed what historians have called forms of 'Catholic Fascism', due to the relationship that evolved between state and Church, as well as to the convergence of specific doctrinal elements of Fascism and of the tradition of Catholic thought into a corporative ideology (E. Collotti, *Fascismo, fascismi*, Milan: Sansoni, 2004, p. 26). On the Iberian dictatorships and generic Fascism see also the sections on Spain and Portugal in S. Payne, *A History of Fascism, 1914–1945* (London: UCL Press, 1995).

107 The government established by Philippe Pétain at Vichy, following the fall of France in May-June 1940, was not simply a product of the military defeat but also of longer-term anti-democratic and pro-Fascist tendencies in French politics and society. During the war, the Vichy regime sought to retain neutrality and to build a 'National Revolution' (which included anti-Semitic laws and the restoration of the role of the Catholic Church in national education) while at the same time collaborating with Nazi Germany. See R. Paxton, *Vichy France: Old Guard and New Order, 1940–1944* (New York: Columbia University Press, 1982), especially chapter 2.

108 *Il Messaggero* was, and still is, the Roman daily newspaper, founded in 1878. On the Italian press during the Fascist period see P. Murialdi, *La stampa del regime fascista* (Rome and Bari: Laterza, 2008; first edn 1980); N. Tranfaglia, *La stampa del regime 1932–1943. Le veline del Minculpop per orientare l'informazione* (Milan: Bompiani, 2005).

109 The monthly magazine of the Italian Touring Club *Vie del Mondo* started its publications in 1922. Its articles, with illustrations, focused on travel, tourism and geography.

110 Francesco Orestano was president of the Italian Philosophical Society. He interpreted Fascism as a doctrine that opposed the Enlightenment, liberalism and historical materialism, and insisted on its ties with Catholicism (*Indice biografico*, vol. 8, p. 2558; G. Turi, *Giovanni Gentile. Una biografia*, Florence: Giunti, 1995, pp. 413, 465).

111 Carlo Scorza, a Fascist since 1920, was Secretary of the Fascist Party between April 1943 and 25 July 1943. At the Grand Council meeting of 24 July, he presented his own motion in favour of reforms (F. Deakin, *Storia della Repubblica di Salò*, Turin: Einaudi, 1963, pp. 448–9; Missori, *Gerarchie*, p. 275).

112 Lorenzo Chierici replaced Senise as Head of the Police from April 1943 until 25 July, when, following Mussolini's demise, Senise returned to his position (Missori, *Gerarchie*, pp. 187–8).

113 This section is followed by a single line.

114 The Ruffo di Calabria were descendants of one of the most ancient Italian aristocratic families. This sentence is followed by a single line.

115 'Trip'.

116 'Vigorous'/'brave'.

117 Capodimonte is on the south-west coast of Lake Bolsena and Valentano a few miles to the west, towards the border between Lazio and Tuscany (still in the province of Viterbo); Pitigliano is in the province of Grosseto in Tuscany, some 15 miles north-west of Valentano.

118 Both small towns are north of Pitigliano (about 5 and 10 miles respectively), still in the province of Grosseto.

119 Four dots in the original.

120 Santa Cristina and San Giorgio are both patron saints of Bolsena, a town on the north-east of Lake Bolsena. The two saints are represented in the Romanesque basilica by a ceramic by the Florentine sculptor Giovanni Della Robbia (1469–1529).

121 The French writer François de La Rochefoucauld (1613–80), also well known for his aphorisms.

122 In fact, in May 1943 the Japanese army sought unsuccessfully to conquer Chungking, an important city in the centre of a rice-growing area in the south-west of China. Chungking had been made temporary capital of nationalist China in 1938 following the fall of Nanjing to the Japanese.

123 This section is followed by a single line.

124 This section is followed by a single line.

125 Montini was indeed elected Pope in 1963 as Paul VI.

126 Michael MacWhite was the official representative of the Irish Free State in Rome from 1938; Raimundo Fernández-Cuesta was the Spanish Ambassador to Italy until 1945.

127 This section is followed by a single line.

128 This sentence was added, at the top of the page, after 25 July.

129 On Rodolfo Graziani see Introduction, note 93, p. 194.

130 Guglielmo Nasi was a general of the Italian army who fought under Graziani in Ethiopia in 1935–6, and Vice Governor of Italian East Africa. During the Second World War, he was the last Italian general to surrender to the British in east Africa in November 1941. After the armistice, he moved to Badoglio's side (Rochat, *Le guerre italiane*, p. 91).

131 Barnes is perhaps referring to the fact that following Allied victory at El Alamein, Churchill ordered that church bells rang in Britain for the first time since the start of the war. It is unlikely that Barnes would have a precise idea of the talks that led to the Casablanca Conference.

132 This section is followed by a single line.

133 This section is followed by a single line and by a blue arrow in right hand margin.

134 Luigi Lojacono was Italian Ambassador to Madrid, a journalist and writer, and a supporter of universal Fascism. See also introduction, note 60, p. 192.

135 As the Allies ejected Axis forces from north Africa and prepared to land on European soil for the first time since 1940, the United States of America Air Force (USAAF) and the Allied supreme command in the Mediterranean agreed on the necessity of air superiority. Throughout May 1943, therefore, the principal airfields of Sicily and Sardinia were bombed often and hard (Baldoli and Knapp, *Forgotten Blitzes*, p. 30).

136 Syria was under French control at the outbreak of the Second World War, but was conquered by the British, who defeated the Vichy troops there

in 1941. Its independence was recognized in January 1944. Barnes highly overestimated the number of Allied troops present in Syria.

137   On 14 May 1943 the American 12th Air Force attacked the port of Civitavecchia, some 40 miles north of Rome. Bombs fell also on the city, hitting the cathedral and the train station and killing at least 295 civilians. See the appendix to M. Gioannini and G. Massobrio, *Bombardate l'Italia. Storia della guerra di distruzione aerea, 1940–1945* (Milan: Rizzoli, 2006), http://rcslibri.corriere.it/bombardatelitalia (last accessed 27 May 2013).

138   In February 1943, diplomat Egidio Ortona became secretary of the Italian Foreign Office Undersecretary Bastianini.

139   On 28 May 1943 the American 12th Air Force attacked the port and marshalling yard of Leghorn. Bombs fell also on the city, killing some 250 civilians (appendix to Gioannini and Massobrio, *Bombardate l'Italia*, http:// rcslibri.corriere.it/bombardatelitalia, last accessed 27 May 2013).

140   This section is followed by a single line.

141   This section is followed by a single line.

142   The Terziari (Terzo Ordine Francescano) are members of a Franciscan Catholic community founded in the fifteenth century. Their headquarters in Rome is in the Basilica Cosma e Damiano (R. Luconi, *Il Terzo Ordine regolare di S. Francesco*, Macerata: Bisson & Leopardi, 1935; M. Mannu, *Il Terzo ordine francescano: orizzonti storici*, Rome: Graphein, 1999).

143   In Italian, *tenuta* means 'estate' and *campagna* 'countryside'.

144   Castel Fusano is a coastal area south-west of Rome.

145   Professor of philosophy and former Minister of Education, founder of the National Institute of Fascist Culture, Giovanni Gentile was killed by partisans in Florence in April 1944. On 24 June 1943 he gave a solemn speech to the nation (broadcast by the Italian radio) from the Campidoglio. In expectation of an imminent Anglo-American landing in Italy, he invited his compatriots to a desperate but proud clash of civilizations from which Rome would have emerged as the moral victor of the war. See G. Gentile, 'Discorso agli italiani', in *La vita e il pensiero*, vol. 4, (ed.) B. Gentile (Florence: Sansoni, 1951), pp. 74–5, 80.

146   Rev. Leo Ward (1893–1984) was an American Catholic philosopher.

147   For a summary of this speech (given on the afternoon of 6 July at Palazzo Venezia to the Comitato Corporativo Centrale), see B. Mussolini, *Opera Omnia di Benito Mussolini*, (eds) E. and D. Susmel, vol. 31, *Dal discorso al Direttorio nazionale del P.N.F. del 3 gennaio 1942 alla liberazione di Mussolini* (Florence: La Fenice, 1951–63), p. 198.

148   *Punch* was a British weekly satirical magazine, published from 1841 to 2002.

149   In fact, according to the Lateran Pacts of 1929, the churches in Rome that were property of the Vatican were the three basilicas of San Giovanni in Laterano, Santa Maria Maggiore and San Paolo, and the Church of San Callisto near Santa Maria in Trastevere. The issue of Vatican property in

relation to the bombing of Rome was discussed by the Allies before the raid on San Lorenzo. See in particular TNA, AIR 20/2565, War Cabinet Chiefs of Staff Committee, Memorandum for the British Foreign Office signed by Anthony Eden, 17 June 1943.

150 The raids were instead deemed successful, from a military point of view, by the American report drafted immediately after the bombardment and based on aerial photo reconnaissance. The latter showed that all the objectives (the San Lorenzo and the Littorio marshalling yards, and the airfields at Ciampino) had been hit and damaged. See TNA, AIR 20/2565, Northwest American Photo Reconnaissance Wing, report of 19 July 1943.

151 For the official reaction of the Vatican, see 'Il Santo Padre tra i fedeli della Sua Diocesi di Roma colpiti dall'incursione aerea', L'Osservatore Romano, 21 July 1943, p. 1.

152 In fact, although the bombing of Rome made a huge impression, authorities from many Italian cities reported widespread reactions of joy to the announcement that bombs had fallen near the palaces of the Duce and the King, demonstrating how by then most Italians only hoped for the dictatorship and the war to end. The manifesto referred to by Barnes might be one of the leaflets that the Allies dropped on Italian cities from aircraft in order to persuade civilians that the British and the Americans had to bomb them because of Mussolini and Hitler, who were responsible for the war (M. Fincardi, 'Anglo-American Air Attacks and the Rebirth of Public Opinion in Fascist Italy', in Bombing, States and Peoples in Western Europe, 1940–1945, (eds) C. Baldoli, A. Knapp, R. Overy, London: Continuum, 2011, pp. 241–55).

153 'Menefreghismo' literally means 'not to care'; thus by 'menefreghisti' Barnes describes those Italians who had become apathetic and were only waiting for peace, whatever the costs.

154 This section is followed by a single line.

155 This section is followed by a single line.

156 Cefalù is a coastal town some 40 miles east of Palermo.

157 Mussolini had referred to Sicily as an impregnable fortress in his propaganda speeches. In particular, on 24 June 1943, at the last meeting of the National Fascist Party in Palazzo Venezia, he uttered a speech, which was reported in posters all over the country, on the supposed impregnability of the Sicilian island to Allied invasion: as soon as the enemy attempted to land, he stated, he would be 'frozen' on the boat-topping line, 'the sea shore, where the water finishes and the land begins'. See 'I doveri imperiosi dell'ora', Opera Omnia di Benito Mussolini, vol. 31, pp. 195–7.

158 The Maddalena is an archipelago in the north-east of Sardinia. Porto Vecchio is in the south-eastern coast of Corsica, and Porto Ferraio on the northern coast of the Elba island in Tuscany.

159 Although Barnes usually names the region of Puglia by its Italian name, he used here the English translation 'Apulia'.

160 Mosciano is a neighbourhood of Scandicci, south west of Florence. 'Finis' means 'The end' in Latin.

161   This section is followed by a single line.

162   The ability to get to things at exactly the right time.

163   This section is followed by a single line.

164   This section is followed by a single line.

165   Anglo-American bombing during Badoglio's 45-day rule was indeed
       designed, together with anti-German propaganda, to intensify the pressure
       on the Prime Minister to sue for peace by suggesting that worse attacks
       could follow (Baldoli and Fincardi, 'Italian Society under Anglo-American
       Bombs: Propaganda, Experience, and Legend', *The Historical Journal*, 52
       (4), 2009, 1017–38).

166   This section is followed by a single line.

167   This section is followed by a single line.

168   'We shall return to where we were – soon'.

169   'Believe, Obey, Fight'.

170   'Rallying cry'.

171   Mainland Italy.

172   This section is followed by a single line.

173   This section is followed by a single line.

174   This section is followed by a single line.

175   This section is followed by a single line.

176   'If Badoglio has enough common sense to understand the need to resist until
       mid-November (in any case), if the possibility to resist until then exists, if,
       as a gifted military man, he is able to devise good defence plans, and at the
       same time, as a good [*illegible*] he shows to be able to [handle] the Italian
       people, then there will be hope to reach a compromise [*illegible*]. Otherwise
       everything will be lost, and the only hope for the salvation of the world will
       reside in the strength of resistance of Germany and Japan. I love Italy more
       than ever; but the Italians have disenchanted me. It is now their turn to
       disenchant my disillusions. In the next months, who will live, will see.'

177   As it is evident in the diary, Barnes's attitude towards the Badoglio
       government was ambivalent until the September armistice. Here he was
       referring to a Cabinet meeting of 5 August, when a commission was created
       to investigate illicit wealth gathered by a number of Fascist leaders. While
       Barnes agreed with this resolution (as well as with other measures, such
       as Badoglio's heavy-handed repression of post–25 July popular protest),
       the dissolution of the Fascist Party, of Corporations and other Fascist
       institutions from as early as 27 July was not so welcome (see for example his
       comments on 31 July). For an analysis of Badoglio's government see G. De
       Luna, *Badoglio. Un militare al potere* (Milan: Bompiani, 1974), pp. 233–48.

178   This section is followed by a single line.

179   On the myth of the Fascist 'corporativist' state and on the supporters of
       Fascist 'trade unionism', see G. Santomassimo, *La terza via fascista. Il mito
       del corporativismo* (Rome: Carocci, 2006); A. Gagliardi, *Il Corporativismo
       fascista* (Rome-Bari: Laterza, 2010).

180 This section is followed by a single line.

181 Four dots in the original.

182 This section is followed by a single line.

183 See Introduction, note 80, p. 193.

184 In the Soviet Union, the GPUS (Ghepeù) was the State Political Direction which in 1922 replaced the Čeka as a service for internal security. This section is followed by a single line.

185 Although rumours reached Barnes on the secret negotiations between Badoglio and the Allies, he could not have any information about the details. The German army was in fact ready to invade Italy. See also below, note 220.

186 This section is followed by a double line.

187 This section is followed by a double line.

188 On the rivalry between Badoglio and Graziani and on Badoglio's final triumph by May 1936, see De Luna, *Badoglio*, pp. 151–9.

189 In Italian, *rifugio* means shelter (an air raid shelter, in this case), and *cantina* basement (generally of a block of flats).

190 In the hope to save Rome from Anglo-American bombing, Marshal Badoglio unilaterally declared it an 'open city' on 14 August 1943. The link between bombing and the special status of Rome continued to be raised by Vatican diplomats too, in attempts to provide the city with immunity. However, the Allies never recognized the status of open city to the Italian capital, which following the Italian surrender of September 1943 was under German occupation until 4 June 1944. See M. Carli and U. Gentiloni Silveri, *Bombardare Roma. Gli Alleati e la città aperta (1940–1944)* (Bologna: Il Mulino, 2007).

191 Admiral Priamo Leonardi was the Italian commander at Syracuse and Augusta. Although it was the best-defended militarily, his stronghold surrendered without fighting. See C. D'Este, *1943. Lo sbarco in Sicilia* (Milan: Mondadori, 1990), pp. 249–50.

192 In fact, Mussolini's last meeting with Hitler before his fall took place at Feltre (in the province of Belluno) on 19 July 1943.

193 Liberal politician Vittorio Emanuele Orlando (1860–1952) was Minister of the Interior from 1916 and Prime Minister after Italy's defeat at the Battle of Caporetto in October 1917. He represented Italy at the Peace Conference in Paris in 1919–20, and was accused by the Fascists of being responsible for what they considered a 'mutilated victory'. Orlando was sympathetic to Mussolini's government until the beginning of the dictatorship in 1925. After the fall of Mussolini, he met the King several times and collaborated with the Badoglio government. He became president of the Chamber in the first anti-Fascist Italian government led by Ivanoe Bonomi, after the liberation of Rome, in June 1944. Orlando's speech to the Sicilian population on 18 August 1943, following the final capitulation of the island to the Allies the previous day, pointed at the responsibilities of Fascism in the disastrous outcome of the war. The reaction of the King was one of

annoyance, and demonstrated the ambiguities of the Badoglio government (see P. Puntoni, *Parla Vittorio Emanuele III*, Bologna: Il Mulino, 1993, p. 156).

194 The Allied Conference of Quebec took place on 17–24 August 1943 to prepare the invasion of France.

195 Between 1932 and 1943 Raffaele Guariglia had been the Italian Ambassador to Spain, Argentina, France, the Vatican and Turkey. He became Foreign Minister under Badoglio's government, between July 1943 and February 1944.

196 Some of the most destructive raids on Italian cities occurred in August 1943: on the 4th, a raid on Naples caused an estimated 700 dead; Turin, Milan and Genoa were attacked on the 7th (with at least 280 dead), and Turin and Milan again on the 12th (with more than 700 victims); in Rome more than 500 people were killed by the raid of the 13th; and on the 15th Milan was again targeted, leaving at least 200 dead. In the second half of August attacks moved south, with hundreds of victims at Foggia, Benevento and, again, Naples. For details on raids on Italian cities during the Second World War, see the appendix to Gioannini and Massobrio, *Bombardate l'Italia* http://rcslibri.corriere.it/bombardatelitalia (last accessed 27 May 2013).

197 This section is followed by a single line.

198 This section is followed by a single line.

199 The Gargano is the northern part of Puglia. Indeed, from November 1943 the US 15th Air Force set up Italian bases in the region around Foggia for use against Axis targets including southern France, northern Italy, Austria, southern Germany, Czechoslovakia, Yugoslavia, southern Poland and Romania.

200 This section is followed by a single line.

201 Count Quinto Mazzolini was Chief of Cabinet of Badoglio's Minister of Popular Culture Carlo Galli.

202 This section is followed by a single line.

203 This section is followed by a single line.

204 King Boris III of Bulgaria died on 28 August 1943. He had allied Bulgaria with the Axis powers in 1941.

205 This section is followed by a single line.

206 Roberto Farinacci was the principal representative of intransigent Fascism in Italy. 'First hour' Fascist, leader of the squads in Cremona in northern Italy, he was Secretary of the Fascist Party in 1925–6, when Mussolini needed a strong Party in order to face the political scandal caused by the murder of Socialist MP Giacomo Matteotti in 1924. He supported Mussolini at the Grand Council meeting of 24 July 1943 and joined the Salò Republic. He was shot by partisans on 28 April 1945. For a biography, see M. Di Figlia, *Farinacci. Il radicalismo fascista al potere* (Rome: Donzelli, 2007). On Farinacci, see also Introduction, pp. 19–21.

207 Those 400,000 Italian workers in Germany (a rough estimate generally confirmed by historians) could hardly have been defined a 'Fascist militia'

ready to support a coup in Italy. When asked by Mussolini and Graziani during the Salò Republic, Hitler refused to allow what he then called 'Badoglio-Truppen' to return to Italy; and out of the 600,000 Italian military internees in Germany (who had been captured after the armistice) only 10 per cent accepted to join the army of the new Fascist regime, despite the tragic conditions they were suffering in German concentration camps. See B. Mantelli, *Camerati del lavoro. I lavoratori emigrati nel Terzo Reich nel periodo dell'Asse* (Scandicci: La Nuova Italia, 1992); G. Hammermann, *Gli internati militari italiani in Germania, 1943–1945* (Bologna: Il Mulino, 2004).

208 This section is followed by a single line.

209 This section is followed by a single line.

210 The Nunziatura Apostolica was the Vatican diplomatic mission both to other states and to their Catholic hierarchies.

211 This section is followed by a single line.

212 The Rubicon is a small river in the province of Forlì-Cesena, which flows into the Adriatic Sea. In the late-Republican Roman age (between 59 and 42 BC) it established the frontier between Roman territory and Cisalpine Gaul, and it was forbidden to cross it with armies. Caesar's decision to cross it in 49 BC is at the origin of the saying.

213 Antonino Pagliaro was a Fascist literary critic and translator who taught linguistics at Rome university and co-edited the *Enciclopedia Italiana* (*Indice biografico*, vo.. 8, p. 2593). Giuseppe Ricciotti was a military chaplain in the First World War and a historian of the Bible; among other works, he wrote a popular life of Christ, *Vita di Gesù Cristo* (Milan: Rizzoli, 1941).

214 A newspaper entitled *Fronte Unico*, founded by the University Fascist Groups, had in fact been published in Rome since 1937 (R. Zangrandi, *Il lungo viaggio*, p. 85). In September 1943 the newspaper, again directed by a group of young Fascists, was revamped, and published articles that were strongly anti-American and anti-Badoglio.

215 Ettore Muti, a Fascist since 1921, was the Secretary of the Fascist Party between October 1939 and October 1940. Probably suspected of being involved in a plan to prepare an insurrection to reinstate Mussolini in power, in August 1943 he was killed in uncertain circumstances by *Carabinieri* who were arresting him. He was remembered as a hero and a martyr during the Salò Republic. The only existing biographies of Muti are either journalistic or neo-Fascist nostalgic accounts.

216 Socialist MP Giacomo Matteotti denounced the means of violence and intimidations used by Mussolini's government during its last general elections in a speech at the Chamber in May 1924. In June he was kidnapped by members of the Fascist secret police. In August, his corpse was found outside Rome. Mussolini's responsibility in this murder was exposed at the time by anti-Fascist clandestine press, and has been confirmed by scholarly research conducted in archives more recently. See in particular the work by M. Canali, *Il delitto Matteotti* (Bologna: Il Mulino, 2004 – first edn 1997). See also *Diary 1944*, note 10, p. 218.

217 This section is followed by a single line.

218 This section is followed by a single line.

219 'Lorry'.

220 The armistice between Italy and the Allies was broadcast on 8 September, although it had been signed at Cassibile (near Syracuse) 5 days earlier. In fact, the process towards the armistice had secretly begun shortly after 25 July. What Badoglio sought to avoid, and what Churchill and Roosevelt instead wanted, was Italy's unconditional surrender. This led to 45 days of negotiations, while Italy was still allied with Germany. Eventually the armistice was concluded on Anglo-American terms, while the Italian army had not prepared any resistance against the likely German invasion. The short message broadcast by Badoglio on 8 September did not specify anything about Italy's new military position towards Germany, and Italy declared war on Germany only on 13 October (one month after the Germans had occupied Rome). On the armistice and its consequences see E. Aga Rossi, *A Nation Collapses: the Italian Surrender of September 1943* (Cambridge: Cambridge University Press, 1999).

221 This section is an interlinear addition by Barnes at the top of the page.

222 Monsignor Luigi Traglia was vicar of the Roman diocese; he became cardinal in 1960.

223 On the Salerno landing and the Italian campaign up to Naples, see below, note 240.

224 Carlo Galli had been an Ambassador to Persia, Portugal, Yugoslavia and Turkey between 1924 and 1938. In August 1943 he was made Minister of Popular Culture by Badoglio.

225 The provinces of Kotor, Split and Zadar constituted the Italian governorate of Dalmatia since June 1941 (while Zadar had been Italian since the First World War, Kotor and Split were occupied between May and June 1941). Following the Italian surrender of September 1943, the German army invaded Italian Dalmatia (except for Zadar), which was annexed to Croatia.

226 This section is followed by a single line.

227 Because of his propaganda for Radio Roma in 1941–3, Ezra Pound was accused of betrayal by the American government and faced the same situation as Barnes if caught by the Allies. During the Salò Republic he continued his pro-Fascist activity, and was finally caught by the partisans, who handed him over to the American army in May 1945. After having spent 12 years in a mental hospital in Washington he returned to Italy, and died in Venice in 1972. Pound's pro-Fascist radio speeches during the Second World War have been published in L. Doob (ed.), *Ezra Pound Speaking: Radio Speeches of World War II* (London: Greenwood Press, 1978).

228 The sentence in brackets was added later at the margin of the line, and encircled. Rapallo is a town in the province of Genoa on the Ligurian coast.

229 On the meaning of 'Lord Haw Haw' see Introduction, p. 1.

230 Cisterna di Latina, south of Rome.

231 'Hotel'.

232 Montesacro is a hill north-west of Rome.

233 Free shooters or guerrilla fighters.

234 This section is followed by a single line.

235 Vittorio Mussolini (1916–97) was Mussolini's second son, and among the founders of the Salò Republic.

236 This section is followed by a single line.

237 This section is followed by a blue arrow in right hand margin.

238 Oswald Mosley, founder of the British Union of Fascists in 1932, was imprisoned in May 1940 under Defence Regulation 18B because of his pro-Nazi views. Although Barnes was on good terms with Mosley, the BUF was closer to Nazi Germany than to Fascist Italy, particularly from 1935 onwards. See R. Thurlow, *Fascism in Britain: A History, 1918–1985* (Oxford: Blackwell, 1987), pp. 163–87; C. Baldoli, 'Anglo-Italian Fascist Solidarity? The Shift from Italo-philia to Nazi-philia in the BUF', in *The Culture of Fascism: Visions and the Far Right in Britain*, (eds) J. Gottlieb and T. Linehan (London: I. B. Tauris, 2004), pp. 147–61.

239 On 12 September 1943 German paratroopers rescued Mussolini, who was held prisoner on the Gran Sasso, in the Abruzzo Apennines, after his arrest in July. See Deakin, *Storia della Repubblica di Salò*, pp. 537–9.

240 The Allies had landed in Salerno on 9 September, but German resistance delayed their progress towards Naples until 1 October. During those weeks, the area in between the two cities became 'no man's land', with towns completely destroyed and thousands of civilians dead, as a result of both Allied bombing and German destruction. See G. Gribaudi, *Guerra totale. Tra bombe alleate e violenze naziste: Napoli e il fronte meridionale, 1940–44* (Turin: Bollati Boringhieri, 2005), pp. 311–16.

241 'Vicarage'.

242 'Disgusting King'.

243 This section is followed by a single line.

244 Mussolini's first public act as head of the new Fascist government was to release five 'orders of the day', which were broadcast by the radio on 15 September. He stated that he was going to reconstruct the Fascist Party and the new state, and to resume the leadership of Fascism in Italy. He ordered Italians to support the German ally and promised exemplary punishment for all those who had betrayed. Although he freed the army from the vow to the King, who had 'given the nation to the enemy', he appeared rather cautious at this point and did not insist too much on the republican aspect of the new regime (see *Opera Omnia di Benito Mussolini*, vol. 32, *Dalla liberazione di Mussolini all'epilogo*, p. 231).

245 This section is followed by a single line.

246 This section is followed by a single line.

247 Italianized word: it should be 'sabotaging'.

248 This section is followed by a single line.

249   On the use of Mazzini and Garibaldi during the Salò Republic, see E. Pala,
       *Garibaldi in camicia nera. Il mito dell'Eroe dei Due Mondi nella Repubblica
       di Salò* (Milan: Mursia, 2011); R. Sarti, 'Giuseppe Mazzini e la tradizione
       repubblicana', in *Almanacco della Repubblica. Storia d'Italia attraverso
       le tradizioni, le istituzioni e le simbologie repubblicane*, (ed.) M. Ridolfi
       (Milan: Bruno Mondadori, 2003), pp. 64–5.

250   On 17 and 18 September 1943 the 12th USAAF successfully bombed the
       airport of Ciampino south of the capital.

251   This section is followed by a single line.

252   Founded in July 1861, *L'Osservatore Romano* was, and still is, the official
       daily newspaper of the Vatican.

253   Poggio Mirteto is a town in the province of Rieti, north of Rome.

254   These were consequences of a raid on 18 September by the African-based
       RAF on the Viterbo area.

255   From Churchill's speech, 21 September 1943 to the House of Commons:
       'We may pause for a moment to survey and appraise the act of the Italian
       Government, endorsed and acclaimed as it was by the Italian nation.
       Herr Hitler has left us in no doubt that he considers the conduct of Italy
       treacherous and base in the extreme – and he is a good judge in these
       matters ... yet I cannot view the Italian action at this juncture as other
       than natural and human. May it prove to be the first of a series of acts of
       self-redemption.' (Churchill, *Onwards to Victory*, pp. 197–204).

256   From Hitler's speech, 10 September 1943 over German radio: 'The collapse
       of Italy was long foreseen ... The pain which I personally experience is
       understandable in the face of this unique injustice that has been done to this
       man [Mussolini], the unworthy handling of one, who for twenty years lived
       only to care for his people, and is now reduced to the level of a common
       criminal. I was and am fortunate to be able to call this great and faithful
       man my friend ...' In M. Domarus, *Hitler: Reden und Proklamationen
       1932–1945: Band II (2): Untergang* (Munich: Süddeutscher Verlag, 1965),
       pp. 2035–9.

257   This section is followed by a single line.

258   Catholic prayer for the dead, *Resquiescat in pace* (in Latin) means 'Rest in
       peace'.

259   Fascist motto, first used publicly in Italy by the nationalist poet Gabriele
       D'Annunzio, which means 'hurray'.

260   This section is followed by a single line.

261   On 25 September 1943 the 12th USAAF bombed the marshalling yard of
       Campo di Marte in Florence. Bombs fell also on surrounding areas of the
       city, causing more than 200 victims (Gioannini and Massobrio, *Bombardate
       l'Italia*, pp. 434–5).

262   Pejorative dialectal expression which means 'among their own dead'.

263   In fact, only 2 per cent of the Italian army joined the Salò army formations,
       which were increasingly taken over by the German army or the Waffen-SS.
       Administrators, prefects, and all those who worked for the Salò Republic

ministries and local councils were proud of having remained on the side of the German ally, although worried that northern Italy might be annexed to the Reich. They found themselves caught between their compatriots, who had by then almost unanimously rejected Fascism, and the arrogance of the Germans, which no amount of propaganda, describing the Germans as trustworthy friends, could disguise. None of the Salò Republic institutions (the special police, the volunteer National Republican Guard, the Republican Fascist Party) had any support among the population, who perceived clearly that the Republic was not able to defend cities from aerial destruction. From a military point of view, the Republic simply reiterated a situation that civilians had faced from the first months of the war. That experience had shown the incapacity of local authorities in protecting the population, and the disaster continued under the Republic. See in particular L. Ganapini, *La repubblica delle camicie nere* (Milan: Garzanti, 2002; first edn 1999) and 'The Dark Side of Italian History, 1943–1945', *Modern Italy*, 12 (2), 2007, 205–24.

264   This section is followed by a single line.

265   Mugello is a valley in north-eastern Tuscany; Faenza and Lugo are towns in the Romagna region, north of Forlì and west of Ravenna.

266   Ravenna was bombed for the first time on 30 December 1943. Positioned on the northern side of the Gothic line, it was mostly bombed in March 1944 and, because of its marshalling yard, in August and September 1944 (D. Molesi, *Ravenna nella Seconda Guerra Mondiale*, Ravenna: Longo, 1974).

267   Naples, liberated on 1 October 1943, was the most bombed city in Italy, targeted more than 100 times by the Allies for its port and industries, from October 1940 until September 1943. After that, Naples was also bombed by the Germans, with the last German attack on the city taking place on 15 March 1944 – the heaviest of German air raids on Italy, resulting in the death of 278 civilians. On Naples during the war, see G. Gribaudi, *Guerra totale*, and 'The True Cause of the "Moral Collapse": People, Fascists and Authorities under the Bombs. Naples and the Countryside, 1940–1944', in (eds) Baldoli, Knapp and Overy, *Bombing, States and Peoples*, pp. 219–37.

268   This section is followed by a single line.

269   On 5 October 1943 the 12th USAAF hit the marshalling yard of Bologna. Bombs fell also on the city, killing 80 civilians. On the bombing of Bologna see *Delenda Bononia. Immagini dei bombardamenti, 1943–1945*, (eds) C. Bersani and V. R. Roversi Monaco (Bologna: Biblioteca Comunale dell'Archiginnasio, 1995).

270   This section is followed by a single line.

271   Celso Luciano was the prefect of Venice.

272   This section is followed by a single line.

273   These words are followed by a single line.

274   In fact Grandi had escaped to Portugal via Spain. In December 1947 he moved to Brazil. See F. Bertagna, *La patria di riserva. L'emigrazione fascista in Argentina* (Rome: Donzelli, 2006), p. 209.

275 This section is followed by a single line.

276 Nino Sammartano was a Fascist writer, the author of a number of books on Fascist pedagogy and textbooks for Italian schools (see for example *Corso di cultura fascista ad uso delle scuole medie inferiori*, Florence: Le Monnier, 1934).

277 This section is followed by a single line.

278 Italy had attacked Greece from its bases in Albania on 28 October 1940. However, by the end of November the Italian army had retreated back to Albania, under Greek counter-attack, forcing Hitler to make the German army intervene to rescue its ally. Germany invaded Greece on 6–7 April 1941, and an armistice, which included Italy, was signed on 23 April. Greece was divided between Italy, Bulgaria and Germany, with Italian occupation extending over most of central Greece and the Peloponnese and over most of the Greek islands. Following the armistice of September 1943, Italian soldiers, who had until then been responsible for war crimes against the Greek population, became themselves victims of vindictive German violence. See D. Rodogno, *Fascism's European Empire*, especially part 2; L. Santarelli, 'Muted violence: Italian war crimes in occupied Greece', *Journal of Modern Italian Studies*, 9 (3), 2004, 280–99; I. Insolvibile, *Kos, 1943–1948. La strage, la storia* (Naples: Edizioni Scientifiche Italiane, 2010).

279 This section is followed by a single line.

280 'Puddies', here used to indicate Buona's feet or shoes, means mittens worn by babies. It can refer to the hands or feet of babies or pets.

281 The Commune of Toscolano Maderno on Lake Garda hosted both the Republic's Ministry of the Interior and the German embassy.

282 Predappio, Mussolini's birthplace and therefore site of 'pilgrimage' during the Fascist regime, is a town in the Forlì province in the Romagna region. See S. Serenelli, '"It was like something that you have at home which becomes so familiar that you don't even pay attention to it": Memories of Mussolini and Fascism in Predappio, 1922–2010', *Modern Italy*, 18 (2), 2013, 157–75.

283 This section is followed by a single line.

284 'College'. Riva del Garda is a town on the northern coast of the lake in the province of Trento.

285 Arco, in the province of Trento, is just north of Riva del Garda, and is home to a twelfth-century castle.

286 During the evening of 5 November 1943, five bombs fell on the Vatican City, without causing any injury but slightly damaging the buildings near St Peter's (including windows of the Basilica and of the Vatican museums).

287 In fact, the opposite had occurred: on 1 November 1943, following the American invasion of the Pacific island of Bougainville, the Japanese attempted to reinforce their garrison there but were driven off by US carrier aircraft. This, as well as Barnes's previous comment on Italian public opinion supposedly rallying to the Salò Republic, is an example of his desperate attempt to believe in Axis victory at the eleventh hour.

288   This section is followed by a single line.

289   A sixteenth-century villa between Salò and Barbarano on Lake Garda.

290   This section is followed by a single line.

291   'I don't think it is either useful or necessary that the radio remains London's monopoly in English language. I could fight their infamous propaganda. I don't need a ministry. but without a microphone I cannot send'.

292   This section is followed by a single line.

293   Passo della Futa is a 903m. mountain pass on the Apennine between Romagna and Tuscany.

294   Ciano was indeed going to be executed on 11 January 1944 following the trial of Verona. See above, note 61.

295   Luigi Federzoni was among the founders of the Italian Nationalist Association in 1910, Minister of the Colonies in 1922–4 and 1926–8, and Minister of the Interior between 1924 and 1926 (Missori, *Gerarchie*, p. 205).

296   The Greek Island of Leros, like other islands of the Dodecanese previously under Italian control, was conquered by the Germans by 16 November 1943. On the Dodecanese during Italian and German occupation see N. Doumanis, *Myth and Memory in the Mediterranean: Remembering Fascism's Empire* (Basingstoke: Palgrave, 1997).

297   Four dots in the original.

298   After the outbreak of war, Oswald and Diana Mosley were detained in Holloway Prison under Defence Regulation 18B. On Churchill's prompting, Minister of Home Security Herbert Morrison decided to release Mosley on house arrest on medical grounds in November 1943, which caused controversy among the British Left. See M. Perry, *'Red Ellen' Wilkinson: Her Ideas, Movements and World* (Manchester: Manchester University Press, 2014), chapter 8.

299   This section is followed by a single line.

300   In the province of Perugia.

301   In Latin, 'family heads'.

302   West of Panicale and south-west of Lake Trasimeno, in Tuscany.

303   'Coach'.

304   Fernando Mezzasoma was Mussolini's Minister of Popular Culture during the Salò Republic. See also Introduction, p. 20.

305   Giovanni Dolfini was Mussolini's private secretary during the Salò Republic.

306   Four dots in the original.

307   This section is followed by a double line.

308   This section is followed by a single line.

309   This section is followed by a single line.

310   This section is followed by a single line.

Diary 1944

1   This section is followed by a single line. Giuseppe Pizzirani was the Head
    of the Republican Fascist Party in Rome until April 1944, when he became
    Vice Secretary of the national Republican Fascist Party. On his difficult
    role, like that of all Fascist authorities at the time of the Salò Republic, see
    A. Osti Guerrazzi, La 'Repubblica necessaria'. Il fascismo repubblicano a
    Roma, 1943–44 (Milan: Angeli, 2004), p. 32.

2   This section is followed by a single line.

3   This section is followed by a single line.

4   This sentence is followed by a large red asterisk in the margin.

5   Italianized word ('insofferenza'): impatience/intolerance.

6   This section is followed by a single line.

7   The Verona trial was held between 8 and 10 January 1944 against the 19
    members of the Grand Council who voted in favour of Grandi's motion on
    25 July 1943. Except for Tullio Cianetti (President of the Fascist Syndicates
    and member of the Grand Council who voted for Grandi but the next day
    wrote to Mussolini that he had repented), who was sentenced to 30 years,
    they were all condemned to death. However, most of them had already
    fled and only five (one of whom was Ciano) were shot. The trial was held
    by an Extraordinary Tribunal set up by Pavolini, in which the judges were
    nominated by the Fascist Party.

8   Three dots in the original.

9   Federzoni (see Diary 1943, note 295, p. 217) voted in favour of Grandi's
    motion at the Grand Council meeting of 24 July, but escaped the Verona
    trial (Missori, Gerarchie, p. 205).

10 Giovanni Marinelli was one of the creators of the Fascist police, the
    illegal 'parallel' police which served to stabilize the regime in the 1920s
    against political opponents, and which came to light in 1924 in relation
    to the Fascist kidnapping and murder of Socialist MP Giacomo Matteotti.
    Marinelli was in fact implicated in the kidnapping of Matteotti, and, when
    brought to a farce trial in 1925, refused to reveal Mussolini's responsibility
    in planning the kidnapping and homicide of the Socialist MP. See M. Canali,
    'The Matteotti murder and the origins of Mussolini's totalitarian Fascist
    regime in Italy', Journal of Modern Italian Studies, 14 (2), 2009, 146–67.

11 Carlo Pareschi was Minister of Agriculture and member of the Grand
    Council from 1941 until 25 July 1943 (Missori, Gerarchie, p. 253).

12 This section is followed by a single line.

13 This section is followed by a single line. On the republic's 'socialization', see
    Introduction, pp. 24–5.

14 This section is followed by a single line.

15 Nettuno is a few miles south of Anzio, where the Allies landed on 22
    January 1944.

16 The Pontine marshes, in the Littoria (today's Latina) province in Lazio,

were reclaimed by the regime in the 1930s and represented one of the most successful pieces of Fascist propaganda: the 'internal colonies', together with the colonies in Africa, were supposed to resolve the problem of Italian emigration abroad. See C. Burdett, 'Journeys to the other spaces of Fascist Italy', *Modern Italy*, 5 (1), May 2000, 7–23; S. B. Fraudsen, '"The war that we prefer": The reclamation of the Pontine Marshes and Fascist expansion', in *International Fascism, 1919–1945*, (eds) R. Mallett and G. Sørensen (London: Frank Cass, 2002), pp. 69–82.

17 *Il Regime Fascista* was Farinacci's daily newspaper, published in Cremona from 1929 (before that year it was entitled *Cremona Nuova*). Although published locally, it represented the views, at a national level, of intransigent Fascism, often attacking Fascists who maintained 'moderate' views or those who were considered potential internal enemies. As a result, it was kept under control by the regime and at times censored (see M. Di Figlia, *Farinacci*, especially chapter 4).

18 On Tullio Calcagno and his clerical-Fascist newspaper *Crociata Italica*, of which Barnes was a contributor, see Introduction, pp. 19–20.

19 This section is followed by a single line.

20 The battle stalled at the Gustav line, from just south of Gaeta (north of Naples) on the Tyrrenic coast to Ortona on the Adriatic coast, via Cassino, from 15 January until 11 May 1944.

21 On 12 February 1944 the seventh meeting of the Republican Fascist government formally approved the 'socialization' of industries. It also sanctioned the death penalty for deserters and anyone who did not respond to conscription. For a chronology of the main events of the Salò Republic, see M. Franzinelli, *RSI. La Repubblica del Duce, 1943–1945* (Milan: Mondadori, 2007), pp. 215–23.

22 This section is followed by a single line.

23 This section is followed by a single line.

24 Emanuele Tornaghi was Farinacci's private secretary during the Salò Republic.

25 Piero Parini was General Secretary of the Italian *Fasci* Abroad from 1928 to 1937. Following the occupation of Greece, in 1941 he became governor of the Ionian Islands until the fall of the Fascist regime in July 1943. He then returned to Italy and from October of that year acted as Podestà (Fascist unelected mayor) of Milan.

26 Agostino Gemelli was the founder of the Catholic University and president of the Vatican Academy of Science.

27 Some of the hardest battles of the Italian campaign took place at Cassino on the Gustav Line. On 15 February 1944 US bombers together with artillery had destroyed the abbey at Monte Cassino, which resulted uselessly in military terms (the German troops were not in the monastery itself) as well as being highly controversial (the monastery had been founded in the sixth century and had both artistic and religious significance).

28 Subhas Chandra Bose was an Indian nationalist who, following Pearl

Harbor, fought on the side of the Japanese as a form of anti-British revolt. Barnes was referring to the Japanese attack on Imphal and Kohima, which, however, ended in Japanese defeat in late May 1944.

29   By March 1944 the Soviet offensive had advanced across the Ukraine to Bukovine.

30   Karl von Rundstedt was a field marshal of the Wehrmacht during the Second World War.

31   During the Salò Republic, Mussolini's nephew Vito (son of the Duce's brother Arnaldo, who died in 1931) and his family lived on Isola del Garda (former property of the Borghese family) with numerous relatives, among whom Count Vanni Teodorani, husband of Arnaldo's daughter Rosa and founder, after the war, of the Republic's veteran association (Consorzio Alberghi Riviera del Garda, *I Luoghi della Repubblica di Salò*, Gardone Riviera: L'Editoriale Grafica, 1997, p. 21).

32   Gilberto Bernabei was deputy chief of cabinet at the Ministry of Popular Culture in the 1930s, and after the armistice followed Mezzasoma to Salò.

33   Giorgio Almirante was among the founders of the neo-Fascist party *Movimento Sociale Italiano* in December 1946.

34   Four dots in the original.

35   Busto Arsizio is a town west of Milan, in the province of Varese.

36   'Memorandum'.

37   This section is followed by a single line.

38   This section is followed by a single line.

39   Barnes was referring to the troops of De Gaulle's Free French employed in the Italian campaign; at their command was General Alphonse Juin, who had achieved an important breakthrough at Garigliano on the Gustav Line on 13 May 1944.

40   German counter-attack delayed the Allied advance at Villers-Bocage in Normandy on 12–14 June 1944.

41   Pun on Badoglio.

42   The battle for the liberation of the Norman port city of Cherbourg lasted from 10 to 27 June 1944, while, on the eastern Front, the Soviet army conquered Vitebsk, in Belorussia, on 26 June, opening the way towards Minsk.

43   Avranches was liberated by American troops on 31 July and Vire on 8 August 1944.

44   Italianized word: it should be 'philo-Russian'.

45   Italianized word: it should be 'philo-American'.

46   Four dots in the original.

47   'Right', 'Very right'. Four dots in the original.

48   Between 29 April and 2 May 1942 Mussolini and Ciano met Hitler and von Ribbentrop at Salzburg to discuss the military situation.

49   The role of the Party was indeed emphasized with its rebirth as the

Republican Fascist Party, in the attempt to return to its early revolutionary rhetoric. See Ganapini, 'The dark side of Italian history', 210–11.

50   The Manifesto of Verona, drafted at the first meeting of the Republican Fascist Party on 14–16 November 1943, had indeed re-established the Lateran Pacts, confirming Catholicism as the state religion, while proclaiming respect of other religions so long as they were not 'against the laws' (article 6). Jewish religion was evidently to be excluded, since article 7 stated that the Jews were 'foreigners and belong to an enemy nation'. A. Fappani and F. Molnari, *Chiesa e Repubblica di Salò. Fonti edite ed inedite* (Turin: Marietti, 1981), pp. 56–8.

51   On the 'socialization' see Introduction, pp. 24–5.

52   Three dots in the original. Catholic Action, founded in 1867, was the most important lay Catholic organization in Italy, particularly active among Italian youth. Despite the Lateran Pacts between the Church and the Fascist regime, Catholic Action came to a clash with the Fascist organization of youth in 1931. On the reasons why *Crociata Italica* was not fully endorsed by Mussolini, see Introduction, p. 20.

53   On this publication by Barnes, see Introduction, pp. 24–5.

54   Official links between the Allies and the Italian Resistance were established from spring 1944, and one of the main Allied contributions to Italian partisans was the launch, by parachute, of provisions and weapons. See T. Piffer, *Gli Alleati e la Resistenza italiana* (Bologna: Il Mulino, 2010), pp. 91–100.

55   This section is followed by a single line.

56   Florence was liberated on 4 August 1944. The delay of the Allied advance after the liberation of Rome was due to the fact that the Italian campaign had by then become a secondary theatre, and six divisions had been withdrawn from Italy in preparation for the landings in southern France.

57   From the origins of the Republic onwards, Graziani sought to organize a new Italian army that would fight with (but remain independent of) the Germans. Because of the lack of volunteers, he had to impose conscription, and Italian divisions were sent to be trained in Germany. However, the Germans preferred to employ Italians as workers (for example for the military engineering group Todt in Italy) rather than as soldiers. On Graziani's failed attempt to create an efficient Republican army see L. Ganapini, *La Repubblica delle camicie nere*, pp. 70–85.

58   On 20 July 1944 an unsuccessful attempt against Hitler's life was endeavoured by Colonel Claus von Stauffenberg at the dictator's headquarters in Eastern Prussia. It was the last of a series of attempts that had marked the history of the German resistance since 1939. Immediately after the assassination attempt there were widespread demonstrations of support for Hitler across Germany.

59   The Battle for Normandy lasted from the landing on 6 June to mid-August 1944.

60   On Mosley's release see *Diary 1943*, note 298, p. 217.

61	While northern-central Italy was under the German-controlled Salò Republic, southern Italy experienced occupation by the Allied Military Government. The complex relationship between Italian civilians and Allied soldiers was exploited in the Fascist press, which sought to depict the situation in the south as one of poverty and chaos. For a thorough study of the experience of southern Italy in 1943–5, see N. Gallerano (ed.), *L'altro dopoguerra. Roma e il Sud 1943–1945* (Milan: Angeli, 1985).

62	The German 'Vengeance weapons' V1 and V2 were respectively flying bombs and rockets used during attacks on southern England, Belgium and France. The V1 assaults on England took place between June 1944 and March 1945, causing the death of 6,184 civilians and forcing Allied bombers to attack the launch sites (Operation Crossbow). The V2s, launched between September 1944 and March 1945, killed 2,754 civilians.

63	This section is followed by a single line.

64	The Florentine bridges were destroyed (with the exception of Ponte Vecchio) because they had been mined by retreating German troops.

65	On 15 August the Allies landed in Provence. Toulon and Marseilles were liberated respectively on 20–26 and 28–29 August.

66	Rudolf Rahn was the German Ambassador to the Salò Republic. The German embassy was located in a nineteenth-century villa (Villa Bassetti) on the lake shore at Toscolano Maderno.

67	Telesio Interlandi was responsible for radio propaganda during the Salò Republic. Until the fall of Mussolini in July 1943, he directed *Il Tevere*, an anti-Semitic daily paper founded by Mussolini in December 1924. In 1938 Interlandi founded the fortnightly *La Difesa della Razza*, the main racist newspaper in Italy (published until June 1943). See M. Michaelis, 'Mussolini's unofficial mouthpiece: Telesio Interlandi – *Il Tevere* and the evolution of Mussolini's anti-semitism', *Journal of Modern Italian Studies*, 3, 1998, 217–40.

68	*Te Deum Laudamus*, a Christian prayer used since the Middle Ages to thank God.

69	Rimini was indeed liberated four days later, on 21 September.

70	Romania capitulated to the Soviet Union on 23 August 1944, and two days later declared war on Germany. Bulgaria signed an armistice with the Soviet Union on 11 September 1944. Besides having developed an organized anti-German resistance, Bulgaria continued the war after its liberation on the side of the Soviet forces in Yugoslavia and Hungary.

71	Fino Mornasco, a small town about 6 miles south of Como.

72	South Tyrol in Italian.

73	'Greetings'.

74	Carlo Emanuele Basile was member of the National Directory of the Fascist Party from 1928; war volunteer in Spain and Ethiopia in the 1930s; General Inspector of the Fasci abroad from 1931, and General Secretary from 1942. During the Salò Republic he was Head of Province of Genoa (1943–4) and Undersecretary of the Armed Forces (1944–5). See M. Franzinelli,

L'amnistia Togliatti. 22 giugno 1946: colpo di spugna sui crimini fascisti (Milan: Mondadori, 2006), pp. 184–6.

75 The *Brigate Nere* ('black brigades') were constituted with a decree of 30 June 1944 as the military arm of the Fascist Party, with the main duty of anti-partisan repression. They were responsible for some of the cruellest acts of violence against partisans and civilians during the civil war. See D. Gagliani, *Brigate nere. Mussolini e la militarizzazione del Partito fascista repubblicano* (Turin: Bollati Boringhieri, 1999).

76 In Latin, 'nothing stands in the way'.

77 Five dots in the original.

78 *Corriere della Sera* is one of the main Italian daily newspapers, founded in Milan in March 1876. Directed by Luigi Albertini during the Liberal period, the paper was brought under Fascist control following the laws of 1926, which outlawed opposition parties and suppressed any newspaper adverse to the Fascist regime. See P. Murialdi, *Storia del giornalismo italiano* (Bologna: Il Mulino, 1996), pp. 131–7.

79 Villa Omodeo at Soiano (near Manerba del Garda, south of Salò) was the headquarters of the Ministry of Defence under Marshal Graziani (Consorzio Alberghi Riviera del Garda, *I Luoghi della Repubblica di Salò*, p. 21).

80 Led by Junio Valerio Borghese, the X Mas was a Fascist Republican irregular military formation made of volunteers. They fought both Allies and partisans and terrified civilian populations suspected of sympathizing with the Resistance. See L. Ganapini, *La Repubblica delle camicie nere*, pp. 60–70. Vittorio Veneto is a town in the province of Treviso.

81 The *Federale* was the local leader of the Fascist Party.

82 On the 'children of Salò' see A. Gibelli, *Il popolo bambino. Infanzia e nazione dalla Grande Guerra a Salò* (Turin: Einaudi, 2005), pp. 366–83.

83 'Pippo' was the best-known legend of Second World War Italy: he was said to be a cunning pilot (or, even, a sort of anthropomorphic plane) who acted in isolation, constantly on the lookout for any small breach of the rules carried out by civilians; if he found any, he was said either to take photographs of the wrongdoer or even drop small bombs on them. For a psychological explanation of the legend of Pippo, see Baldoli and Fincardi, 'Italian society under Anglo-American bombs', 1030–2.

84 Virle Treponti is a hamlet of the commune of Rezzato, in the province of Brescia.

85 Fasano del Garda is a hamlet of the commune of Gardone Riviera, on the west coast of the lake just north of Salò. The German presence was particularly strong there: while not far from the German embassy, it hosted Luftwaffe personnel, representatives of the German press, German radio installations, the German consulate, a German hospital and a large air raid shelter. Rahn's personal residence was at Villa Cristofori, just above the town, and, whenever he visited the Salò Republic, Field Marshal Kesselring resided in another villa in the town centre (Consorzio Alberghi Riviera del Garda, *I Luoghi della Repubblica di Salò*, pp. 11–13).

86   This section is followed by a single line.

87   The rumour about explosive objects allegedly dropped by the Allies with the aim at killing children was invented and spread by the Fascist press in the spring of 1943. The propaganda campaign proved counter-productive as it spread panic across Italy, undermining morale instead of strengthening it. Indeed, between 18 May and 2 June 1943 Ministry of Popular Culture directives to the press sought to limit the psychological reaction, asking the newspapers to end publications on the subject. Moreover, many began to believe that it was the Fascists or the Germans who had spread the objects with the purpose of blaming the enemy (Baldoli and Fincardi, 'Italian society under Anglo-American bombs', 1033–4). In May 1943, another British subject living in Italy, Marquess Iris Origo, also commented in her diary on Italian press reports of 'fountain-pens, pencils, watches, lipsticks, and even dolls and cough-drops' that were allegedly dropped by Allied aircraft with the intention of mutilating women and children (I. Origo, *War in Val d'Orcia: An Italian War Diary, 1943–1944*, London: Alison and Busby, 2005; 1st edn 1947, p. 47).

88   Although the British government intended to extend Britain's political influence on Greece after the war, the War Office and Special Operations Executive had to support the Greek Communist-dominated Resistance movement for military reasons. For an analysis of the British attitude towards Greece at this time, see P. Papastratis, *British Policy towards Greece during the Second World War 1941–1944*, Cambridge: Cambridge University Press, 1984, pp. 129–216.

89   This section is followed by a single line.

90   Between 16 December 1944 and 25 January 1945 the Germans launched an offensive through the Ardennes. They made rapid progress at first because bad weather grounded Allied air power, but by late December Allied reinforcements and aircraft halted the offensive and drove the German army back to its starting point.

91   Five dots in the original. This section is followed by a single line.

92   The *Befana*, Epiphany, is represented in Italy as an old good witch who, coming down from a chimney hood, brings sweets to children in the night between 5 and 6 January.

93   This section is followed by a single line.

Diary 1945

1   By the beginning of January 1945 the Soviet army had moved the frontline into Bielorussian, Ukrainian, Hungarian and Yugoslav territories. Barnes is referring to the consequences of a major offensive that began on 12 January and that was going to bring the Soviet armies to the Czech border some 35 miles east of Berlin by early February.

2   The fourteenth cabinet meeting of the Republic took place on 18 January 1945, and established lines along which to organize the Fascist trade

unions. This, as well as more generally the so-called 'socialization' of the Republic, did not have any impact on the organization of northern Italian workers, who were by then in the overwhelming majority anti-Fascist. Alongside German repression, Fascist trade unionism during the Republic failed in the attempt to counteract Communist organization in the factories. The workers' strikes that had continued from the beginning of the Salò Republic had indeed demonstrated that the Communist Party was able to coordinate action between partisan bands and workers. Favoured by the population's general hostility towards the Republic, the most significant strikes occurred in Turin in November 1943, in Milan that December, and in Genoa in January 1944, culminating in the general strike in most of northern Italy in March 1944. A last general strike occurred on 18 April 1945, preceding the armed confrontation with the Germans that led to the liberation by Italian partisans of northern Italian cities. See S. Peli, *La Resistenza in Italia. Storia e critica* (Turin: Einaudi, 2004).

3   Gioacchino Nicoletti was a journalist and writer; he fought in the African campaign and returned to Italy after the armistice. His best-known book was *Sotto la cenere* (Milan: Treves, 1927), on his experience in the First World War.

4   The Teheran conference, to coordinate the future strategy between the Western Allies and the Soviet Union, took place between 28 November and 1 December 1943. The conference Barnes was referring to in fact took place at Yalta (Crimea) between 4 and 11 February 1945. The Allies discussed the last phase of the battle for Germany and the future occupation of the country by the three victors and by France.

5   Following the German invasion of France and Pétain's armistice with Germany in June 1940, French General Charles de Gaulle broadcast from London the first appeal for the organization of the French resistance. He set up the Free French movement, which during the war became coordinated with the French Committees for National Liberation. In June 1944 he had landed in France, and in August, after the liberation of Paris, was acclaimed in the capital. In October 1944 the United States and Britain recognized his administration as provisional French government. He was President of the French Republic until 1946 and from 1958 to 1969.

6   This section is followed by a single line.

7   This section is followed by a single line. At Yalta, Stalin agreed that the Soviet Union would wage war on Japan within three months after German surrender. Indeed, the Soviet-Japanese war began on 8 August 1945, in between the two atomic bombs on Hiroshima and Nagasaki, and precisely three months after the German armistice of 8 May 1945.

8   Edvige Mussolini Mancini was the third child (after Benito and Arnaldo) of Alessandro Mussolini and Rosa Maltoni.

9   Barbarano is a hamlet of the commune of Salò on Lake Garda.

10   The San Francisco Conference, formally known as the United Nations Conference on International Organization, established the United Nations between April and June 1945.

11 Although no mass resistance or sabotage materialized in Germany during the war, in the last year the home front moved from endurance to apathy, and issues of personal survival prevailed over national interest. By early 1945 the German war economy was close to collapse because of intensive bombing and large-scale evacuation which involved 9 million people by the end of the war. On the German home front in the last year of the war, see I. Kershaw, *The End: Hitler's Germany, 1944–45* (London: Allen Lane, 2011).

12 This section is followed by a single line.

13 Alberto Mellini Ponce de León was Mazzolini's chief of Cabinet at Salò. He wrote a book of memoirs: *Guerra diplomatica a Salò* (Milan: Cappelli, 1945).

14 On historian and anti-Fascist exile Gaetano Salvemini see Introduction, note 25, p. 189. In 1910, in his book *Il ministro della malavita*, Salvemini denounced the corruption and the lack of democracy in Italian politics under Liberal Prime Minister Giovanni Giolitti.

15 This section is followed by a single line.

16 Sir Arnold Talbot Wilson, author of numerous books on the British Empire, was acting civil commissioner in the Persian Gulf after the First World War, and a conservative MP in 1933–40. In his book *The Suez Canal: Its Past, Present, and Future* (London: Oxford University Press, 1939) he provided a history of the Suez Canal from the perspective of British interests, in the attempt to persuade public opinion about its importance as the key to India and for the British Empire more generally.

17 This section is followed by two single lines.

18 This section is followed by a single line.

19 'Faith & hope'. This section is followed by a single line.

20 Joachim von Ribbentrop was German Ambassador to London in 1936–8 and the Reich's Foreign Minister in 1938–45.

21 Although Germany, as well as the Allies, possessed chemical warfare weapons, no serious plan to use them was developed because of fear of retaliation. The only time Churchill considered the possibility of using chemical bombs against German cities was after the V1 attacks on London in June 1944, but the idea was rejected by the Chiefs of Staff. See R. Harris and J. Paxman, *A Higher Form of Killing: The Secret History of Chemical and Biological Warfare* (London: Chatto & Windus, 1982), pp. 125–7.

22 This section is followed by a single line.

23 See *Diary 1943*, note 15, p. 197.

24 Passo dello Stelvio is a 2,758 metre pass in the province of Bolzano in South Tyrol.

25 Alfred Rosenberg was responsible for the Nazi Party's foreign relations between 1933 and 1945.

26 Ernest Bevin was Churchill's Minister of Labour, and became Foreign Minister in the post-war Labour Government. Mussolini was referring to a speech delivered by Bevin at the Yorkshire Regional Conference of the Labour Party in Leeds on 7 April 1945, when he provoked an outburst of controversies in the press over the need to reveal to the public the difficulties of holding the three Allied powers together (also by providing opposition parties with the government's foreign policy documents).

27 British Labour politician Clement Attlee was Churchill's deputy Prime Minister during the war Coalition Government in 1940–5, and after the war he became Britain's Prime Minister. Herbert Morrison, also from the Labour Party, was a member of Churchill's cabinet from 1941, first as Minister of Supply, then as Home Secretary, and finally as Minister of Home Security.

28 Labour Party MP Arthur Greenwood had been Minister of Health in 1929–31 and member of the War Cabinet (without portfolio) in 1940–2.

29 Conservative politician Sir Samuel Hoare was Secretary of State for Air in the 1920s; Secretary of State for India in the early 1930s; Foreign Minister over the international crisis provoked by the Italian invasion of Ethiopia in 1935; and Ambassador to Spain from May 1940 to December 1944. His diplomatic activity in Madrid was successful in establishing a satisfactory relationship with the Spanish authorities and in securing the release from Spain of some 30,000 Allied prisoners of war.

30 Lord Emanuel Shinwell was a Trade Union delegate and a Labour politician; Sir Richard Stokes was a Labour politician, and in 1951 became Lord Privy Seal; they were critical of Churchill's Coalition Government and did not occupy any position in it.

31 Mussolini was probably referring to Hastings William Sackville Russell, 12th Duke of Bedford, a pacifist, and thus accused of pro-fascist sympathies, during the Second World War; and to novelist Rhys Davies, who worked at the War Office in 1939–40.

32 Harold Harmsworth, Viscount Rothermere, was newspaper proprietor. In the early 1930s some of his newspapers, such as the *Daily Mail* and the *Daily Mirror*, were sympathetic to the British Union of Fascists. He was a supporter of appeasement before the Second World War.

33 In fact Maurice Drummond Peterson was born in Dundee, although he was educated in Canada (where he moved because of his father's job) and at Oxford. He entered the British Foreign Office in December 1913, and then served as a diplomat at Washington, Prague, Tokyo, Cairo and Madrid; he was Undersecretary of State (Foreign Office) in 1942, Ambassador in Ankara in 1944–6 and in Moscow in 1946–9 (when he retired).

34 At the end of the Casablanca Conference in January 1943, Roosevelt and Churchill agreed on requesting unconditional surrender to the Axis countries. In December 1942 they had agreed also on warning the Axis states that after the war their military leaders would be brought to court and would have to respond to any war crimes committed.

35 Four dots in the original.

36 This section is followed by a single line.

37 Filippo Anfuso was the Salò Republic's Ambassador to Berlin from

September 1943 and, from 26 March 1945, Undersecretary of Foreign Affairs.

38 Indeed, Germany could not possibly regain the mastery of the air at this stage. The Luftwaffe had lost the air war by summer 1944, not because of lack of aircraft production but because of lack of fuel and inadequate aircrew training which resulted in exceptionally high loss rates. The Luftwaffe had high expectations of the new Messerschmitt Me262 jet fighter, but it could not be produced in sufficient numbers before the end of the war.

39 This section is followed by a single line.

40 This section is followed by a single line.

41 In Latin, 'nothing should be said about the dead except good things' (from the ancient Greek historian Diogenes Laertius).

42 This section is followed by a single line.

43 The guest-quarters of the Italian National Institute for Tourism.

44 Alfredo Cucco was Undersecretary of Popular Culture during the Salò Republic from February 1944, and among the founders of the neo-Fascist party *Movimento Sociale Italiano* in December 1946.

45 It is not clear to whom Barnes is referring, but not to Gioacchino Volpe, Fascist Italy's best-known historian, who had been one of the regime's most important intellectuals but did not take part in the Salò Republic.

46 Madonna di Campiglio is a touristic locality in the province of Trento at 1,550 metres above sea level.

47 Nicola Bombacci was a Fascist journalist (although only from 1935) and a supporter of Fascist trade unionism during the Salò Republic, when he also acted as one of Mussolini's advisers. Mussolini, Petacci, Pavolini, Bombacci and the other 14 Fascists who were with them were shot at Dongo in the province of Como, where they had been caught by partisans as they were seeking to escape towards Switzerland. On the same day, Farinacci was shot by partisans at Vimercate, in the Brianza region north of Milan.

48 On 2 May 1945 the German forces in Italy signed the unconditional surrender to the Allies.

49 Italianized word for 'crucifixion'.

50 This section is followed by two single lines.

51 This section is followed by two single lines.

BIBLIOGRAPHY

Archival sources

Archivio Centrale dello State, Rome (ACS)
Archivi di famiglie e persone, James Strachey Barnes: b. 1 (Barnes, *Promemoria*, 1947; correspondence); b. 2 (correspondence); b. 3 (correspondence); b. 4 (unpublished manuscript of Diary 1943, 1944 and 1945; unpublished manuscript of Diary 1913; unpublished manuscript of memoir *Life Made Whole*).
Ministero della Cultura Popolare, 'Reports (1922–1945)'.
Ministero dell'Interno, Direzione Generale Pubblica Sicurezza, IIGM, A5G.

Fondazione Ugo Spirito, Rome
Archivio Storico, Fondo Pellizzi, Serie V, b. 33, b. 30 (Barnes's correspondence with Camillo Pellizzi).

The National Archives, Kew (TNA)
WO 204/12841; AIR 8/777; AIR 20/2565.

The British Library
Barnes, J. S., Fascism and the International Centre of Fascist Studies, CINEF (Centre International d'Études sur le Fascisme), unpublished typescript (Lausanne, 1929).

Newspapers and periodicals

The British-Italian Bulletin (1935–1936)
Bulletin of International News (1935)
Educazione Fascista (1928)
Fronte Unico (1943)
L'Osservatore Romano (1943)
Il Secolo d'Italia (1960)
La Stampa (1940)
The Times (1952; 1955)

Published primary sources

Barnes, J. S., *The Universal Aspects of Fascism* (London: Williams and Norgate, 1928).
—*Half a Life* (London: Eyre & Spottiswoode, 1933).
—*Half a Life Left* (London: Eyre and Spottiswoode, 1937).
—*Io amo l'Italia. Memorie di un giornalista inglese* (Milan: Garzanti, 1939).
—*Giustizia sociale attraverso la riforma monetaria* (Venice: Ministero della Cultura Popolare, 1944).
Benini, Z., *Vigilia a Verona* (Milan: Garzanti, 1949; republished as *Carcere degli scalzi*, Florence: Ponte alle Grazie, 1994).
Churchill, W. S., *Onwards to Victory: War Speeches of the Right Hon. Winston S. Churchill, 1943*, (ed.) C. Ede (London: Cassell, 1944).
Ciano, G., *The Ciano Diaries, 1939–1943: The Complete, Unabridged Diaries of Count Galeazzo Ciano, Italian Minister for Foreign Affairs, 1936–1943*, (ed.) H. Gibson (Garden City, NY: Doubleday, 1946).
Currey, M., *A Woman at the Abyssinian War* (London: Hutchinson, 1936).
Currey, M. and Goad, H., *The Working of a Corporate State* (London: Nicholson and Watson, 1933).
Domarus, M., *Hitler: Reden und Proklamationen 1932–1945: Band II (2): Untergang* (Munich: Süddeutscher Verlag, 1965).
Doob, L. (ed.), *Ezra Pound Speaking: Radio Speeches of World War II* (London: Greenwood Press, 1978).
Eden, A., *The Reckoning: The Eden Memoirs* (London: Cassell, 1965).
Escott, T. H. S. (ed.), *Pillars of the Empire: Sketches of Living Indian and Colonial Statesmen, Celebrities, and Officials* (London: Chapman and Hall, 1879).
Farinacci, R., *Realtà storiche* (Cremona: Cremona Nuova, 1939).
Fuller, J. F. C., *The First of the League Wars: Its Lessons and Omens* (London: Eyre and Spottiswoode, 1936).
Gentile, G., *La vita e il pensiero*, vol. 4, (ed.) B. Gentile (Florence: Sansoni, 1951).
Goad, H., *What is Fascism? An Explanation of its Essential Principles* (Florence: Italian Mail and Tribune, 1929).
—*The Making of the Corporate State: A Study of Fascist Development* (London: Christophers, 1932).
Jerrold, D., *Jeorgian Adventure* (London: Collins, 1937).
—*Britain and Europe, 1900–1940* (London: Collins, 1941).
Lojacono, L., *Il Fascismo nel mondo* (Rome: L'Economia Italiana, 1933).
Mellini, A., *Guerra diplomatica a Salò* (Milan: Cappelli, 1945).
Mussolini, B., *Opera Omnia di Benito Mussolini*, (eds) E. and D. Susmel, vol. 31, *Dal discorso al Direttorio nazionale del P.N.F. del 3 gennaio 1942 alla liberazione di Mussolini*; vol. 32, *Dalla liberazione di Mussolini all'epilogo* (Florence: La Fenice, 1951–63).
Nicoletti, G., *Sotto la cenere* (Milan: Treves, 1927).
Origo, I., *War in Val d'Orcia: An Italian War Diary, 1943–1944* (London: Alison and Busby, 2005; 1st edn 1947).
Pellizzi, C., *Problemi e realtà del fascismo* (Florence: Vallecchi, 1924).
—*Fascismo-aristocrazia* (Milan: Alpes, 1925).

Petrie, C., *Mussolini* (London: The Holme Press, 1931).
—*Monarchy in the Twentieth Century* (London: Dakers, 1952).
—*The Modern British Monarchy* (London: Eyre and Spottiswoode, 1955).
Polson Newman, E. W., *The New Ethiopia* (London: Rich and Cowan, 1938).
Puntoni, P., *Parla Vittorio Emanuele III* (Bologna: Il Mulino, 1993).
Ricciotti, G., *Vita di Gesù Cristo* (Milan: Rizzoli, 1941).
Salvemini, G., *Il ministro della malavita* (Florence: Edizione della Voce, 1910; most recent edn Bari: Palomar, 2006).
—*The Fascist Dictatorship in Italy* (New York: H. Holt, 1927).
Sammartano, N., *Corso di cultura fascista ad uso delle scuole medie inferiori* (Florence: Le Monnier, 1934).
Senise, C., *Quando ero capo della polizia, 1940–1943* (Rome: Ruffolo, 1946).
Villari, L., *The Awakening of Italy: The Fascista Regeneration* (London: Methuen, 1924).
—*The Fascist Experiment* (London: Faber & Gwyer, 1926).
Wilson, A. T., *The Suez Canal: Its Past, Present, and Future* (London: Oxford University Press. 1939).

Secondary sources

Aga Rossi, E., *A Nation Collapses: The Italian Surrender of September 1943* (Cambridge: Cambridge University Press, 1999).
Albanese, G., *La Marcia su Roma* (Rome and Bari: Laterza, 2006).
—'Reconsidering the March on Rome', *European History Quarterly*, 42 (3), 2012, 403–21.
Albanese, G. and Isnenghi, M. (eds), *Gli italiani in guerra. Conflitti, identità, memorie del Risorgimento ai nostri giorni*, vol. 4 (Turin: UTET, 2009).
Baldoli, C., *Exporting Fascism: Italian Fascists and Britain's Italians in the 1930s* (Oxford and New York: Berg, 2003).
—'Bombing the eternal city: The Allies and Rome in the Second World War', *History Today*, May 2012, 10–15.
Baldoli, C. and Fincardi, M., 'Italian society under Anglo-American bombs: Propaganda, experience, and legend, 1940–1945', *The Historical Journal*, 52 (4), 2009, 1017–38.
Baldoli, C. and Knapp, A., *Forgotten Blitzes: France and Italy under Allied Air Attack, 1940–1945* (London: Continuum, 2012).
Baldoli, C., Knapp, A. and Overy, R. (eds), *Bombing, States and Peoples in Western Europe, 1940–1945* (London: Continuum, 2011).
Bersani, C. and Roversi Monaco, V. R. (eds), *Delenda Bononia. Immagini dei bombardamenti, 1943–1945* (Bologna: Biblioteca Comunale dell'Archiginnasio, 1995).
Bertagna, F., *La patria di riserva. L'emigrazione fascista in Argentina* (Rome: Donzelli, 2006).
Bettin, C. M., *Italian Jews from Emancipation to the Racial Laws* (Basingstoke: Palgrave, 2010).
Blet, P., *Pius XII and the Second World War According to the Archives of the Vatican* (Hereford: Gracewing, 1999).

Bradshaw, D. '"Those extraordinary parakeets": Clive Bell and Mary Hutchinson', part 1, *The Charleston Magazine*, Autumn–Winter 1997, 16, 5–12; part 2, *The Charleston Magazine*, Spring–Summer 1998, 17, 5–11.

Bradshaw, D. and Smith, J., 'Ezra Pound, James Strachey Barnes ("The Italian Lord Haw-Haw") and Italian Fascism', *Review of English Studies*, 64 (266), 2013, 672–93.

Breschi, D. and Longo, G., *Camillo Pellizzi. La ricerca delle elites tra politica e sociologia, 1896–1979* (Soveria Mannelli: Rubbettino, 2003).

Burdett, C., 'Journeys to the other spaces of Fascist Italy', *Modern Italy*, 5 (1), May 2000, 7–23.

Canali, M., *Il delitto Matteotti* (Bologna: Il Mulino, 2004; 1st edn 1997).

—'The Matteotti murder and the origins of Mussolini's totalitarian Fascist regime in Italy', *Journal of Modern Italian Studies*, 14 (2), 2009, 146–67.

Carli, M. and Gentiloni Silveri, U., *Bombardare Roma. Gli Alleati e la 'città aperta' (1940–1944)* (Bologna: Il Mulino, 2007).

Colarizi, S., *L'opinione degli italiani sotto il regime, 1929–1943* (Rome and Bari: Laterza, 1991).

Collotti, E., *Fascismo, fascismi* (Milan: Sansoni, 2004).

Collotti, E. and Klinkhammer, L., *Il fascismo e l'Italia in guerra. Una conversazione fra storia e storiografia* (Rome: Ediesse, 1996).

Consorzio Alberghi Riviera del Garda (ed.), *I Luoghi della Repubblica di Salò* (Gardone Riviera: L'Editoriale Grafica, 1997).

Deakin, F., *Storia della Repubblica di Salò* (Turin: Einaudi, 1963); 1st English edn, *The Brutal Friendship: Mussolini, Hitler and the Fall of Italian Fascism* (New York: Harper and Row, 1962).

De Felice, R., *Rosso e nero* (Milan: Baldini e Castoldi, 1995).

—*Mussolini l'alleato, 1940–1945*, vol. 2: *La guerra civile, 1943–1945* (Turin: Einaudi, 1997).

De Grand, A., *Bottai e la cultura fascista* (Rome and Bari: Laterza, 1978).

De Grazia, V. and Luzzatto, S. (eds), *Dizionario del Fascismo* (Turin: Einaudi, 2003).

De Luna, G., *Badoglio. Un militare al potere* (Milan: Bompiani, 1974).

De Rosa, G. and Malgeri, F., *Giuseppe Bottai e 'Critica Fascista'* (S. Giovanni Valdarno: Landi, 1980).

Del Boca, A., *I gas di Mussolini. Il fascismo e la guerra d'Etiopia* (Rome: Editori Riuniti, 1996).

—*Mohamed Fekini and the Fight to Free Libya* (Basingstoke: Palgrave, 2011).

D'Este, C., *1943. Lo sbarco in Sicilia* (Milan: Mondadori, 1990).

Di Figlia, M., *Farinacci. Il radicalismo fascista al potere* (Rome: Donzelli, 2007).

Dordoni, A., *Crociata Italica: Fascismo e religione nella Repubblica di Salò* (Milan: Sugarco, 1976).

Doumanis, N., *Myth and Memory in the Mediterranean: Remembering Fascism's Empire* (Basingstoke: Palgrave, 1997).

Duggan, C., *Fascist Voices: An Intimate History of Mussolini's Italy* (Oxford: Oxford University Press, 2013).

Dunnage, J., *Mussolini's Policemen: Behaviour, Ideology and Institutional Culture in Representation and Practice* (Manchester: Manchester University Press, 2013).

Fappani, A. and Molinari, F., *Chiesa e Repubblica di Salò. Fonti edite ed inedite* (Turin: Marietti, 1981).

Fondazione Luigi Micheletti (ed.), *1943–45. L'immagine della Repubblica Sociale Italiana nella propaganda* (Milan: Mazzotta, 1985).

Franzinelli, M., *Squadristi. Protagonisti e tecniche della violenza fascista, 1919–1922* (Milan: Mondadori, 2003).

—*L'amnistia Togliatti. 22 giugno 1946: colpo di spugna sui crimini fascisti* (Milan: Mondadori, 2006).

—*RSI. La Repubblica del Duce, 1943–1945* (Milan: Mondadori, 2007).

Gagliani, D., *Brigate nere. Mussolini e la militarizzazione del Partito fascista repubblicano* (Turin: Bollati Boringhieri, 1999).

Gagliardi, A., *Il Corporativismo fascista* (Rome and Bari: Laterza, 2010).

Gallerano, N. (ed.), *L'altro dopoguerra. Roma e il Sud 1943–1945* (Milan: Angeli, 1985).

Galli Della Loggia, E., *La morte della patria: la crisi dell'idea di nazione tra Resistenza, antifascismo e Repubblica* (Rome and Bari: Laterza, 1996).

Ganapini, L., *La repubblica delle camicie nere* (Milan: Garzanti, 1999 and 2002).

—'The dark side of Italian history, 1943–1945', *Modern Italy*, 12 (2), 2007, 205–24.

Gentile, E., *La grande Italia. Ascesa e declino del mito della nazione nel ventesimo secolo* (Milan: Mondadori, 1997).

—*E fu subito regime. Il fascismo e la Marcia su Roma* (Rome and Bari: Laterza, 2012).

Germinario, F., *L'altra memoria. L'estrema destra, Salò e la Resistenza* (Turin: Bollati Boringhieri, 1999).

—*Estranei alla democrazia. Negazionismo e antisemitismo nella destra radicale* (Pisa: Biblioteca Franco Serantini, 2001).

Gibelli, A., *Il popolo bambino. Infanzia e nazione dalla Grande Guerra a Salò* (Turin: Einaudi, 2005).

Gioannini, M. and Massobrio, G., *Bombardate l'Italia. Storia della guerra di distruzione aerea 1940–1945* (Milan: Rizzoli, 2007).

Goebbels, J., *Diario intimo* Milan: Mondadori, 1948).

Gooch, J., *Mussolini and His Generals: The Armed Forces and Fascist Foreign Policy, 1922–1940* (Cambridge: Cambridge University Press, 2007).

Gottlieb, J. and Linehan, T. (eds), *The Culture of Fascism: Visions and the Far Right in Britain* (London: I. B. Tauris, 2004).

Gregor, A. J., *Mussolini's Intellectuals: Fascist Social and Political Thought* (Princeton, NJ: Princeton University Press, 2006).

Gribaudi, G., *Guerra totale. Tra bombe alleate e violenze naziste: Napoli e il fronte meridionale, 1940–44* (Turin: Bollati Boringhieri, 2005).

Griffin, R., *Modernism and Fascism: The Sense of a Beginning under Mussolini and Hitler* (Basingstoke: Palgrave, 2007).

Hammermann, G., *Gli internati militari italiani in Germania, 1943–1945* (Bologna: Il Mulino, 2004).

Harris, R. and Paxman, J., *A Higher Form of Killing: The Secret History of Chemical and Biological Warfare* (London: Chatto & Windus, 1982).

Imbriani, A. M., *Gli italiani e il Duce. Il mito e l'immagine di Mussolini negli ultimi anni del fascismo, 1938–1943* (Naples: Liguori, 1992).

Insolvibile, I., *Kos, 1943–1948. La strage, la storia* (Naples: Edizioni Scientifiche Italiane, 2010).

Isnenghi, M., *Intellettuali militanti e intellettuali funzionari. Appunti sulla cultura fascista* (Turin: Einaudi, 1979).

—(ed.), *I Luoghi della memoria: Personaggi e date dell'Italia unita* (Rome and Bari: Laterza, 1997).

—(ed.), *I luoghi della memoria: Strutture ed eventi dell'Italia unita* (Rome and Bari: Laterza, 1997).

Kenny, M., *Germany Calling: A Personal Biography of William Joyce, 'Lord Haw-Haw'* (Dublin: New Island, 2003).

Kershaw, I., *The End: Hitler's Germany, 1944–45* (London: Allen Lane, 2011).

Knox, M., *Hitler's Italian Allies: Royal Armed Forces, Fascist Regime, and the War of 1940–43* (Cambridge: Cambridge University Press, 2000).

Koon, T., *Believe, Obey, Fight: The Political Socialization of Youth in Fascist Italy* (Chapel Hill, NC: University of North Carolina Press, 1985).

Labanca, N. (ed.), *I bombardamenti aerei e l'Italia nella Seconda Guerra Mondiale* (Bologna: Il Mulino, 2012).

Legnani, M. and Vendramini, F. (eds), *Guerra, guerra di liberazione e guerra civile* (Milan: Franco Angeli, 1990).

Luconi, R., *Il Terzo Ordine regolare di S. Francesco* (Macerata: Bisson & Leopardi, 1935).

Luzzatto, S., *The Body of Il Duce: Mussolini's Corpse and the Fortunes of Italy* (New York: Metropolitan Books, 2005).

Lyttelton, A. (ed.), *Liberal and Fascist Italy* (Oxford: Oxford University Press, 2002).

Malgeri, F., *La chiesa italiana e la guerra (1940–1945)* (Rome: Studium, 1980).

Mallett, R. and Sørensen, G. (eds), *International Fascism, 1919–1945* (London: Frank Cass, 2002).

Mancini, C. M., *Le carte del maggiore James Strachey Barnes R. F. C.* (Rome: typescript, 2007; latest edn with CD Rom, 2012).

Mannu, M., *Il Terzo ordine francescano: orizzonti storici* (Rome: Graphein, 1999).

Mantelli, B., *Camerati del lavoro. I lavoratori emigrati nel Terzo Reich nel periodo dell'Asse* (Scandicci: La Nuova Italia, 1992).

Martin, S., *Sport Italia: The Italian Love Affair with Sport* (London: I. B. Tauris, 2011).

Martland, P., *Lord Haw Haw: The English Voice of Nazi Germany* (Richmond, Surrey: National Archives, 2003).

Mazzantini, C., *A cercar la bella morte* (Venice: Marsilio, 1995).

Michaelis, M., 'Mussolini's unofficial mouthpiece: Telesio Interlandi – *Il Tevere* and the evolution of Mussolini's anti-Semitism', *Journal of Modern Italian Studies*, 3 (3), 1998, 217–40.

Missori, M., *Gerarchie e statuti del PNF* (Rome: Bonacci, 1986).

Molesi, D., *Ravenna nella Seconda Guerra Mondiale* (Ravenna: Longo, 1974).

Monelli, P., *Roma 1943* (Rome: Miglioresi, 1943).

Monteleone, F., *Storia della radio e della televisione in Italia. Società, politica, strategia, programmi 1922–1992* (Venice: Marsilio, 1992).

Moseley, R., *Mussolini's Shadow: The Double Life of Count Galeazzo Ciano* (New Haven, CT, and London: Yale University Press, 1999).

Murialdi, P., *Storia del giornalismo italiano* (Bologna: Il Mulino, 1996).

—*La stampa del regime fascista* (Rome and Bari: Laterza, 2008).

Nappo, T. (ed.), *Indice biografico italiano* (Munich: Saur, 2002).

Nello, P., *Dino Grandi* (Bologna: Il Mulino, 2003; first edn 1993).

Osti Guerrazzi, A., *La 'Repubblica necessaria'. Il fascismo repubblicano a Roma, 1943–44* (Milan: Angeli, 2004).

Overy, R., *Russia's War* (London: Penguin, 1998).

Painter, B., *Mussolini's Rome: Rebuilding the Eternal City* (Basingstoke: Palgrave, 2005).

Pala, E., *Garibaldi in camicia nera. Il mito dell'Eroe dei Due Mondi nella Repubblica di Salò* (Milan: Mursia, 2011).

Papastratis, P., *British Policy towards Greece during the Second World War 1941–1944* (Cambridge: Cambridge University Press, 1984).

Pavone, C., *Una guerra civile. Saggio storico sulla moralità nella resistenza* (Turin: Bollati Borighieri, 1991). English edn, *A Civil War: A History of the Italian Resistance* (London and New York: Verso, 2013).

Payne, S., *A History of Fascism, 1914–1945* (London: UCL Press, 1995).

Paxton, R., *Vichy France: Old Guard and New Order, 1940–1944* (New York: Columbia University Press, 1982).

Peli, S., *La Resistenza in Italia. Storia e critica* (Turin: Einaudi, 2004).

Perry, M., *'Red Ellen' Wilkinson: Her Ideas, Movements and World* (Manchester: Manchester University Press, 2014).

Petese, L. (ed.), *L'archivio Pellizzi: il percorso di un intellettuale tra fascismo e Repubblica* (Rome: Fondazione Ugo Spirito, 2003).

Piffer, T., *Gli Alleati e la Resistenza italiana* (Bologna: Il Mulino, 2010).

Pollard, J., '"Clerical-Fascism": Context, overview and conclusion', *Totalitarian Movements and Political Religions*, 8 (2), 2007, 433–46.

Rainero, R. H. (ed.), *L'Italia in guerra. Il quarto anno – 1943* (Gaeta: Stabilimento Grafico Militare, 1994).

Ridolfi, M., *Almanacco della Repubblica. Storia d'Italia attraverso le tradizioni, le istituzioni e le simbologie repubblicane* (Milan: Bruno Mondadori, 2003).

Roberts, D. D., 'Myth, style, substance and the totalitarian dynamic in Fascist Italy', *Contemporary European History*, 16 (1), 2007, 1–36.

Rochat, G., *Italo Balbo: lo squadrista, l'aviatore, il gerarca* (Turin: Utet, 1986).

—*Guerre italiane in Libia e in Etiopia. Studi militari, 1921–1939* (Treviso: Pagus, 1991).

—*L'esercito italiano in pace e in guerra. Studi di storia militare* (Milan: RARA, 1991).

—*Le guerre italiane, 1935–1943. Dall'impero d'Etiopia alla disfatta* (Turin: Einaudi, 2005).

Rodogno, D., *Fascism's European Empire: Italian Occupation during the Second World War* (Cambridge: Cambridge University Press, 2006).

Sanford, G., *Katyn and the Soviet Massacre of 1940: Truth, Justice and Memory* (New York: Routledge, 2005).

Santarelli, L., 'Muted violence: Italian war crimes in occupied Greece', *Journal of Modern Italian Studies*, 9 (3), 2004, 280–99.

Santomassimo, G., *La terza via fascista. Il mito del corporativismo* (Rome: Carocci, 2006).

Serenelli, S., '"It was like something that you have at home which becomes so familiar that you don't even pay attention to it": Memories of Mussolini and Fascism in Predappio, 1922–2010', *Modern Italy*, 18 (2), 2013, 157–75.

Suzzi Valli, R., 'Il fascio italiano a Londra. L'attività politica di Camillo Pellizzi', *Storia contemporanea*, 6, 1995, 957–1001.

Tarchi, M., *Esuli in patria. I fascisti nell'Italia repubblicana* (Parma: Guanda, 1995).

Thurlow, R., *Fascism in Britain: A History, 1918–1985* (Oxford: Blackwell, 1987).

Tonning, E., Feldman, M. and Addyman, D. (eds), *Modernism, Christianity, and Apocalypse* (Leiden: Brill Academic Publishers, 2014).

Tranfaglia, N., *La stampa del regime 1932–1943. Le veline del Minculpop per orientare l'informazione* (Milan: Bompiani, 2005).

Turi, G., *Giovanni Gentile. Una biografia* (Florence: Giunti, 1995).

—*Lo stato educatore. Politica e intellettuali nell'Italia fascista* (Rome and Bari: Laterza, 2002).

Venè, G. F., *Mille lire al mese. Vita quotidiana della famiglia nell'Italia fascista* (Milan: Mondadori, 1988).

Wrench, J. E., *Francis Yates-Brown, 1886–1944* (London: Eyre and Spottiswoode, 1948).

Zangrandi, R., *Il lungo viaggio attraverso il fascismo. Contributo alla storia di una generazione* (Milan: Feltrinelli, 1971; 1st edn Turin: Einaudi, 1948).

Zimmerman, J. D. (ed.), *Jews in Italy under Fascist and Nazi rule, 1922–1945* (Cambridge: Cambridge University Press, 2005).

INDEX

Aberystwith 45
Abruzzo 17
Abyssinia *see* Ethiopia
Addis Ababa 8
Acerbo, Giacomo 42
Adriatic, sea, coast and ports 9, 28,
    67, 71–2, 82, 90, 102. 140, 151
Aegean, islands 67, 119
Africa, Italian empire in, 2, 3
    war front in, 11–12, 27, 29–30, 47,
      49–54, 59–60, 64–5, 73, 165,
      171–2
Albania 11, 28, 55, 67, 81
Albini, Umberto 43, 66
Allies
    and air mastery 36, 65, 155
    and Barnes 13
    and the bombing of Italy 2, 11, 14,
      18, 36, 161, 165
    'hypocrisy of' 14, 65, 162, 167
    invasion of Italy by 17, 19, 23, 28,
      77
    military strategy of 27–9, 55, 67,
      71–2, 78, 119, 127, 129, 138–42,
      151–2, 154–5, 157, 168–9
    and propaganda 172
    and shipping war materials 27
Almirante, Giorgio 137, 141, 182
Alps 140
Altieri, Donna Lodovica (mother of
    Buona Barnes), 8
Altieri Pasolini, Camilla (cousin of
    Buona Barnes) 33, 37, 55, 67,
    111
Alto Adige *see* South Tyrol
Ambrosio, Vittorio 43
Amery, Leo 2
Ampleforth 48
Ancona 102, 139, 151

Anfuso, Filippo 180
Anglican Church 4, 69, 109
Anglo-Persian Oil Company 5–6
anti-Semitism 20, 25, 32, 34, 44, 69–70,
    79, 81–2, 92, 103, 118, 129,
    167–8, 172, 174, 177–8, 180
Apennines, mountain and frontline
    127, 139–41, 148
Arco 115
Argentina 82, 114
Armistice (Italian surrender, September
    1943) 9, 12–13, 16–17, 20, 81,
    98, 100–1, 109–10, 122, 140
Arno, river 109
Asia 148, 179
Atlantic, charter (1941) 167
Atlantic, ocean and battles 72
Attlee, Clement 177
Augusta 86, 89
Auristi, Carmine 35–6, 43, 46, 63, 88,
    95, 97, 120–1
Australia 27, 29, 148, 178
Austria 8, 24
Avranches 140, 143, 153
Axis, Barnes's opinions of 10, 59, 63
    and Italian public opinion 11
    Italian 'plot' against 21, 122, 167,
      179
    military developments 28–9, 35,
      41–2, 46–7, 49, 52, 65, 91–2,
      119, 135, 141, 152, 157, 165

Badoglio, Pietro 73–9, 81, 87, 97,
    104, 131, 142
    appointed as prime minister 14–15,
      17, 21, 25
    and the armistice 16, 98, 100, 110
    Barnes's views about 15, 17, 21,
      25, 73, 79, 84, 104, 106–7

www.ingramcontent.com/pod-product-compliance
Lightning Source LLC
Chambersburg PA
CBHW071851270326
41929CB00013B/2185